GRACE HOPPER AND THE INVENTION OF THE
INFORMATION AGE

LEMELSON CENTER STUDIES IN INVENTION AND INNOVATION

ARTHUR P. MOLELLA AND JOYCE BEDI, GENERAL EDITORS

Arthur P. Molella and Joyce Bedi, editors, *Inventing for the Environment*

Paul E. Ceruzzi, *Internet Alley: High Technology in Tysons Corner, 1945–2005*

Robert H. Kargon and Arthur P. Molella, *Invented Edens: Techno-Cities of the Twentieth Century*

Kurt Beyer, *Grace Hopper and the Invention of the Information Age*

GRACE HOPPER AND THE INVENTION OF THE INFORMATION AGE

KURT BEYER

THE MIT PRESS

CAMBRIDGE, MASSACHUSETTS

LONDON, ENGLAND

For information on quantity discounts, email special_sales@mitpress.mit.edu.

Set in Engraver's Gothic and Bembo by SNP Best-set Typesetter Ltd., Hong Kong. Printed and bound in the United States of America.

Library of Congress Cataloging-in-Publication Data

Beyer, Kurt W.
Grace Hopper and the invention of the information age/Kurt W. Beyer.
    p. cm.—(Lemelson Center studies in invention and innovation series)
Includes bibiographical references and index.
ISBN 978-0-262-01310-9 (hardcover : alk. paper)
1. Hopper, Grace Murray. 2. Women computer engineers—United States—Biography. 3. Computer science—United States—History. I. Title.
QA76.2.H67B49   2009   004.092—dc22   2008044229

10 9 8 7 6 5 4 3

for my late father, Karl Beyer

CONTENTS

SERIES FOREWORD

Invention and innovation have long been recognized as significant forces in American history, not only in technological realms but also as models in politics, society, and culture. They are arguably more important than previously thought in other societies as well. What there is no question about is that they have become the universal watchwords of the twenty-first century, so much so that nations are staking their futures on them.

Since 1995, the Smithsonian's Lemelson Center has been investigating the history of invention and innovation from such broad interdisciplinary perspectives. So, too, does this series, the Lemelson Center Studies in Invention and Innovation. Books in the series explore the work of inventors and the technologies they create in order to advance scholarship in history, engineering, science, and related fields that have a direct connection to technological invention, such as urban planning, architecture, and the arts. By opening channels of communication between the various disciplines and sectors of society concerned with technological innovation, the Lemelson Center Studies aim to enhance public understanding of humankind's inventive impulse.

Arthur Molella and Joyce Bedi

ACKNOWLEDGEMENTS

I first came across Admiral Grace Murray Hopper when I was a teenager attending my sister's graduation from the College of William and Mary. The fiery speaker stoked my imagination and influenced my own career choices, first as a naval officer, then as an academic, and finally as an information technology entrepreneur. Hopper was a well-known figure in the Navy, but when I arrived at the University of California at Berkeley I found, to my surprise, that many people there did not know about her accomplishments. Berkeley in the late 1990s was at the epicenter of the "dot com" boom, a phenomenon dominated by young male entrepreneurs who slept under their desks, dreamed of stock options, and believed they were inventing the Information Age for the first time.

Under the guidance of Cathryn Carson, Jack Lesche, Todd La Porte, Roger Hahn, and Thomas Hughes, I began piecing together the evolution of the Information Age.

Not only did Grace Hopper play a pivotal role in creating the foundation for the computer industry; she was surrounded by remarkable men and women whose contributions have been overlooked or forgotten. I have woven their story into this book, with Hopper's early career serving as the binding thread.

Cathy Carson influenced me greatly during my time at Berkeley. Her work ethic and her dedication to this project will forever be appreciated. I also felt very fortunate to spend quiet summer afternoons learning from one of the founders of the field of the history of technology, Thomas Hughes. He helped me understand how technologies evolve and grow, and what role system builders such as Hopper play in the process of technical innovation.

Over the years I spent many hours in archives throughout the country. The help of the archivists at these repositories in sifting through documents was invaluable. In particular, the good people at the Archives Center at the Smithsonian's National Museum of American History in Washington, at the Charles Babbage Institute's Center for the History of Information Technology at the University of Minnesota, at the Harvard University Archives in Cambridge, and at the Van Pelt Library of the University of Pennsylvania in Philadelphia must be commended. Special thanks to Alison Oswald at the Smithsonian and to Jeffrey Yost and Arthur Norberg at the Charles Babbage Institute. I especially enjoyed Arthur's insights based on his Remington Rand research.

It takes a village to turn research into a manuscript, and many people helped to forge this work along the way. My wife Johanna was a constant springboard for ideas and put up with many late nights. Tim Kasta was a valuable sounding board as we discussed the intricacies of technical innovation over California wine. Colleagues at the Naval Academy, especially Bob Artigiani and David Peeler, keenly commented on drafts. Paul Cerruzi, W. Bernard Carlson, and Kathleen Williams provided valuable support and feedback. During the final preparation of the manuscript, Joyce Bedi and Art Molella of the Smithsonian's Lemelson Center were indispensable. Joyce in particular must be thanked for long discussions over cracked crab in Annapolis. Her unwavering support during my transition to fatherhood will also not be forgotten.

GRACE HOPPER AND THE INVENTION OF THE INFORMATION AGE

Recently I typed "Grace Hopper" into a popular Internet search engine and came up with more than a million "hits." Though this number pales in comparison with those for other twentieth-century icons, say John F. Kennedy (11 million) or Elvis Presley (8 million), Hopper is unquestionably the most numerically popular computer pioneer on the Web.[1] The top results are an assortment of adoring websites dedicated to "Amazing Grace" or "The Grandmother of Cobol" and numerous quotations from Hopper herself. An image search produces hundreds of pictures of the petite, heavily wrinkled computer programmer proudly wearing her Navy uniform in the twilight of her career.

There is no denying that Grace Murray Hopper became a minor celebrity during the autumn of her career, or that she came to personify computer programming and the programming profession. But Hopper's career may have gone unnoticed by the public had it not been for an interview broadcast on the popular CBS television show *60 Minutes* in March 1983. In that interview (conducted by Morley Safer), the irreverent Hopper, then a captain, playfully reflected on her life. Hers was a classic Hollywood-style tale: a young, bright-eyed mathematics professor leaves her job to serve her country during World War II and serendipitously finds herself at the forefront of the computer revolution, facing technical challenges and gender discrimination. With hard work and perseverance bordering on obstinacy, she helps to drive the new technology forward. The result is a superlative career that follows the meteoric trajectory of the information age.

Among the millions of people who saw the *60 Minutes* interview was U.S. Representative Philip Crane (R-Illinois). He promptly initiated a bill to have the contributions of this extraordinary woman properly recognized. The bill, passed by the House of Representatives, promoted Captain Grace Hopper by special appointment to the lofty rank of Commodore. Later she was promoted to Rear Admiral and was accorded further honors and awards. In 1985 the Navy's newest Data Automation Center was renamed the Grace Murray Hopper Center, and in 1997 the Navy's latest and most advanced guided missile destroyer was named the *USS Grace Hopper*.

The accolades precipitated by the *60 Minutes* interview were well deserved, but the interview also marked a growing chasm between rhetoric and reality. The public discourse since 1983 has preserved and perpetuated the "myth" of Grace Hopper, depicting her as a heroic pioneer who was single-handedly responsible for the invention of computer programming. And, as evidenced by interviews, articles, and speeches in her final years, Hopper enjoyed the limelight to a great extent, which only helped to further her myth. The intention of this book is to strip back the layers of rhetoric and to uncover a more authentic Grace Hopper in the context of the early computer industry. The young, vibrant Grace Hopper portrayed in these pages is far more complex and human then the popular press's portrayals of the aging admiral.

HOPPER IN HER PRIME: THE COLLABORATIVE REBEL

Anecdotes abound of the late Admiral Hopper, the majority highlighting her most lauded trait: irreverence bordering on insubordination. Nonetheless, the first 36 years of her life were marked by a certain amount of conventionality. In the 1920s it was not uncommon for privileged women from the Northeast to seek higher education. In fact, the percentage of women receiving doctorates in mathematics during the 1920s and the early 1930s was not achieved again until the 1980s.[2] This reminds us that the history of women's emancipation in America has not been linear.

Rather than steady progress, there have been waves of opportunity and retrenchment—for example, increasing opportunity in the 10 years after World War I, then retrenchment during the Depression. Hopper came of age during the 1920s, and both her public choices and her private ones coincided rather than conflicted with the desires of her family and her community.

The attack on Pearl Harbor and the ensuing mobilization created unprecedented career opportunities for women. The large-scale reorganization of labor opened a wide variety of occupations that before 7 December 1941 were reserved for men. The most iconic cultural image of this period, Rosie the Riveter, represented the millions of women who replaced men in the workforce as they deployed to Europe and the Pacific. Like millions of other women of her generation, Hopper benefited from this labor shift. And Pearl Harbor was a watershed in Grace Hopper's personal life as well as in her career. In the months following that fateful day, she divorced her husband, left a secure tenure-track position at Vassar College, and joined the Navy. She then became an officer in one of the most gendered organizations of its day. Her military rank endowed her with the external trappings of authority: uniform, title, pay, privilege. Military rank, protocol, and tradition helped to neutralize societal prejudices against women in positions of public responsibility. The benefits of military rank were evident as newly minted Lieutenant (j.g.) Hopper was assigned to Commander Howard Aiken's Harvard Computation Laboratory during the war. Aiken, a difficult man who would be classified as a "male chauvinist" by today's standards, found a kinship with Hopper not because she was a rebel but because of her ability to ingratiate herself to Aiken and her fellow workers. Of course she was a talented mathematician and computer programmer, but more importantly she was loyal to her boss and helped to organize and control his laboratory. She actively erased gender differences through her clothing, her language, her drinking habits, and her humor, gaining the trust and respect of Aiken and her peers to the point that she became the most prominent person in the Harvard Computation Laboratory apart from the fiery Aiken.

The pattern of collaboration rather than rebellion continued when Hopper left Harvard and joined the Eckert-Mauchly Computer Corporation (EMCC) in 1949. Far from shunning organizational politics and attempting to garner respect entirely on the basis of her technical talents, Hopper actively participated in and even shaped the organizational culture of the EMCC and that of the greater programming community. The alliances she cultivated supported her career initiatives and protected her during times of turmoil. Indeed, she was so good at understanding institutions and their unwritten rules that she remained influential in male-dominated military and business organizations throughout the postwar period, during which women were encouraged to retreat from the public sphere. All things considered, it was Hopper's collaborative abilities rather than her rebellious nature that created the space for her independent thought and action within potentially hostile organizations. Hopper's professional freedom also was facilitated by the novelty of the computer profession. The fact that computing was a new discipline afforded her the flexibility to define her role within the emerging computing community. More established fields often have gender-defined roles and responsibilities.[3] Hopper's programming knowledge and expertise stood her in good stead with her peers, regardless of gender. And as the relevance of programming grew, so did Hopper's stature.

It is important to note that when relatively well-established companies such as Remington Rand and IBM became involved in computing, they brought with them a masculine business culture that negatively affected the evolving gender-neutral programming profession. Betty Snyder Holberton and Betty "Jean" Jennings Bartik experienced the sea change at Remington Rand, which effectively ended their private-sector careers, and John Backus (the inventor of FORTRAN) described the programming culture at IBM in the late 1950s as that of an elite male fraternity.[4]

The exceptional challenges that Grace Hopper and her female peers faced as they attempted to forge careers after the war reminds us that "success" as defined by one's society often come at a personal price. Hopper, like other women during her era, consciously traded marriage and family for a career. Though she filled the emotional gap with colleagues, Hopper's most common method of dealing with personal loneliness was to throw herself into her work. The stress of being a pioneer exploring uncharted intellectual territory in an adolescent field weighed heavily on her at times. The burden of constantly peering into an uncertain future became so daunting during the late 1940s that Hopper reached a breaking point. Close friends and family rescued her from alcoholism and dissuaded her from suicide. Rather than tarnishing her enduring reputation, Hopper's personal struggles highlight her achievements and remind us that even the best and brightest among us are sometimes overwhelmed by life's challenges.

PROGRAMMING AS INVENTION

Most stories of invention revolve around a particular physical artifact, such as the airplane or the automobile. The physical artifact lends itself to description by the author and evolves physically over time, and its importance within the context of the history of technology is readily evident. Writing a book about the invention of programming comes with its own challenges. Though programs are "physical" in the sense that they can be printed out or viewed on a computer screen, "programming" is the active process of making programs, so the invention of programming entails describing the invention of an action or an activity as much as it has to do with a thing.

It is no surprise, then, that historians have largely overlooked the history of programming. It was not until the 1980s and the early 1990s that William Aspray, Nancy Stern, Michael Mahoney, Paul Ceruzzi, and others began exploring computer history.[5] Their early works, for the most part, concentrate on machines and the men who created them. In retrospect, the emphasis on hardware is paradoxical insofar as by 1970 the vast majority of the computer industry's productive resources went into programming and software development. By 1985, software constituted 90 percent of the cost of a computer system, and Microsoft soon eclipsed IBM in market capitalization and influence.[6]

The first coordinated effort to promote the history of programming was a 1978 conference sponsored by the Association for Computing Machinery. Led by the longtime programmer Jean Sammet, the three-day conference asked programming pioneers to dig into their personal notebooks and diaries and attempt to reconstruct a computing past of which they had been a part. The keynote speaker for the event was none other than Grace Hopper. The ACM held a second History of Programming Languages conference in 1993. Once again, the makers of history rather than professional historians presented papers and discussed the historical significance of their work. Fortunately, the historical community has demonstrated a growing interest in computers and programming since the last ACM conference, and in April 2001 a well-attended conference on the history of software was held in Palo Alto.[7]

Programming was an afterthought during the process of designing the first generation of large-scale computers. Consequently, the complexities of programming caught the pioneering inventors off guard. In programming the Mark I and Mark II computers, teams of specialists[8] had to reduce each problem to a series of mathematical steps. Each step was then represented in code, producing a line-by-line translation that was transferred onto paper tape and manually checked and rechecked for errors. Not until a 1953 paper by John Mauchly and Grace Hopper concerning programming's influence on future computer development did hardware design begin to take the exigencies of programming into account.[9]

The first three modern "programmers" were Robert Campbell, Robert Bloch, and Grace Hopper. As early as 1944 the Harvard trio began to search for ways to write and run code more efficiently. Under wartime pressure, they developed a systematic approach to coding that was relatively efficient and accurate. In particular, Hopper and Bloch experimented with the earliest instances of subroutines, branching techniques, code compression, and debugging procedures, and they applied their techniques to a diverse range of scientific and engineering problems. Furthermore, Hopper and Bloch established an information-processing organization that achieved remarkable rates of efficiency and accuracy while operating around the clock, seven days a week.

The programming techniques developed by Hopper, Campbell, and Bloch at Harvard did not come into their own until wedded with hardware advances made at the University of Pennsylvania. Electronic computing, as first demonstrated in the Electronic Numerical Integrator and Calculator (ENIAC), decoupled calculating speed from the realm of the physical. Whereas Howard Aiken's mechanical hardware could complete three calculations per second, the ENIAC could handle 5,000. For all of its marvelous internal speed, however, the ENIAC was not programmable in the present-day sense of the word.

It would take the dynamic mind of John von Neumann to imagine a technology that melded the benefits of Mark I's programming with the ENIAC's electronic circuitry. After spending the fall of 1944 in Cambridge working with Hopper and Bloch on the nuclear implosion problem for the Manhattan Project and the winter and spring in Pennsylvania brainstorming with J. Presper Eckert Jr. and John Mauchly on the next-generation ENIAC, von Neumann put pen to paper and captured an evolving revolutionary computer architecture. The "First Draft of a Report on EDVAC," dated 30 June 1945, outlined the structural design of a general-purpose stored-program computer and became the working blueprint for the next generation of computers, including the EDSAC and ACE machines in England and the UNIVAC and IAS machines in the United States.

Internal memory allowed long and complicated sequences of operations to be executed at electronic rather than mechanical speed. This stored-program architecture married the electronic speed of the ENIAC with the automatic sequence control and programming capability of Mark I. The subsequent "von Neumann architecture" was the theoretical underpinning of the computer revolution, yet Grace Hopper and the programming crew at Harvard have not previously been identified as important participants in the concept's creation. This does not mean that we should discount von Neumann's intellectual capacity to generate original ideas. Creative concepts, however, do not appear out of a vacuum, and during the fall of 1944 von Neumann had a distinctly broad perspective on the nascent computing field. He could identify the strengths and weaknesses of computer projects and could fashion a new technical variation with shared elements. "Von Neumann," Aiken recalled, "had this marvelous ability to absorb and make big jumps, and then he talked about things, talked about concepts without worrying about where they came from."[10] (Interestingly, von Neumann cites Aiken in the "First Draft" but does not cite either Eckert or Mauchly.)

After the war, Hopper permanently resigned from her position at Vassar College, joined the Naval Reserve, and remained with Aiken to establish the Harvard Computation Laboratory. Apart from being placed in charge of Mark I and writing that machine's manual of operation, Hopper emerged as Aiken's most trusted deputy. She engaged visiting scholars, businessmen, and military officials interested in developing their own computing capabilities, represented the Computation Laboratory during visits to other large-scale computing projects, and spoke for Aiken in his absence. She also helped to organize two landmark computer conferences at Harvard, one in 1947 and one in 1949. Remarkably, Hopper's rise to prominence at Harvard occurred at a time when many women were forced from public life under the pressure of postwar demobilization.

Hopper's most important contributions as an inventor, however, occurred not on Harvard's campus but rather in Philadelphia at the Eckert-Mauchly Computer Corporation from 1949 to 1960.[11] Though Hopper continued to be associated with EMCC until 1971, the years 1949–1960 are critical for a number of reasons. First and foremost, that period coincides with Hopper's seminal papers on programming and computer design.[12] Those papers describe a series of programming advances that permit humans to communicate with computers in terms other than ones and zeros.[13] Hopper's achievements established the field known during the 1950s as *automatic programming*, which influenced the direction of programming and software development from that point forward and which served as the foundation for future high-level computer languages. Second, the period marks the point when programming transitioned from ancillary work assigned primarily to women to the main "reverse salient"[14] impeding the further development of the computer industry. It made no difference how fast hardware could compute if programming efficiency did not improve at a similar rate. Moreover, most users were prevented from exploiting the machines' computational power by the lack of useful program applications and the cost and scarcity of a labor force skilled enough in advanced mathematics to create such applications. Hopper's inventions broke down the communication barrier between man and machine, "democratizing" the field of computer programming, which aided mass adaptation of the technology during the 1960s.

Though it is sometimes difficult to identify the motivation behind particular inventions, it appears that a dearth of talented programmers, a personal frustration with the monotony of existing programming techniques, and the lack of resources made available by senior management at Remington Rand to support computer clients led Hopper to invent the technologies and techniques, such as the compiler, that allowed the computers to, in effect, help program themselves. Interestingly enough, as her A-0 compiler evolved into the A-1 and the A-2, Hopper's reasoning in regard to the invention changed. Compilers became less about relieving programmers of the monotony of coding and more about reducing programming costs and processing time.

Hopper's dynamic representation of her invention is matched by an evolving approach to innovation, which I refer to as *distributed invention*. This term describes Hopper's unique style of program development, wherein prototypes were farmed out to an ever-widening circle of programmers and users. This growing network of invention crossed organizational boundaries and provided Hopper with a variety of feedback that she then incorporated into more advanced prototypes.

During the 1950s, Hopper established herself as a spokesperson for the evolving computer industry. As a tireless advocate for her inventions, Hopper provided a particular vision of the future, not only for those working in the computer industry, but also for potential users. Building a new technology is only half the battle; getting people to use it instead of an alternative is the other half. "In my view," said Jean Sammet in her welcoming remarks at the first ACM History of Programming Languages Conference in 1978, "Grace Hopper did more than any single individual to sell the concepts of the higher-level languages from both a technical and an administrative viewpoint."[15] That assertion was met with overwhelming applause.

PRIMARY SOURCES

Historians of computing are fortunate in that many of the early pioneers were fastidious in saving work documents, memos, notes, and letters. One can speculate that Grace Hopper and her peers had a sense of destiny. Or maybe they were detail-oriented people, on the verge of obsessive-compulsive. In either case, historians and posterity benefited. The starting point for researchers seeking primary source material is the Grace Murray Hopper Collection in the Archives Center of the Smithsonian Institution's National Museum of American History in Washington. Eight boxes contain technical notes and manuals, operating instructions, descriptions of projects, press clippings relating to computers, photographs, academic articles, and a "humor file." The material is indexed chronologically, and much of it is annotated in Hopper's own hand.

Harvard University and the Charles Babbage Institute at the University of Minnesota hold the papers of many pioneering figures of the computer industry. Harvard's Aiken Collection contains a wealth of personal correspondence, memos, reports, notes, studies, news clippings, and photographs. Associated with Howard Aiken's papers are the records of the Computation Laboratory for the period 1944–1961. The Charles Babbage Institute manages a vast collection of personal papers, most notably those of Walter Anderson, Isaac Auerbach, Edmund Berkeley, Margaret Fox, and Betty Holberton. The Charles Babbage Institute also holds the records of the 1978 History of Programming Languages Conference. That conference was organized by the

Special Interest Group in Programming Languages of the Association for Computing Machinery; the participants included a number of people who were involved in the development of COBOL, and Grace Hopper was the keynote speaker.

Other notable primary sources are housed in the Hagley Museum and Library in Wilmington, Delaware (the Sperry Rand records), the Library of Congress (the John von Neumann papers), the Van Pelt Library at the University of Pennsylvania (the John Mauchly papers), and the IBM Corporation Archives in Somers, New York.

Also located at the Archive Center of the Smithsonian's National Museum of American History in Washington is the Computer Oral History Collection,[16] a rich assortment of interviews with computer pioneers collected in 1972 under the sponsorship of the American Federation of Information Processing Societies and the Smithsonian Institution. The collection includes five restricted interviews with Grace Hopper and a rare tape of a Hopper lecture, which I was fortunate to acquire through the assistance of the Smithsonian archivist Alison Oswald. The oral history collection holds about 70 further interviews relevant to the project, including four with John Mauchly and one with Howard Aiken (used extensively by I. Bernard Cohen in the preparation of *Howard Aiken: Portrait of a Computer Pioneer,* MIT Press, 1999). Other interviewees include Richard Bloch and Robert Campbell (Hopper's fellow programmers on Mark I), Hopper's colleagues at the Harvard Computation Laboratory (Morris Rubinoff, Robert Burns, An Wang), Hopper's colleagues at the Eckert-Mauchly Computer Corporation (Jean Bartik, Betty Holberton, Isaac Auerbach), and a wide variety of computer pioneers who interacted with Hopper throughout her career (among them Irving Reed, Mina Rees, Herman Goldstine, and Robert Patrick).

The Computer Oral History Collection also contains transcripts of panel discussions held during a 1967 meeting of the Association for Computing Machinery titled "In the Beginning, Reminiscences of the Creators." Notable participants included Grace Hopper, John Mauchly, Herman Goldstine, Richard Bloch, Maurice Wilkes, Betty Holberton, and Isaac Auerbach. And the collection also contains transcripts from a 1972 computer forum held at the U.S. Military Academy, the keynote speakers at which were Grace Hopper and Herman Goldstine.

Other sources of oral histories are the Charles Babbage Institute (already mentioned) and the Schlesinger Library at the Radcliffe Institute for Advanced Study in Cambridge, Massachusetts. The Charles Babbage Institute is home to an extensive interview, conducted by Christopher Riche Evans in 1976, in which Hopper discusses her involvement with Aiken at the Harvard Computation Laboratory, the programming of Mark I, and her work with J. Presper Eckert Jr. and John Mauchly. Among the other interviewees are Eckert, Mauchly, Margaret Fox, Betty Holberton, William Norris, and Walter Anderson. In the Schlesinger Library (dedicated to the study the history of women in the United States), I located a very useful interview with Adele Mildred Koss, a programmer who worked with Hopper at the Eckert-Mauchly Computer Corporation. I also uncovered the video and transcript of Grace Hopper's interview with Morley Safer on the television program *60 Minutes* in 1983.

RECONSTRUCTING THE PAST: THE USE OF ORAL HISTORIES AND OTHER ARTIFACTS

Historians, like archeologists, are detectives, uncovering clues while attempting to reconstruct a probable past. The analogy holds especially true for historians of technology, for we have access to artifacts and objects sculpted by the minds and hands of our protagonists. A wonderful depiction of this special relationship between object and inventor is captured by a video interview with J. Presper Eckert Jr. that I uncovered. The interview was conducted in front of the ENIAC, the computer that the young Eckert patiently designed and constructed during the 1940s.

The ENIAC itself was an extension of its creator. The materials chosen for the machine reflect Eckert's understanding of cutting-edge concepts in electronics. Its organization and its flow echo Eckert's design philosophy. In the video interview, one can see the aging inventor being transported back through the decades, remembering in an instant why certain dials were placed in such arrays, why color codes were used, and how humans interacted with the ENIAC to produce calculations at the speed of light.

So, too, can we learn about Grace Hopper by studying her programs, manuals, operating instructions, professional publications, and flow charts. At the dawn of the computer age, Hopper's work laid the foundation for the programming profession. Principles of code preparation, logical program design, documentation, and testing flowed from her work on Mark I, Mark II, Mark III, and UNIVAC. Her training as a mathematician enabled her to communicate with and to master the new machines. The individuals who came to be known as programmers in the 1940s and the 1950s shared this crucial educational attribute with her, and the budding profession became an early "priesthood" of math wizards who held the key to the powerful new technology.

Paradoxically, Hopper's mathematical mind constantly rejected mathematics to a great extent. Hopper could speak the language of the machine as well as anyone, but she always found herself trying to move the early profession beyond mathematics. It wasn't enough to write programs that could be understood by only a few people. At Harvard, Hopper created documentation standards that explained each segment of code, and at EMCC she drew graphical representations that explained the mathematical logic behind her code and could be understood by the less mathematically gifted. Eventually, Hopper created a compiler that permitted humans to communicate with computers in non-mathematical terms. Much like Eckert's hardware designs, Hopper's programs mirrored what she held dear, which in her case was the overarching need to help others learn to communicate with these wondrous mechanical creations. In this respect, Hopper the "college professor" aligned with Hopper the inventor, for she never stopped teaching.

Among the richest sources of information about Hopper and her peers were the oral histories located at the Archive Center of the Smithsonian's National Museum of American History and the Charles Babbage Institute. Because of the foresight of a variety of historical and computing organizations, academics, and computer pioneers, I was fortunate enough to have access to interviews with Hopper and many of her colleagues spanning 50 years. Paradoxically, what I see as good fortune other academics sometimes criticize as "soft" evidence. They protest that oral histories are highly inaccurate, limited by the fragile nature of memory. Oftentimes the interviews were conducted well after the events transpired and were further corrupted by the agendas of the interviewer, the interviewee, or both. These scholars would prefer concrete evidence, such as time cards, company memorabilia, and office memos. Such evidence carries an aura of fact, because it was generated while events transpired and because it is not dependent on the limitations of memory.

Of course original documents from the period under study are essential when reconstructing past events, because they serve as a skeleton for the historical narrative. I argue that the rich volume of oral histories available in this instance helps to flesh out those structural bones. And that flesh is what makes this story so juicy, for we quickly realize that invention as a human endeavor is complex and messy. Logic and reason are the twin pillars of technology, but they do not in and of themselves explain the act of invention. Why humans create and why those creations happen at particular times and places are far more complicated then the cliché notion that invention is the mother of logical necessity.

The thousands of pages of oral history I reviewed in writing this book provide insight into the motivations behind people's actions. Childhood insecurities, ambition, jealousy, the need to please, stubbornness, and patriotism all drive the creative spark. We also get a real sense of the conditions under which Hopper and her peers worked. The strain and stress of wartime research and development at the Harvard Computation Laboratory is described in detail by Grace Hopper, Howard Aiken, Robert Campbell, Richard Bloch, and Edmund Berkeley in a way that time sheets and organization manuals cannot capture. The memories of John Mauchly, J. Presper Eckert Jr., Betty Holberton, Jean Bartik, and many others provide a window into the world of the first computer start-up company as it was half a century before Silicon Valley's "dot com" boom of the 1990s brought the culture of the "start-up" company to the attention of the popular press.

This does not mean that all oral histories are created equal. Part of the researcher's job is to develop a keen eye for identifying quality. Quality starts with the interviewer, and the computing community should feel fortunate that the majority of the oral histories held by the Smithsonian, the ACM, and the Charles Babbage Institute were conducted by professionals who understood both the techniques of interviewing and the technical subject at hand. For the most part they knew what questions to ask and in what order to ask them, and they had a good sense of when to give their interviewees enough line to run with a topic and when to reel them in.

The sheer volume of interviews available afforded me the ability to look at a given historical experience from a variety of different perspectives. Hopper's memories could be compared and contrasted with the memories of many others who were witness to the same events in question. Likewise, Hopper was interviewed many times over 40 years, and it became apparent that with time she became accustomed to telling a given story. But how Hopper "scripted" the past also provides insight into how she viewed the world and herself within that world. The depth and breadth of oral histories, combined with other primary and secondary sources, allows for the accurate plotting of the past, despite the fallibility of memory.

DISTRIBUTED BIOGRAPHY

For much of the twentieth century, biography was an accepted and widely utilized genre within the history of technology. Early texts praised the pioneers of various technologies, including Thomas Edison and the Wright brothers.[17] The ideal of the self-less individual inventor tinkering in a basement or a garage for the benefit of society resonated with both academics and lay readers. This hagiographic approach served to advance the virtue of individual achievement while legitimizing the value of technological change.

Books that highlighted specific technologies employed the biographical genre as well. Hugh Aitken's tribute to radio and Thomas Hughes's detailed account of the electrification of Western society anchor the narrative to a few individuals responsible for the technical achievement.[18] In fact, one could argue that the cornerstone of Hughes's influential systems methodology is not the system itself but rather its builder. The system builder is a sovereign individual who, through leadership, intuition, and technical prowess, superimposes order on the raw material of nature and the surrounding society. The system builder is *sovereign* in the sense that actions are willful and effect change. Hughes identifies Henry Ford, Elmer Sperry, Thomas Edison, and Samuel Insull as archetypal system builders.

With the growing influence of sociology, women's studies, and anthropology on historical literature during the 1980s, anthropocentric accounts of technology came under fierce attack. The focus of the history of technology shifted toward social and political structures that directed and determined the construction of technological knowledge. Wiebe Bijker, Trevor Pinch, Ruth Schwartz Cowan, and Donald MacKenzie established the social construction of technology as the field's dominant methodology. The result—a precipitous decline of biography as a compelling genre—was reflected by the majority of winners of the Dexter Prize and the Usher Prize in the 1990s.[19] For these authors, individual engineers and inventors had become reflections of larger social factors and institutional structures. Their choices were over-determined by and limited to the restricted

possibilities of action offered by the historical trends within a
given society.

A few academics on the frontiers of the history of technology,
including David Nye, Donald Reid, and Bruno Latour, went so
far as to question the very notion of human agency. In *The
Invented Self: An Antibiography, from Documents of Thomas A. Edison*,
Nye asserts that individuals are "divided selves who remain
essentially unknowable in their endless variations."[20] Nye concludes that it is futile for the historian to attempt to construct
a definitive person. The naive realist conception of personal
coherence is but a myth, for the agent is decentered and dispersed
by language. The best a historian can do, as in Reid's attempts
in *Paris Sewers and Sewermen*,[21] is emphasize the centrality of
rhetoric in communicating, interpreting, and representing
objects and people, and in uncovering the unsystematic incoher-
ence and flux of perceived reality. In the post-structuralist view
of technology, biography as an effective tool of historical study
is limited at best.

In view of the social constructivist and post-structuralist challenge, is there a place for biography in the history of technology?
Before we agree to condemn the multitude of historical biographies to the methodological ash heap, let us consider some of
the arguments.

In response to the post-structuralist challenge, self-inspection
suggests that certain physical and mental continuities can be
discerned apart from language. These continuities can be identified in others living around us, and also in those who came before
us. When I began to study Grace Hopper, there appeared to be
unlimited possibilities concerning what constituted her person.
But as Hopper the historical figure is examined further, options
are eliminated, patterns emerge, and identity surfaces. Granted,

the essence of Hopper changes over time, gaps in her personality exist, and contradictions abound, but in the end much of her identity and her uniqueness can be salvaged.

If we accept that people are unique entities who can be recovered by historians, the next step is to identify their place in relation to the greater currents of social history. Though I believe that social constructivism provides a better understanding of society's role in the development, dissemination, and implementation of technological knowledge, I suspect that this is only part of the story, for there is no society external to and separate from the individual. Every institution, every organization, and every government is an aggregate of unique individuals, each with his or her own "personal society" that is continuously refined and updated. Most importantly, when people become conscious of greater social trends, they have the capacity to press up against them, and, with time, even break through them. As Anthony Giddens writes in *Modernity and Self-Identity* (1991), "the self is not a passive entity, determined by external influences: in forging their self-identities, no matter how local their specific contexts of action, individuals contribute to and directly promote social influences that are global in their consequences and implications." I believe that Grace Hopper is such an individual, and that a biographical approach is the best methodological approach to her uniqueness and achieve greater understanding of the human condition. But I also have learned the lessons of the past 30 years, and I accept that Hopper is an individual embedded in an ever-changing historical landscape. Therefore, the narrative of this work has a distributed nature to it that attempts to highlight Hopper's achievements from 1945 to 1960[22] within the context of the people and events that surrounded her. Sometimes the computer pioneer is the centerpiece of a chapter or subchapter; at other times her role is tangential to the story line. In this sense the literary style of *distributed biography* mirrors and supports my notion of *distributed invention*.

In the end, the career of this influential college professor turned naval officer turned inventor turned business executive serves as the ideal conduit for exploring the rise of the computer industry and the invention of computer programming in what we refer to today as the information age.

"I can still remember December 7," said Grace Hopper, reflecting on that fateful day in 1941. "The two of us were up in our study. We had a great double desk and we each had a window and solid books all around but there was a little radio up in the shop and I can remember the announcement of Pearl Harbor."[1] Hopper and her husband Vincent sat in utter disbelief as trusted voices described the surprise aerial attack by the Japanese that killed 2,403 Americans, wounded 1,178, destroyed 188 aircraft, and sent a significant part of the Pacific Fleet to the bottom of the harbor.

How could this occur? What happened to our homeland defenses? Why couldn't we track the movements of the Japanese fleet? Didn't we have adequate intelligence to warn of an attack? What does this mean for the nation? What does this mean to us? These were the immediate questions that weighed heavily on Grace and Vincent Hopper as they stayed glued to their radio like so many Americans. With each passing hour more complete details of the attack were reported, and in the months to follow history unfolded at a dizzying pace.

On 8 December, the United States and Britain declared war on the Japanese Empire. Three days later, Germany declared war on the United States. The Third Reich had consolidated its hold on Western Europe and had moved its forces to within 19 miles of Moscow in the East. In January, Germany launched "Operation Drumbeat," a devastating submarine offensive against American shipping along the eastern coast of North America. In the Pacific, Japanese expansion spread to Hong Kong, Guam, Wake Island, Midway Island, and Singapore. In May 1942, U.S. forces surrendered the Philippine Islands.

On the home front, life transformed just as rapidly. In January the Emergency Price Control Act and Stabilization Act was passed, authorizing the president to control prices, wages, and public utility rates. The government initiated a system of rationing, which extended eventually to food and gasoline, while certain consumer goods, such as automobiles, were no longer produced. Finally, the War Powers Act granted the federal government draconian powers ranging from the control of the country's transportation systems and the unlimited acquisition and disposition of property to the forced purchase by Federal Reserve Banks of government obligations.

Indeed, the events in Hawaii that Sunday morning profoundly changed America. Moreover, 7 December would also be the chronological fulcrum from which Grace Hopper's own life would pivot. In the months that followed that fateful day, Grace Murray Hopper would leave her position as a tenured professor at Vassar College, divorce her husband, and join the U.S. Navy at the age of 36 years.

GRACE MURRAY HOPPER: MATHEMATICIAN AND TEACHER

Like many highly educated young American women during the 1930s,[2] Grace Brewster Murray came from a well-established

Anglo-Saxon family. Grace's mother was an accomplished mathematician, and her father, a life insurance executive, made no distinction when it came to educating his son and his two daughters. The Murray home at 316 West 95th Street in New York City, filled with books, provided an environment in which young Grace's academic ambitions were supported and encouraged.[3]

When Grace matriculated at Vassar College in 1924, it was customary for an affluent young American woman to complete her education, work a few years, then marry and start a family. Yet the thrill of academic achievement at Vassar led Grace to pursue a graduate degree in mathematics and physics at Yale University. By continuing her studies, Grace joined a growing minority of women who strove for more visible public positions.[4]

But even among this exceptional group of scholarly women, Grace stood out. First, she was one of only 396 Americans to be awarded doctorates in mathematics between 1930 and 1934, and the first woman to receive a mathematics degree from Yale. Second, whereas the vast majority of educated women found employment in elementary or secondary schools, Grace went on to become a college professor. Finally, many of the women who did secure college and university positions remained unmarried. Though the position of professor garnered respect, the broader society questioned a woman's ability to balance a career with family life.[5]

In June 1930, Grace married Vincent Hopper, a quiet, studious man who supported his wife's career ambitions. The two had first met in Wolfeboro, New Hampshire, where the Murray and Hopper families had summer homes. It has been suggested that Vincent had been dating Grace's sister.[6]

At the time of their marriage, Vincent Hopper was a doctoral candidate in comparative literature at Columbia and was teaching at New York University. Together, the two academics created a life that permitted each to grow personally and professionally. During the academic year, they occupied an apartment on the same city street on which Grace had grown up. Among their neighbors were Grace's brother and his wife, Grace's sister and her husband, and Grace's parents. Summers were spent in New Hampshire fixing up an old farmhouse the couple had bought with wedding money. When not working on the house, they were playing badminton and golf, or Grace was hooking rugs for the farm or knitting sweaters for friends.[7]

Supported by a loving family, Grace Murray Hopper completed her dissertation in 1934 and (as I have already noted) became the first woman to graduate from Yale with a doctorate in mathematics in the school's 233-year history. Upon graduation she accepted a full-time academic position at her undergraduate alma mater, Vassar.

BUILDING A CAREER: TEACHING AT VASSAR

In 1861, Matthew Vassar, a brewer and a businessman, established Vassar College in Poughkeepsie, 75 miles north of New York City. Vassar's vision at the time was to offer women a liberal arts education comparable to those offered by the best men's colleges of the day. As a former Vassar student and professor, Grace Hopper followed in the footsteps of many pioneering alumni, including Ellen Swallow Richards (the first woman to graduate from the Massachusetts Institute of Technology) and Maria Mitchell (the first woman to be elected to the American Academy of Arts and Sciences).

For a young professor beginning her academic career, Vassar offered a variety of advantages. The college provided a friendly environment with a significant proportion of female faculty. Furthermore, women occupied positions of authority within the administration. Though during the 1930s most women's colleges emphasized teaching above research, Hopper would have ample opportunity to build a career that fulfilled her academic ambitions.

Like all new professors, Hopper would spend her first years working her way up the seniority ladder. "[O]f course [I] started with all of the courses nobody else wanted to teach," she recalled.[8] In addition to basic trigonometry and calculus, she taught the entire technical drawing curriculum, which included mechanical and architectural drawing and a lab on shading and perspective.

Aware of the harsh economic climate outside of the Vassar campus, Hopper did not complain even when faced with a teaching load of five or six courses per semester. Instead, Hopper took what came to her and turned it to her advantage. "[The courses] had gotten into terrible doldrums," she recalled, "and I brought in new texts and new materials, and above all I brought in new applications. I began dumping in a little non-Euclidean [geometry] so they could begin to understand the new concepts of space. See, all of that was new then—all the Einstein stuff was brand new and exciting, and it was fun to try and bring it into the courses."[9]

Hopper's interdisciplinary approach to teaching sprang from her wide-ranging academic interests. Vassar faculty members were permitted to audit classes, and Hopper did not hesitate to do so. She attended classes in astronomy, physics, chemistry, geology, biology, zoology, economics, architecture, philosophy, and the history of scientific thought. Newfound knowledge quickly found its way into her courses. "[T]here was a continuing tendency throughout all those years of not just pure mathematics," she recalled. "They learned their pure mathematics all right, but also I kept bringing in applications of it and uses of it."[10]

Hopper's innovative pedagogical approach had a dramatic effect on both students and faculty members. Students from a variety of departments flocked to her classes. Classes that had traditionally drawn few students began to attract 75 or more. Hopper had succeeded in making the sometimes-esoteric field of mathematics relevant for a wide array of majors. The mathematician Winifred Asprey, a Vassar undergraduate in the 1930s who had shared many mathematics classes with Grace Hopper, remembered her as "the most inspirational [person] you can possibly imagine."[11]

Surprisingly, many faculty members were not pleased with Hopper's approach. She recalled: "The younger group—older than I was but younger still—they disapproved of practically everything I did because I wasn't doing the right things, and I was going off into things which were not mathematics."[12]

In order to push through her curriculum revisions, Hopper allied herself with senior members of the faculty, including the department chair and the dean. "The dean liked it because it was interdisciplinary, which was just beginning to be talked about," she recalled, ". . . and here was the math department which they had thought of as the most isolated of all beginning to draw people from the other departments and interrelate the work, so they liked that too." Even Hopper's former calculus professor from her days as a Vassar undergraduate, Gertrude Smith, approved of her unique approach: "She was probably the most old-fashioned of the lot . . . but she just viewed her child's adventures with delight so to speak. She wasn't quite sure it was orthodox, but it delighted her."[13]

Hopper's first nine years as a college professor formed a foundation that would serve her well in the years to come. Intellectually, she had broken down traditionally rigid disciplines and had mastered a wide range of academic subjects. All the while, she saw mathematics as the link across all disciplines, and she found practical ways for her students to experience those connections directly. Moreover, she learned to be an effective public speaker, and she was credited by both students and fellow teachers as a great communicator and motivator. Astute at navigating Vassar's bureaucracy, she became an agent of change in the face of institutional inertia.

By 1940, Professor Hopper had established herself as a respected member of the Vassar faculty. She had mastered the art of teaching, but part of her still yearned to move beyond the Poughkeepsie campus and rub shoulders with the elite in her field. That year she decided to apply for the Vassar faculty fellowship, which permitted recipients a one-year sabbatical in order to pursue research or coursework at another institution. Hopper chose to study with the celebrated mathematician Richard Courant at New York University.

Courant had been the director of the renowned Mathematics Institute at the University of Göttingen when Hitler had come to power. Because of his Jewish ancestry, the talented mathematician had been placed on leave in the spring of 1933, then temporarily reinstated in recognition of his distinguished service in the German Army during World War I. In the spring of

1934, with conditions deteriorating, Courant resigned. He left Germany and accepted a full professorship at NYU, where in 1936 he set out to build a department of applied mathematics in the Göttingen tradition.[14]

In the fall of 1941, Hopper began to work closely with Courant in the emerging field of partial differential equations. This particular type of equation was the mathematical foundation for an array of cutting-edge scientific and engineering disciplines, including aerodynamics (the study of gases in motion), hydrodynamics (liquids in motion), electrical engineering, and quantum mechanics. These techniques could be applied to, among other things, aircraft design, weather prediction, traffic flow, and the propagation of radio waves.

Hopper admired Courant's mathematical genius, and she gained from him the ability to glimpse at the obscured numerical tapestry underpinning the physical world. "He [was] just one of the most delightful people to study with I've ever known in my life," she recalled, "Of course, he scolded me at intervals . . . because I kept on doing unorthodox things and wanted to tackle unorthodox problems."[15] But after Japan attacked Pearl Harbor, the lighthearted mood of the NYU mathematics department changed. For the rest of her time there, Hopper's work was dedicated to somber problems concerning national defense.

IN SEARCH OF A NEW PATH

"I finished that year [with Courant], and then of course when we were in the thick of it, my brother and my husband and everyone wanted in," Hopper recalled.[16] Vincent Hopper left NYU and desperately tried to get an officer's commission. Because of his age and his poor eyesight, he was rejected. Grace's brother Roger, who had just completed a doctorate in economics, also had poor eyesight. Both men then put their promising academic and business careers on hold and enlisted. Both served the entire extent of the war in the Army Air Corps, Roger Murray eventually receiving a commission and rising to the rank of captain.[17]

By the summer of 1942, Grace Hopper's husband, her brother, her cousins, and many of her friends had joined the military. "Our whole family was in," she recalled. "Everybody except my sister, who had small children and wasn't acceptable."[18] Grace, too, aimed to do her part. In the summer of 1942, not wanting to go back to Vassar, she took a position at Barnard College, where she taught an improvised summer school course designed to prepare mathematicians for the war effort.[19] The unprecedented attack on American soil had awakened a deep patriotism in Grace and others, but traumatic events also affect individuals on a deeper level. Often they lead to introspection. For Grace, Pearl Harbor became the external catalyst that led to a series of changes in her personal life.

Though her tenured position at Vassar appeared ideal, deep down Grace wanted to escape a job that was secure and respected but no longer challenging. She wanted to break away from the mundane 75-mile commute to Poughkeepsie from New York City, and from the 35 summers she had spent with family members in New Hampshire. At last facing the fact that her marriage had failed, she decided to leave everything behind and join the Navy.

On 30 July 1942, President Roosevelt signed the Navy Women's Reserve Act, which authorized the formation of the WAVES (Women Accepted for Volunteer Emergency Service). WAVES were assigned to non-combat positions as aircraft mechanics, pilots, radio operators, medical personnel, and so on. Mildred McAfee, president of Wellesley College, was named the new organization's first director. By 1945 the WAVES numbered 8,000 officers and 76,000 enlisted personnel.[20]

Hopper returned to Vassar in the fall, but she had lost the desire to teach undergraduates. "I was beginning to feel pretty isolated sitting up there, the comfortable college professor," she recalled. "All I was doing was more teaching, and I wanted very badly to get in [to the Navy], so I finally gave Vassar an ultimatum that if they wouldn't release me I would stay out of work for 6 months because I was going into the Navy, period."[21]

The dissatisfied mathematician eventually arranged a leave of absence from her teaching position, but she quickly discovered that joining the Navy was not a simple matter. Aside from the fact that she was considered too old and too small for naval service, her chosen profession as a mathematics professor had been declared crucial to the war effort. Undeterred, Hopper obtained waivers for her weight and age. In December 1943, on the eve of her 37th birthday, she reported to the United States Naval Reserve Midshipmen's School in Northampton, Massachusetts.

Midshipmen's School, designed to transform civilians into future naval officers, was a harrowing experience for most young recruits. "When we first got there we had to pack up all of our civilian clothes and ship them home," Hopper recalled. "They wouldn't let us wear silk, so we had to wear those horrible [cotton] stockings."[22] Recruits were fitted for uniforms (cotton stockings and all), given haircuts, and separated from their family and friends. The first days were dedicated to learning proper military protocol: how to wear a uniform, how to carry oneself, how to address superiors and subordinates. Each recruit was expected to memorize a wide assortment of facts and figures, including the ranks and rates of officers and enlisted personnel and the names and capabilities of various ships and weapon systems.

The training environment was deliberately made stressful in order to fortify a recruit's resolve when faced with obstacles. Amenities were few, personal time limited, and opportunities for sleep and relaxation restricted. In the classroom, Hopper and her peers learned about naval history, navigation, tactics, naval organization, and the basic principles of leadership. Naval etiquette, from wearing the proper attire at functions to the correct way to write business letters, was also emphasized.[23] Despite all the rigors, Midshipman Grace Hopper remembered an unexpectedly pleasant experience:

When I got there I'd been teaching all these courses, doing all this outside work, running back and forth from New York to Poughkeepsie and teaching at Barnard and Vassar and umpteen other things trying to take courses, write stuff . . . and all of a sudden, I didn't have to decide anything, it was all settled. I didn't even have to bother to decide what I was going to wear in the morning; it was there. I just picked it up and put it on. So for me all of a sudden I was relieved of all minor decisions. All the minor stuff was gone. I didn't even have to figure out what I was going to cook for dinner. . . . It's all gone, and I just reveled in it. I had the most complete freedom I'd ever had. . . . I just promptly relaxed into it like a featherbed and gained weight and had a perfectly heavenly time.[24]

Midshipmen's School was so agreeable to Hopper, in fact, that she was named battalion commander, the highest-ranking position within the school. She graduated first in her class.

THE FIRST DAY OF THE REST OF HER LIFE

When Lieutenant (junior grade) Grace Hopper graduated from Midshipmen's School, in the summer of 1944, it became the responsibility of the Bureau of Naval Personnel in Washington to decide how best to utilize her talents. During peacetime, assignment decisions usually took into consideration the desires of the officer in question. But during wartime, the needs of the Navy usually superseded the needs and wants of the individual.

When Hopper entered officer training, she was under the impression that upon graduation she would be assigned to the Navy Communications Annex. The Communication Annex consisted of a covert cadre of mathematicians and logicians tasked with breaking enemy codes. Modern warfare's dependence on wireless communications for command and control augmented the status of these technical elites, for knowledge gleaned from intercepted enemy communications could influence a war's outcome as much as traditional determinants such as superior weaponry and manpower. It seemed logical that Hopper's mathematical expertise would best serve the war effort in such a capacity. Furthermore, the head of the Communication Annex, Captain Howard Engstrom, had been one of Hopper's mathematics professors at Yale. "I had talked to Engstrom, and so far as I knew it was set up that I would be assigned to the Communications Annex," she recalled. In fact, during the fall of 1943,

Grace Hopper on the day of her graduation from the Naval Reserve Midshipmen's School in Northampton, Massachusetts, 27 June 1944. Courtesy of Archives Center, National Museum of American History, Smithsonian Institution.

while Hopper was waiting for her age and weight waivers, she took a course in cryptographic analysis in preparation for working with Engstrom.[25] But while Hopper had been at Midshipmen's School, a one-of-a-kind calculating machine had been shipped to Harvard University from IBM's laboratory in Endicott, New York. The mysterious machine, placed under the auspices of the Navy's Bureau of Ships, was a computer, though it was not called that at the time. "Instead of being ordered to the Communications Annex, I was ordered to Harvard, and my orders were changed during the time I was at Midshipmen's School," Hopper stated.[26] Through no choice of her own, Lieutenant (j.g.) Grace Hopper was about to become the third programmer of the world's first computer.

The Automatic Sequence Controlled Calculator, as the machine was officially called, was the brainchild of Lieutenant Commander Howard Aiken.[27] Before the war, Aiken had been a physics graduate student at Harvard. While working on his dissertation, he had formulated plans for a distinctive mechanical arithmetic machine. The concept was supposedly born out of Aiken's aggravation as he struggled through the calculations that supported his doctoral thesis on the propagation of radio waves. The scope and complexity of the mathematics that describe Aiken's work weighed down upon the physicist, and even a small sampling would have taken him years to work out by hand. Aiken's practical disposition led him to consider the possibility of automating the calculating process, and in 1937 he began privately circulating a paper titled "Proposed Automatic Calculating Machine."[28] The paper describes in detail Aiken's vision of an automated arithmetic machine able to solve any problem that could be reduced to numerical analysis, including ordinary and non-linear differential equations.

The culmination of Aiken's seven-year search for relief from tedious calculations stood 8 feet high, 3 feet wide, and 51 feet long, weighed 9,445 pounds, and had 530 miles of wiring. The Automatic Sequence Controlled Calculator, officially donated to Harvard University by the IBM Corporation on 7 August 1944,[29] was capable of addition, subtraction, multiplication, and division. It was also hard-wired for logarithms, trigonometric functions, and exponentials, much like today's hand-held calculators. The massive machine's most noteworthy feature, however, was a paper-tape mechanism. The tape was pre-coded with step-by-step instructions that dictated the machine's operation and guided it toward a solution without the need for further human

The newly dedicated Automatic Sequence Controlled Calculator (referred to by the Harvard crew as Mark I), 1944. Courtesy of Archives Center, National Museum of American History, Smithsonian Institution.

intervention. Aiken's creation was one of the first examples of a programmable machine. Up to that time, machines had been passive tools used by humans to extend some human physical attribute, as a telescope or a typewriter does. Aiken endowed his machine with the ability to take autonomous action. Granted that a human had to specify the parameters of that action, the Automatic Sequence Controlled Calculator was intended to augment not the arm or the eye but the mind.

Mark I, as Aiken called the peculiar "land-based ship" he commanded,[30] was now charged with a much more serious task than helping Aiken to complete his doctoral dissertation. It was a new

The original crew in charge of Mark I, August 1944. From left to right, top: Seaman Bissell, Seaman Calvin, Seaman Verdonck; bottom: Ensign Bloch, Lieutenant Commander Arnold, Commander Aiken, Lieutenant (j.g.) Hopper, Ensign Campbell. Courtesy of Archives Center, National Museum of American History, Smithsonian Institution.

type of secret weapon that could change the outcome of the war. It was to be used to calculate solutions for rocket trajectories, proximity fuses, and mines, and to generate tables of mathematical functions that could be used to solve general engineering problems ranging from radio wave propagation to ship hull design. Staffing these efforts had become Aiken's main concern, and he had begun to seek out mathematicians who had joined the Navy. Lieutenant (j.g.) Grace Hopper seemed to fit the bill.

Hopper reported to Aiken's Harvard command in the basement of Harvard University's Cruft Physics Laboratory on 2 July 1944. If being escorted down to the basement by an armed guard wasn't disquieting enough, the presence of her physically intimidating boss was. "I was a little bewildered and at that point of course thoroughly scared," Hopper recalled. Years later, she distinctly remembered the first words uttered to her by Aiken: "Where have you been?" Aiken had expected Hopper months earlier and had not seen the point of sending a female mathematician to Midshipmen's School.[31]

Aiken proceeded to give his new recruit a tour of the Automatic Sequenced Controlled Calculator. Hopper arrived before IBM had installed the smooth steel casing, so the machine's thousands of moving parts were fully exposed. "All I could do was look at it. I couldn't think of anything to say at that point," she remembered. At the end of the tour, Aiken ordered his new assistant to put off finding a place to live for another day and to get to work immediately. Her first task was to compute the interpolation coefficients for the arctangent to an accuracy of 23 decimal places within a week.[32]

Hopper's frosty reception was an early indication of the antagonistic environment she had just entered. Howard Aiken was disappointed that the Navy had assigned him a female officer to be second in command, an opinion that he openly shared with the rest of the men on his staff. "Well, there was Aiken and then there was the boys," recalled Robert Campbell, one of the two ensigns who arrived at the Computation Laboratory before Hopper.[33] Richard Bloch, the other ensign, also shared Aiken's misgivings. "I later found out that they [Campbell and Bloch] had been . . . trying to bribe each other as to which one would have the desk next to me," Hopper recalled.[34]

Gender tensions aside, Hopper was faced with a technical obstacle of imposing proportions. Aiken had given her a week to solve a fairly straightforward math problem. Arctangents (the inverse of a tangent function) were covered in most high school geometry curricula and were child's play for a former college mathematics professor. The issue was not the problem's complexity, but its scope. Solving for a huge array of numbers to 23 decimal places was humanly impossible within the time frame Aiken had provided. To assist her, Hopper had to rely on a machine the likes of which she had never encountered. She could not turn to previous experience. She could not review work done on other calculating machines, since Mark I was unique.[35] There was no manual of operation, and no customer support. In fact, Hopper did not even know how to refer to her new occupation; the term "programmer" would not enter the language until years later.[36]

"Well, they gave me a code book and told me to do it," Hopper recalled.[37] The "code book" was a crudely tabulated notebook containing instructional codes for the machine. To the untrained eye, the notebook was nothing more than a list of unintelligible numbers. Robert Campbell had quickly thrown it together in the spring of 1944 while running test problems on Mark I after it was brought from IBM's laboratory in Endicott to Harvard.

Not only was Campbell Mark I's first programmer; during 1943 and the first half of 1944 he also served as manager of the project. Aiken had been called up to active duty and assigned to the Naval Mine Warfare School in Yorktown, Virginia. Aiken had chosen the clever young physicist from a list of Harvard graduate students, and during his absence Campbell oversaw the completion of the machine, kept Aiken informed, and served as the bridge between Harvard and IBM. Upon Aiken's return, in May 1944, Campbell was commissioned an ensign in the Naval Reserve and became a full-time member of Aiken's staff.[38]

The techniques Campbell had compiled in the "code book" had been gleaned during the programming of the initial three problems. The first problem (referred to simply as Problem A[39]) involved solving trigonometric functions in connection with antenna design for Professor Ronald King of Harvard's Physics Department.[40] Problem B, requested by the astronomer and telescope lens designer James Baker, concerned refraction angles for rays passing through a multi-component optical system. Problem C, requested by the Navy Bureau of Ships, concerned the effects of small impurities on the physical characteristics of steel. Problem C, in particular, demonstrated to Campbell the true power and potential of the machine, as ten equations were solved simultaneously.[41]

Hopper quickly recognized that to succeed in communicating with Mark I she would have to rely on the experience that Bob Campbell and Richard Bloch had acquired. "Whenever I got in trouble, I would yell at Bloch and Campbell and [they] would tell me how to get out of it," Hopper remembered.[42] Bloch also recalled those early days tutoring the "professor": "I remember sitting down . . . long into the night, going over how this machine worked, how to program this thing, and so on. As I like to remind her, she didn't know a computer from a tomato basket at the time."[43] In fact, as of July 1944 the 23-year-old Bloch knew little more than his pupil; he had acquired only 3 months of coding experience before Hopper's arrival.

What Bloch lacked in experience he made up for in drive and determination. A consummate overachiever, he had majored in mathematics, minored in physics, and played in the Harvard band, and in 1941 he had won the Dexter Award for the top-ranking freshman. Bloch envisioned becoming a college professor, but (as happened for so many young men of his generation) the repercussions of Pearl Harbor translated into an unintended career choice. Upon graduation, he reported for midshipman training at the University of Notre Dame in Indiana, and in September 1943 he was stationed at the Naval Research Laboratory in Washington. "We all wanted to do our thing, and my idea was to get on the biggest ship possible, so I applied for duty as a navigator on a battleship," he recalled.[44] Upon review, the Bureau of Naval Personnel concluded that Bloch's mathematical aptitude would best serve the war effort if applied to analytic and computational work associated with antenna design in the Naval Research Laboratory's Radio Division.

It was at the NRL, in January 1944, that Bloch first met Commander Howard Aiken, whom he had been assigned to escort on a tour of the facilities. "When he heard of my background at Harvard, he asked me would I like to get involved," Bloch recalled. "He told me about this fabulous machine that he had designed and asked if I would like to spend my Naval duty up at Harvard. Of course it sounded intriguing to me, so I jumped at it."[45] At the time Bloch hadn't a clue what Aiken was actually talking about, but on a leap of faith the ensign reported for duty in March 1944. When Bloch arrived at Harvard,

Mark I had recently arrived from Endicott. What Ensign Bloch saw on his first day at Harvard was much more spectacular than he had expected.[46]

So Mark I—the most complex, unique computing machine ever created—was placed in the care of a 37-year-old newly minted naval officer and her 23-year-old sidekick. Howard Aiken and the engineers at IBM had turned a Harvard graduate student's idea for an automated computing machine into a physical reality. It was now up to Grace Hopper and Richard Bloch to communicate with the hulking machine and make it do their bidding. Little did the two know at the time that their work over the next year not only would strongly assist the war effort but also would demonstrate to America's military, academic, and business elites the viability of large-scale automated computing machines, otherwise known as computers.

How does one go about programming the world's first operational computer? With mentors of limited knowledge and experience, Lieutenant Hopper was faced with the daunting task of making the Harvard Mark I's 750,000 parts move with purpose and generate accurate solutions. These solutions, far from academic curiosities, were answers to problems with immediate military applications. In the face of unusual wartime pressures, Hopper relied on her ability to stay calm and rationally think through problems.

The neophyte coder realized that she needed to understand the hardware of Mark I in all its intricate detail if she hoped to have the machine calculate according to her will. This meant quickly educating herself in electronics, despite her limited engineering background. During her first 2 months at Harvard, Hopper spent nights combing through the machine's basic blueprints and circuit diagrams. If she could not understand the purpose of a certain switch or relay, she tracked down Bob Hawkins, an electrical and mechanical maintenance engineer who quickly became known to the early Mark I crew as "Mr. Fixit."

Hopper's resolute effort to understand the machine's hardware provides insight into an aspect of her innovative style.[1] The former college professor was not one to back down from an intellectual challenge, even when the subject matter lay outside her realm of expertise. Nine years at Vassar auditing assorted classes and teaching non-math courses had given her confidence that she could learn just about anything. The new knowledge, when mixed with what she already understood, made Hopper a potent problem solver. To be a better programmer, she first needed to comprehend the peculiar physical nature of Aiken's creation. Hopper's diligence would pay dividends in avoiding coding pitfalls in the coming months and years.

Lieutenant (j.g.) Hopper and Seaman White inspecting Mark I's hardware, 1944. Courtesy of Archives Center, National Museum of American History, Smithsonian Institution.

During her impromptu education in hardware design, Hopper was astonished by the machine's sheer complexity and size. Mark I contained more than 3,500 electromechanical relays, 2,300 storage counters, and thousands of back-wired relay terminals. The myriad of parts was orchestrated by a unique 3-inch-wide punch tape that sequentially entered coded instructions into the machine. Unlike IBM calculating machines based on punch-card technology, the continuously fed coded patterns could, in theory, execute a problem from start to finish without the intervention of an operator. The instructions on the punch tape were "fixed" in the sense that there was no way to modify the sequence of instructions that the machine was to obey without direct human intervention. This innovation was captured in Mark I's official name: Automatic Sequence Controlled Calculator.[2]

Each sequence of coding on the punch tape was broken down into three sections of eight round holes no more than 1/16 inch in diameter. The first section instructed the machine where to find its data; the second indicated where to place the results; the third dictated the process to be applied. The holes were punched according to an eight-bit code that spatially correlated to the numbers 1 through 8 (the number 9 represented a "minus" sign). For example, the code "753" was represented by holes in the 7, 5, and 3 places on the tape. Automatic codes directed the machine to perform specific operations, such as punching output into punch cards and printing on a typewriter. Automatic codes were contained in a codebook or were memorized by the crew.

Though far more complex, Mark I's coded tapes worked in a similar fashion to a variety of other automated devices that appeared with increased regularity during the nineteenth century and the first half of the twentieth.[3] Player pianos, glockenspiels, and semi-automated textile looms all followed the principle of sequenced information embedded in a control mechanism that manipulated the outcome. These machines were hardware specific, however; for example, a player piano could play a fugue or a sonata on the basis of data entered, but it could do no more. What made Mark I unique was that both data and operations could be changed, thus allowing the machine to "simulate" the trajectory of a rocket, the movement of a ship, or even the notes played by a piano. Mark I was the first general computer in the sense that it could become whatever the operator wanted it to become.

But Mark I's flexibility was limited by its processing speed. The cycle time for the thousands of parts was determined by a central driveshaft that spun at 200 rpm. The shaft's rotation translated into a basic computational speed of 300 milliseconds. That is, the main shaft completed a revolution every 3/10 second. The shaft drove the complete skeleton of gears, which manipulated the counter wheels. Therefore, the actual insertion of information, or the addition or subtraction of two digits, was a *mechanical process* done by the rotation of the counter wheels. Multiplication and division, on the other hand, were computed in a separate multiplication section of the machine.[4]

The cycle time of 300 milliseconds corresponded to the execution of one line of coding. This also equaled one addition operation or one subtraction operation. (The laptop computer used to write this book has the capacity to make 1 billion additions per second, and can process information 333 million times as fast as Mark I.) More complex mathematical processes were even slower. A single multiplication could take just under 10 seconds to complete; a single division took nearly 16 seconds. For logarithms, Mark I's main shaft had to spin 298 times, thus taking 90 seconds for this one operation.[5]

By modern computing standards, Mark I's memory capacity was also severely limited. Mark I had 72 storage registers, each capable of holding a 23-digit decimal number and its algebraic sign. Just as an automobile's odometer stores mileage information on numbered wheels connected by a system of toothed gears, Mark I used a system of gears, but with ten stable positions to represent numerical information. The storage registers allowed the machine to maintain intermediate results internally and proceed with further calculations. The machine could also call upon other inputs via switches, data tapes, and punch cards. Output was captured on punch cards or with automated type-writers. Ultimately, the entire 81 feet of gears, switches, wheels, rods, shafts, wires, and tapes was attempting to mimic a human "computer" equipped with a pencil and a pad of paper.[6]

TAMING THE MECHANICAL BEAST

After a month or two working with Aiken's "Automatic Sequence Controlled Calculator," it was apparent to both Hopper and Bloch that the machine was anything but automatic. Automation of Mark I did not occur without a great deal of planning and coding. Bloch thought the process was analogous to a supervisor "calling off the shots—calling the sequence of operations to take place."[7] For example, in any given run, Hopper had to define output accuracy to the decimal (e.g., tenth, hundredth, thousandth). This was accomplished by means of an associated plug wire array that had to be re-plugged from problem to problem. In fact, every machine function had an associated plug wire array, and plug instructions had to be specified accurately for every run of the machine. An error in plugging instructions would cause a given run to abort, and, as Hopper discovered through experience, an inadvertent crossing of wires would have disastrous results.[8]

In an attempt to reduce the time needed to code the machine, Mark I contained built-in mathematical functions. These included multiplication, division, and three functions that are commonly seen on hand-held calculators today: logarithms, the sine function, and scientific notation (10^x). In fact, these functions were responsible for a considerable fraction of the machine's relays, and Aiken had expended a great deal of energy designing them. For all his efforts, Hopper concluded that it was best to code for these manually. The hard-wired functions required approximately 200 machine cycles, or about a minute, to produce a result accurate to 23 places; manual coding required a fraction of that time. Most of the time saving was attributable to the flexibility of manual coding. If, for a given problem, variable x represented the angle of roll of a ship, common sense dictated that the problem only needed to be solved for a limited range of values. Harvard's mechanical brain was not savvy enough to differentiate between capsized ships and ones that floated.

Hopper discovered other odd hardware peculiarities that further limited the machine's automated nature. A nine in the 24th column of the register represented a negative quantity. Because of the end-around carry circuit, each register enabled a carry from the 24th column to the first column. This meant that whenever a problem resulted in a carry, nines had to be supplied to the left of the most significant digit in the shifted result if the quantity were negative, or else a huge negative number would result. If all nines were in the storage register, a negative zero would result. If all zeros where in the register, a positive zero would result. Keeping track of negative zeros, positive zeros, and nines became a task in and of itself, yet was critical in order to bring a problem to a successful conclusion. In the end, the coding practices developed by Hopper and Bloch during the war would have to be adapted to the machine's bizarre hardware design.

Hopper's immediate interest in the hardware of Mark I highlights the fact that hardware and software were not clearly demarcated at the genesis of modern computing. This blurring of hardware and software was far more apparent in the other major American wartime computer, the ENIAC (Electronic Numerical Integrator and Computer),[9] a fully electronic calculating machine developed by John Mauchly and J. Presper Eckert Jr. at the University of Pennsylvania with financial support from the US Army. Instead of electromechanical relays, Eckert and Mauchly employed 18,000 vacuum tubes as computing switches, thus allowing speeds of up to 5,000 computations per minute. Since the electronic speeds were far greater than the speeds at which instructions and data could be fed into the machine via tape, the ENIAC had to be physically reconfigured to represent the problem to be solved. That is, its hardware was re-wired in order to solve ballistics problems for which it was specifically designed. Hence, there was no coding, just hardware manipulation.[10]

"The system design of the ENIAC," Robert Campbell correctly points out, "derived more from analog techniques than it did from anything else. It was sort of a translation into digital terms of the analog type of system design."[11] In other words, the "programming" of the machine was primarily the way one interconnected the physical units of the machine. In this sense the ENIAC was much like Vannevar Bush's differential analyzer, a sophisticated mechanical computing device that the renowned MIT engineer invented during the 1930s. The design similarity was no accident: the University of Pennsylvania had a differential analyzer, and both Eckert and Mauchly had been trained on it.

Hopper's firsthand experience with the ENIAC in 1945 during a visit to Philadelphia reiterates this point:

When I visited ENIAC, the tremendous contrast between Harvard and the activities of Eckert and Mauchly was the programming. You see ENIAC was—you plugged the pieces and essentially you built a special computer for each job, and we were used to the concept of programming and controlling it by our program; there was a very sharp contrast between the automatically sequenced and the plugboard system of ENIAC.[12]

To assist in the time-consuming task of reconfiguring ENIAC hardware for each problem, Eckert and Mauchly hired six women from the U.S. Army's Ballistic Research Laboratory. The BRL employed about 200 "computers," the majority of them recent female college graduates from the Philadelphia and Baltimore area, to calculate firing tables for artillery. Much like Campbell, Hopper, and Bloch at Harvard, the women of ENIAC soon realized that the only way to accurately program the machine was to be intensely familiar with its hardware and circuit design. The pioneers of software, were, essentially, hardware experts.

THE WORLD'S FIRST DATA-PROCESSING CENTER

Six days after Lieutenant (j.g.) Grace Hopper was introduced to the Harvard Mark I, Allied troops stormed the beaches of Normandy. This daring landing, involving more than 5,000 ships, 11,000 planes, and 160,000 troops, attacked a 50-mile stretch of heavily defended French coastline. History has certified the D-Day invasion as the beginning of the end of Hitler's grip on the European continent, but for Hopper and the staff at the Computation Laboratory the outcome of Operation Overlord was still in the balance through the early summer of 1944. Moreover, the outcome in the Pacific was undetermined, as the Japanese continued their offensive through the spring of 1944 in China and New Guinea.

World War II created a surplus of practical computational problems that required rapid and accurate solution. Hopper remembered the difficulty of meeting computational demand with the limited laboratory staff, and the anxiety it created for the small team of programmers: "On the Mark I there was Dick Bloch and Bob Campbell and myself. We later acquired two more lieutenant commanders who worked on it. But by and large the three of us did the bulk of the programming."[13] In fact, by the winter of 1944 coding responsibilities almost exclusively fell upon the shoulders of Hopper and Bloch. Campbell spent the majority of his time developing the blueprints for a new computation machine, Mark II. In a desperate attempt to address the ever-growing demand, Hopper and Bloch developed a systematic approach to coding and batch processing that was efficient, accurate, and relevant for future generations of programmers. The wartime demands on the Harvard Computation Laboratory had inadvertently become the engine for programming innovation.

In typical fashion, Hopper later downplayed the complexities associated with mastering the machine: "You simply step by step told the computer exactly what to do. Now get this number and add it to that number and put the answer there. Now pick up this number and multiply it by that number and put it there. You simply broke down all of your processes of mathematics into a series of very small steps of add, multiply, divide, and make a test, and put them in sequence."[14] Theoretically the concept was not difficult to grasp, but the realities of coding were much more

Commander Aiken, Lieutenant (j.g.) Hopper, and Ensign Campbell standing before Mark I, 4 August 1944. Hopper is holding a sequence-control tape. Courtesy of Harvard University Archives.

complicated, and the organizational demands substantial. The time sensitivity of the wartime problems only added to the inherent pressures associated with creating technical innovation.

INVENTING A SYSTEM OF CODING

DEFINING THE PROBLEM
Hopper and Bloch often found that the problem's originator could describe the desired results but was at a loss concerning the particular equations that needed to be solved. Conversely, Bloch and Hopper knew little about the context from which

problems came. "We had to learn their vocabularies in order to be able to run their problems," Hopper recalled. "I learned languages of oceanography, of this whole business of mines-weeping, of detonators, of proximity fuses, of biomedical stuff. We had to talk to these people—all we had to begin with was mathematics."[15]

Indeed, Hopper's mathematical background prepared her to break down verbal problems into elementary mathematical parts. She could even handle the complicated partial differential equations associated with heat and fluid flow problems, thanks to her training under the mathematician Richard Courant.[16] If she got stuck, Aiken would often help to define a method of solution. "Aiken," the programmer Harry Goheen recalled, "was a genius at figuring out dirty methods."[17]

Hopper and Bloch soon realized that pre-determining parameters for solution accuracy saved coding time and made results more relevant. "On the first early problems, when we were computing how much accuracy we were having, it was an appallingly rough computation," Hopper recalled. "We didn't know much about it yet."[18] Mark I was accurate to 23 decimal places.[19] This was necessary when partial differential equations were involved. But more often then not, such extreme accuracy was superfluous. For instance, most ballistic problems required solutions to no more than four decimal places.

Hopper and Bloch also had to consider the effects of round-off errors. Luckily, Hopper's diverse educational background and her 8 years as a professor had prepared her to deal with a wide range of intellectual challenges. "I was unusual because most mathematicians didn't know anything about round-off errors and truncation errors and the reason I did was because I had taken a course on chemistry," she recalled. "That is where I had learned about round-off errors and computational errors, not in mathematics."[20]

CONSTRUCTING A CODING BLUEPRINT

Once the equations were identified, the blueprint of the finalized code had to be planned. This included the mapping of instruction and data tapes and the positioning of decimal places. As previously mentioned, decimal places were controlled by precise plugboard configurations. The limits of storage, physically embodied by the 72 23-decimal registers, severely affected the planning of instruction and data tapes. The result was the necessary segmentation of problems. Intermediate results had to be captured on punch cards and then reentered into the machine as input for the next sequence. Each series of inputs and outputs required the orchestration of multiple instruction tapes and continuous human intervention.

At first Hopper and Bloch ran their own problems. "I got to the point where I knew that machine like the back of my hand," Bloch enthusiastically recalled, "whether it was a plugging or electrical question, or questions of circuitry, debugging, or programming."[21] But the time spent running problems meant time away from defining and coding other problems. Operating Mark I quickly became the responsibility of enlisted Navy personnel,[22] as the Harvard team turned to division of labor as a means of maximizing the machine's output.

The personnel assignments made at Harvard during the war set important precedents for future labor divisions within the general computing industry. "Coding" (later to be called "programming") became the work of highly skilled mathematicians like Hopper and Bloch. Rudimentary tasks such as tape punching and plugboard manipulation were allocated to less skilled operators. The difference in status between coders and operators at Harvard was formally captured by military rank: coders were officers, while operators were enlisted personnel.[23]

CREATING OPERATING INSTRUCTIONS

Hopper and Bloch codified the roles and responsibilities of the new "operator" position.[24] Operators managed the computation process from start to finish. They were aided by directives known as "operating instructions" that were written by Hopper and Bloch. The operating instructions, much like the main instruction tape for the machine, described the sequential steps to be performed by the operator. Plugging charts were drawn for all plugboards. For instance, the plugboard for the printer controlled the printing machine's decimal columns. This set tab positions, vertical spaces, and horizontal spaces, and it eliminated non-significant zeros. Other plugboards controlled input card feeds, output card punches, and multiplying and dividing units. In addition, for each run a series of switches had to be set. Data switches introduced constants into the problem, while control switches controlled various machine units.

Not only did operators have to manually set initial register, switch, and plugboard settings; these settings had to be changed after a certain number of runs. Each run required the proper manual sequencing of instruction and input tapes. Certain actions were required if an output variable reached a particular threshold value. The active involvement of operators discounted the claim that Mark I was a fully automatic calculation machine, as its official name suggested. There is no doubt that Aiken had the concept of automation as a guiding principle, but in reality the limitations inherent in the machine's hardware required human intervention. This human–machine symbiosis produced the final results.

The imposed division of labor permitted Mark I to operate 24 hours a day, 7 days a week. As in naval shipboard organization, operators "stood watch" for three eight-hour shifts, including midnight to 0800. Hopper and Bloch managed the watch schedule, made sure personnel were properly trained, and stepped in to deal with problems beyond the expertise of the operators. Most calls in the middle of the night dealt with troubleshooting, which effectively placed Hopper and Bloch on call 24 hours a day. The operator Robert Burns remembered in particular Bloch's tendency to fall asleep on the other end of the phone at 2 or 3 a.m. "You'd whistle, scream, you couldn't wake him up," Burns recalled.[25]

A sequence-control tape for Mark I, 1945. Courtesy of Harvard University Archives.

CODING SEQUENCE CONTROL AND DATA TAPES

Transferring code from code sheets to tapes was the most arduous part of the coding process. Hopper made the process less monotonous by assigning small teams to punch each tape. During problem L, in December 1944, Hopper assigned sequence tapes to Livingston and Verdonck and value tapes to Knowlton, Brendel, Bissel, and White. New teams were then created for quality assurance purposes. Knowlton, Brendel, and Calvin were responsible for the accuracy of the sequence tapes, and Hawkins, Bissel, and Calvin checked value tapes. The entire process, as written by Hopper in the operating instructions, was "computed, designed, coded, babied, nursed, pleaded with, and mothered by Lt. (j.g.) Grace Murray Hopper, USNR."[26]

TESTING

With the control and data tapes produced and the operator instructions written, the moment of truth arrived. The initial run of the problem was known as a "test." Regardless of the care and accuracy that went into coding preparation up to this point, the cool logic of the crew gave way to blind faith. To lighten the tense "moment of truth," operator Robert Burns recalled, after a tape was prepared and placed on the machine, the crew brought out an Islamic prayer rug, faced east, and prayed that their work was not in vain.

The "test" began with a "starting tape" that, with a single pass, enabled initial values to be fed into the 72 storage registers before the problem was run.[27] Operators set and checked preliminary plugboard and switch settings, and the main sequence control tape and data tapes were loaded onto the feed mechanisms of the machine. When the Start button was pressed, the driveshaft turned, the relays clattered, and Mark I came to life.

On test runs, the melodious sounds of the machine usually lasted no longer than 30 seconds before clattering to a stop. First-time successes were elusive. Instead, operators obtained complete readouts of all pertinent storage positions, which were then analyzed by Hopper and Bloch for clues. The detective work uncovered why the machine had stopped, and the process was repeated until the problem ran to completion and results were obtained.

PACKAGING THE OUTPUT

Two electric typewriters captured Mark I's output. During the fall of 1944, answers streamed forth from the machine in a chaotic mass of numbers. "We hadn't fully learned how to control the typewriter that would print an amount across a page and in blocks," Hopper recalled. "There was so much of the techniques of handling the typewriter that had to be invented and all of the dress-up we had to learn how to do."[28]

Hopper was the first to realize that Mark I could format the presentation of results by typewriter, an minor insight at the time but one that would have considerable implications. If a computer could be used to control a typewriter, it could be used to control just about any mechanical process. One of Hopper's initial experiments was to generate page numbers for a table of mathematical functions that the machine was producing. "At lunchtime, when Aiken was out of the office, I put a routine on which did nothing but add one and print the number and space, and made it print out just a sequence of numbers," she recalled. "But he [Aiken] came in and found us with all $750,000 worth of Mark I adding one and printing digits—waste of computer time—oh, he went through the ceiling."[29] Eventually, Hopper convinced Aiken that it was much faster to enlist the Mark I to create page numbers and format text than sitting down at the typewriter and manually recreating the presentation of the information. Moreover, removing the human from the output process would help preserve accuracy.

The system of coding developed by Hopper and Bloch under wartime pressure quickly and accurately defined a given problem, distilled it into mathematics that could be represented by machine code, created operating instructions to sequence an array of plugboards and switches, produced sequence control and data tapes, provided quality assurance for those tapes, tested the problem, and packaged the output. The system was embedded in a differentiated organizational structure that borrowed from shipboard and factory operations and took advantage of the efficiencies derived from the division of labor. The end result was a data-processing center that generated accurate solutions 24 hours a day, seven days a week. It is the earliest example of the type of data-processing centers that dominated the computer industry up until the 1960s and before the invention and implementation of time sharing.[30]

THE FIRST HACKERS

Within 6 months of her arrival, Lieutenant (j.g.) Grace Hopper transformed herself from a computing neophyte to an emerging expert in the field. The system of coding she developed and implemented with Richard Bloch successfully met the ever-growing demand generated by the necessities of modern warfare. The wartime setting demanded the Harvard team to work at a pace rarely experienced during peacetime. By the winter of 1945 Mark I was up and running 95 percent of the time, which was astonishing in view of the operational problems that plagued the ENIAC project at the University of Pennsylvania during roughly the same period.[31]

Regardless of these advances in reliability, Mark I's hardware imposed theoretical limits on speed. The rotation of the main driveshaft set the processing speed at 300 milliseconds. The rate of data and instruction input was limited to the mechanical speed of the feed mechanisms, and information had to be entered sequentially—that is, tapes could not reverse themselves in order to input a previous command or number.

Out of sheer necessity, Hopper and Bloch began to create innovative coding techniques to augment hardware performance. "As early as 1944 we started putting together things which would make it easier to write more accurate programs and get them written faster," Hopper recalled.[32] And like so many of her computing advances throughout her career, "educated" trial and error translated into innovation. "There was no theorizing, there was no higher mathematics," Hopper remarked. "There was no future of computers, there was nothing but get those problems going."[33] War had indeed become the mother of invention.

With their knowledge of hardware, Hopper and Bloch realized that a little bit of programming ingenuity could maximize the machine's processing power in the minimal number of driveshaft rotations. For instance, for an operation requiring 25 cycles, only five actually produced activity in the main bus of the machine. Hopper and Bloch began to embed additional operations within instructions, making certain that the embedded codes did not adversely affect the primary operation in progress. For instance, printing commands could be implanted within a multiplication operation. Soon it became standard practice to write programs that maximized the number of embedded instructions. As a result, processing time decreased by as much as 36 percent. Because of the relatively slow processing speed of Mark I, 36 percent could easily translate into weeks of saved run time.

This earliest form of "hacking,"[34] which produced some ingeniously efficient code, had detrimental consequences as well. For instance, the logical flow of programs embedded with extra code became extremely complicated. The flow was so complex, in fact, that often it was impossible for the operator to decipher what was happening. Hopper admitted that she was even at a loss in her attempts to deal with Bloch's hacking. "Dick used to change the instructions on the Mark I overnight," she recalled. "If he thought up a nice instruction to make one of his problems easier, he'd put it in and none of our tapes would run the next morning."[35]

Complex code also made it difficult to analyze the causes of machine stoppages. Both Hopper and Bloch had difficulty deciphering their own handiwork, especially if enough time had passed between writing the code and executing it. To address the problem, Hopper developed a system of documentation within her code. On the master code sheet that was used to punch the tape, she wrote notes and equations that corresponded to each line of code. Bloch and others soon picked up this practice as the Harvard team expanded, and program documentation eventually became standard practice for coders and programmers.

Other techniques for speeding up processing time were not as refined. Hopper had a particularly interesting way to deal with "rounding off" to fewer than 23 decimal places. Instead of coding for the limited accuracy, Hopper applied her knowledge of hardware to create the desired round-off effect by reconfiguring the machine: "I pulled the relays. I pulled the lower twelve position relays in the unit."[36] This practice served her well until one night she forgot to reconnect the machine. The operators on the next shift, perplexed by Mark I's misbehavior, called in Howard Aiken to diagnose the problem. An irate Aiken forbade

Hopper or anyone else from reconfiguring the hardware to meet their coding needs.

MOTHS IN THE MACHINE

Of the many anecdotal stories surrounding Grace Hopper, one of the most famous concerns the discovery of the first computer "bug." The term "bug" had been used by engineers since the time of Thomas Edison to describe mechanical malfunctions. Hopper should be given the credit for introducing the term into the language of computing and, in particular, programming. She described the events surrounding the now-infamous moth as follows:

When we were debugging Mark II, it was over in another building, and the windows had no screens on them and we were working on it at night, of course, and all the bugs in the world came in. And, one night she [Mark II] conked out and we went to look for the bug and found an actual large moth, about four inches wing span, in one of the relays beaten to death, and we took it out and put it in the log book and pasted Scotch tape over it.[37]

From that moment on, it was common practice for Hopper and the rest of the Harvard crew to inform Aiken that they were "debugging" the computer when either the hardware or the coding went amiss.

The myth of the moth puts a playful spin on what would become a grave matter for generations of programmers. "Bugs" hidden in hardware and in software threatened to infect the early machines to such an extent that their very utility came into question. In his memoirs, the English computer pioneer Maurice Wilkes recalled the moment in 1949 when he became conscious of the debugging quandary:

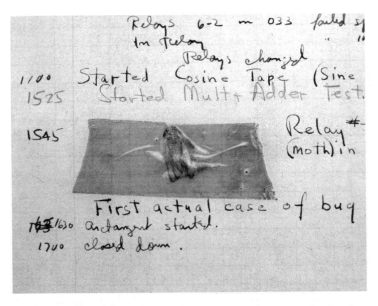

"First actual case of bug being found" as recorded in the Mark II log book on 9 September 1945. Courtesy of Smithsonian Institution.

I well remember when this realization first came on me with full force. The EDSAC was on the top floor of the building and the tape-punching and editing equipment one floor below I was trying to get working my first non-trivial program, which was one for the numerical integration of Airy's differential equation. It was on one of my journeys between the EDSAC room and the punching equipment that 'hesitating at the angles of stairs' the realization came over me with full force that a good part of the remainder of my life was going to be spent in finding errors in my own programs.[38]

Wilkes's observation had significance for the future of comput-ing because the EDSAC (Electronic Delay Storage Automatic Computer) was the first operational electronic computer with stored-program capability. But it is noteworthy that the Harvard

crew came to the same conclusion 5 years earlier. Recalling the
precarious period during the war, Robert Campbell lamented
that bugs jeopardized the entire Mark I project: "For a while it
was a very touch-and-go thing as to whether we could really
keep the machine going in any kind of satisfactory way. It would
seem that a new bug would develop before the bug we were
looking for was found."[39] Hopper added that Mark I was subject
to Murphy's Law: anything bad that could happen to the machine
did happen.[40]

Hopper, Campbell, and Bloch invested substantial energy
in developing practices and procedures for debugging. Like
physicians, they identified symptoms, made diagnoses, and
prescribed treatments. Sometimes symptoms were obvious, as
when Mark I would come to a crashing halt: "The crash of
that thing sounded as if a plane had run into the building,"
Hopper recalled. "You never heard such a crash in your life."[41]
But most symptoms were far subtler. Incorrect results were
the most troubling outcome, and the verification of output
accuracy became a chore in and of itself. If accurate values
previously established existed, then results were compared. But
for the most part, the team needed to generate results via an
alternate computation. At times Bloch went so far as to check
results with a mechanical desk calculator. "The task of performing divisions accurate to 51 places on a ten-decimal digit desk
machine," he noted, "could have been termed cruel and unusual
punishment!"[42]

But checking every result on a desk calculator defeated the
purpose of having a large, automated machine. Hopper concluded that the machine should be used to check itself as much
as possible. Problems were run in two different ways, and the
answers were compared. The likelihood that bugs would generate

the same wrong answer was minute. This form of double check-ing was initiated by operators at intermediate steps throughout a problem's run. When an error was found, Hopper and Bloch provided "rollback" procedures to find the point at which the problem went astray.

HARDWARE BUGS

If the operator determined that the code was "clean" and operat-ing procedures were accurate, then the bug was in the hardware. This required inspecting the thousands of relays and counters, a difficult task because of the machine's size and design. Hopper remembered that the vanity mirror in her handbag became the preferred tool to inspect the $750,000 machine:

I always had a small mirror and one way to find the bugs in Mark I was that they were very often caused by the fraying of the brushes on the counters in which case they would spark. So they would turn out all the lights and then they would borrow my mirror and they would go along and run it and they would look for the sparks in the counters and the mirror would pick up the sparks.[43]

If bugs could not be seen with Hopper's mirror, often the trained ear could hear them. A distinct sound was emitted by Mark I's clutch mechanism as it engaged and released every revolution. Bloch compared the sound to the clatter of a horse's hooves on a paved street. This steady hum was accompanied with the orderly clatter of storage counters and relays banks. Different bugs resulted in distinct asynchronous rhythms. Frederick Miller, a coder who joined the Harvard crew in 1946, remembered being able to pinpoint the problem in the hardware just from the different sounds emanating from the churning machine.[44]

Much to the dismay of the rest of the staff, the distinct sounds generated by hardware bugs also served as an alarm system for Howard Aiken. Aiken's desk was adjacent to the machine, and often he kept his door open so he could hear the hum of the machine "makin' numbers" (as he liked to call it). No matter how busy the Commander seemed to be, if there was an unusual noise emanating from the machine, in no time he would be demanding answers from Hopper or Bloch. Aiken's overzealous nature caused Hopper to do much of her debugging after hours in the peace and privacy of the night.

The concerted effort to lower the frequency of hardware failures not only increased hardware efficiency; it also made debugging easier by isolating potential errors to coding and operating problems. Many hardware bugs related specifically to the relay design of Mark I. Relays registered either 1 or 0 (open or closed), depending on the flow of electricity to the relay switch. If a relay did not function properly, the cause was interference with the electricity flow controlling its action. Relays sometimes sparked when metal flaked off and got caught between contacts. At other times, deficient wiring caused the relays to make no contact at all. The potential for problems was exacerbated by the machine's sheer size and complexity—it had 750,000 moving parts. During the summer and the fall of 1944, faulty and marginal hardware devices were weeded out and replaced with more reliable parts. Because of material shortages attributable to the war, wire salvaged from old pianos had originally been substituted for more optimal materials. Piano wire against brass contacts produced a higher resistance than was desirable, resulting in unreliable relay contacts.

Aiken had picked electromechanical relays over other available technologies because of their proven reliability in the telephone industry. Deployed as the switching backbone in telephone networks for years, relays had first been employed for counting by George Stibitz in the mid 1930s. Stibitz, then a research mathematician at the Bell Telephone Laboratories, had created a circuit of relays that added in binary. Binary arithmetic represented base-ten numbers as a series of ones and zeroes, with one represented by 0001, two by 0010, three by 0011, and so on.[45]

The tradeoff for electromechanical relay dependability was speed. For telephone relays, speed was dictated by the rate in which human fingers could dial. The vacuum tubes used in the ENIAC were thousands of times faster than Mark I's relays. The first vacuum tube, constructed in 1904, was a variation on the light bulb. The invention permitted engineers to regulate and amplify the flow of electricity, but, as John Mauchly discovered, a vacuum tube could also be employed as a binary counter, because it could stop and start the flow of electricity like a gate. A rudimentary vacuum tube has two states (on and off), just as an electromechanical relay has two states (open and closed). But electricity flows through wire at nearly the speed of light, whereas armatures of relays are subject to the limits of mechanical motion. Hence, a tube could perform as a binary switch in the same fashion as an electromechanical relay, but much faster.

In the 1940s a vacuum tube had an operational life of only a few hundred hours. Thus, a machine with a few thousand vacuum tubes would be subject to failure after a minute or two of run time. ENIAC had 18,000 vacuum tubes, and Aiken cautiously assumed that such a machine could never run. He was willing to accept the manageable bugs associated with electromechanical relays in light of the theoretical complications associated with vacuum tubes.[46]

CODING BUGS

If hardware bugs could be ruled out, the most likely source of error was the coding of a problem. Unfortunately, Richard Bloch recalled, coding was subject to a variety of oversights and blunders. A coder could call for the wrong operands or the wrong arithmetic operations. Errors could appear in the coder's calculation of input constants or starting values. Omissions and duplications were common as the coder translated instructions into machine language, while preparation of punch tape, punch cards, and plugboard instructions were subject to human error. "We had to go through the operation step by step," Campbell affirmed, "until we found something which wasn't right, and then look at the circuit diagram and try and figure out what the problem was."[47] This was not a straightforward, linear process, for a coding error could masquerade as a plugging error or vice versa.

Mark I coding required thinking through a vast number of minute steps, then writing the instructions to carry them out. For instance, let us use the analogy of leaving one's house to get one's mail. An equivalent set of instructions in a high-level computer language would be analogous to stating "Walk out the front door, follow the walkway to where it intersects the street, and on your left is the mailbox." The equivalent in Mark I machine language might sound more like "Find your right foot, place your right foot forward, find your left foot, place your left foot in front of your right foot, repeat this twenty times, etc." To minimize errors, Hopper had to keep the details of coding in her head without confusing steps along the way.

The solution required the development of preventive tools, practices, and procedures. Code was initially handwritten in pencil, line by line, on a standardized coding sheet.[48] Coding sheets had a place for annotation, which allowed Hopper and Bloch to attach clarifying equations and written explanations next to each line of code. A fully annotated coding sheet provided a neat, accessible record of the problem that could be double-checked by a second person.

Machine operators were given explicit instructions that helped them to manage the process from start to finish. It became standard operating procedure to double-check all plugboards against plugging charts and to reset control and data switches. In the case of a stoppage, rerun instructions were followed closely, and preliminary printouts on punch cards were compared by hand against source data before being reentered. As Bloch recalled, the best programming techniques called for keeping operator intervention to a minimum, both to reduce manual operational errors and to reduce run time.

What the Harvard team did not do during the war years was explore the possibility of hardware that ran automated checking. Though aware that at the Bell Labs considerable energy was being devoted to creating self-checking circuits, Campbell and Aiken initially did not see the need for such design additions, even in future machines. "I think we felt that with sufficiently reliable components . . . we could make out all right without mechanical self-checking characteristics," Campbell recalled.[49]

Bug-free punch tapes and operator instructions did not guarantee successful results. Hardware manipulation brought its own set of potential errors. Erroneous switch and register settings, improper plugging, failure to follow rerun instructions, and improper arrangement of data punch cards all contributed to the significant challenge of obtaining fast, accurate results. Improper hardware manipulation could even turn fatal, as was nearly the case when an operator named David Green got his tie caught in the sequence mechanism and was nearly strangled.[50]

The infestation of hardware bugs, coding bugs, and operation bugs threatened the success of the first computational machines. The only things separating the Harvard Mark I from failure were the unique abilities and efficient operating procedures developed by Grace Hopper, Richard Bloch, Robert Campbell, and the rest of the Harvard crew. By the spring of 1946, Robert Burns recalled that Bloch "got to the point where he knew the program so well that he could tell you what relay was failing, what counter was bad."[51] They had mastered Mark I while enduring the unrelenting pressures of war.

The person most responsible for the Harvard Computation Laboratory's unique culture was Howard Hathaway Aiken. Aiken's leadership style was more akin to that of a foreman on a factory floor than to that of an Ivy League academic. This can probably be attributed to the fact that he had worked for the electric utilities industry for 13 years before matriculating as a doctoral candidate at Harvard. Aiken's laboratory also differed markedly from more traditional academic environments because of its close relationship with the U.S. Navy. Unlike Robert Oppenheimer, who struggled to preserve civilian control of culture at Los Alamos, Aiken purposely blurred the lines between academia and the military. According to Hopper, Aiken saw himself first as a Navy officer and second as the head of an academically affiliated research facility. Aiken's martial attitude and industry-based sensibilities affected both the nature of the laboratory's research and the technical choices made by its personnel.

Aiken was born 8 March 1900 in Hoboken, New Jersey. His hard personality was forged under extreme conditions. As a teenager (when the family lived in Indianapolis) he became financially responsible for his mother after permanently driving his alcoholic father out of the house with a fireplace poker.

To pay the bills, Aiken held a night job as an electrician's helper for the Indianapolis Light and Heat Company while attending Arsenal Technical High School during the day. Upon graduation, Arsenal's superintendent helped his industrious student obtain a job at the Madison Gas and Electric Company so that he could afford to attend the University of Wisconsin.[1]

Howard and his mother packed their bags for Madison, and in 1923 Howard completed a bachelor's degree in electrical engineering. Upon graduation he accepted a full-time position with Madison Gas and Electric Company as an operating engineer in a gas and electric plant. He was soon placed in charge of the design and reconstruction of the company's main electric generating station. In 1927 he and his mother moved to Chicago, where he designed electric generating stations for the Westinghouse Electrical and Manufacturing Company. The two moved again in 1928 so Howard could become the district manager of the Line Material Company in Detroit.[2]

Management improved Howard's financial situation but brought him farther away from hands-on technical problem solving. In 1932 he decided to return to school, but he left the University of Chicago after two semesters because he thought it was "a lousy institution."[3] Howard and his mother left Chicago and moved into a small apartment at 8 Plympton Street in Cambridge, Massachusetts, so Howard could pursue his doctorate in physics at Harvard. Throughout his years as director of the Computation Laboratory, Howard would leave the lab precisely at noon each day to find a hot lunch and two cold martinis waiting for him at 8 Plympton Street.[4]

But the journey from a graduate student with an idea for a calculating machine to head of the Harvard Computation Laboratory had a number of twists and turns. In the spring of

1941, when Aiken left Harvard to serve in the Navy, many at Harvard saw his machine as marginal and Aiken as dispensable. On 8 December 1939, Frederick Saunders, chairman of the Department of Physics, sent a letter to Harvard's president, James Bryant Conant, summarizing his department's position concerning Aiken and his machine: "We do not feel committed to the promotion of H.H. Aiken in this Department on account of his activities in connection with the calculating machine or the building proposed to house it." Saunders further relayed the department's indifference to the machine: "The machine and the building are both desirable if money can be found, but not necessarily more desirable than anything else."[5] That same month, Conant called for a committee to determine the fate of the proposed machine and its inventor. The Calculating Machine Committee met on 18 December 1939 and agreed that if the school were to go ahead with the computation project, multiple departments, including physics, mathematics, communication engineering, geophysics, and astronomy, should share the costs for housing and maintenance. Regarding Aiken, the committee said this:

A good deal of discussion was devoted to the problem of Mr. Aiken and his future. Representatives of the Department of Physics were rather divided in their feeling as to the possibility of his attaining a professorship in physics. There seemed to be a general agreement that if Mr. Aiken is asked to raise funds and in general to promote the project, it should be made quite clear to him that such activity did not increase his chances of promotion to a professorship.[6]

The "problem" of Howard Aiken became a very sticky issue. In a private letter to Dean George H. Chase, Dean John H. Van Vleck wrote: "If the computing machine is a success,

the University presumably is under something of a moral obliga-
tion to see that Dr. Aiken is retained to man it. However, this is
no doubt a delicate question which can well be omitted from
the minutes."[7]

By the spring of 1940, Aiken's own department had some
interest in the machine, but the department refused to back Aiken
unequivocally. "Assuming that the machine goes forward and
Aiken remains in charge of it," Frederick Saunders wrote, "the
Department agrees to provide from its budget a sum not to
exceed one quarter of Aiken's salary, under the provision that, at
the discretion of the Department, one-quarter of the operating
time of the machine be made available for the solution of problems originating within the Department." Saunders also offered
to house the calculating machine if money could not be found
to build a separate facility.[8]

Feeling that Aiken was being hung out to dry by the Department of Physics, astronomy professor Harlow Shapley wrote
Dean Chase a "bombshell" letter to "stir the physics department
to greater activity."[9] As a stopgap measure, Shapley suggested that
Aiken be retained at least another 2 years as a faculty instructor.
If the money could be found to establish a separate laboratory
for the machine, Shapley recommended, Aiken should be named
director for a 5-year period without any assurance thereafter.
If Aiken could not accept the anemic salary of a faculty instructor with no guarantees beyond 2 years, Dean Chase informed
President Conant, "Shapley is sure that Cunningham and one or
two others would prove quite capable of managing it, perhaps
not quite so well as Dr. Aiken could, but satisfactorily enough at
a much smaller expense."[10]

On 26 April 1940, President Conant wrote to Aiken and
offered him the position of temporary faculty instructor for 2

years at a meager $3,000 the first year and $3,300 the second. At some point during the academic year 1941–42, Conant stated, a decision would be made concerning whether or not a more permanent position would come available "if your work here justifies us in promoting you to a permanent rank." Maintaining an impartial position, Conant ended the letter by suggesting to Aiken that he speak with Dean Westergaard and then "let me know whether you wish to continue at Harvard or not under this arrangement."[11] On 2 May, a disappointed Aiken replied that he hoped to continue at Harvard, and that he would "endeavor to be worthy" of a more permanent position. "Conant said that I was one of these 'faculty instructors' . . . that was a bitter letter," Aiken later recalled.[12] Aiken agreed to continue teaching a course in applied mathematics and to assist with Professor Emory L. Chaffee's course in electron physics. But during the summer the dissatisfied but resourceful Aiken utilized his reserve officer status to further his ties within the Navy. In addition, Aiken initiated a correspondence with his former calculus professor at Wisconsin, Dr. Warren Weaver, who had recently been named the director of the Applied Mathematics Panel of the Office of Scientific Research and Development. Aiken informed Weaver about the invention that he had designed and was constructing with the help of International Business Machines Corporation. In a letter to Weaver dated 5 September 1940, Aiken declared: "It is just possible that my calculating machine or other experience might be useful in your projected research." With regard to issues of military security, Aiken wrote: "You may be interested in knowing that I am at present a member of the United States Naval Reserve with rank of Lieutenant Commander."[13] Aiken's reestablished relationship with Weaver would prove useful in the coming years.

A SOLUTION FOR THE "PROBLEM OF DR. AIKEN'S FUTURE"

"Problem of Dr. Aiken's Future" was the title of a memo generated by a Harvard committee that met 12 March 1940 to
make recommendations about Aiken's fate to President Conant.
The committee concluded that "Dr. Aiken's future is largely
dependent on the success of the calculating machine" and
recommended that Harvard should make no long-term com-
mitments to him.[14] The ambiguity of Aiken's arrangement at
Harvard was cleared up with the Japanese attack on Pearl Harbor.
As the United States mobilized for war, Aiken was called to
active service and given orders to the Mine Warfare School in
Yorktown, Virginia, during the spring of 1941. Aiken asked
physics graduate student Robert Campbell to serve as the liaison
between Harvard and IBM while he was away and to monitor
the construction of the machine. Aiken also maintained contact
with Harlow Shapley, who kept him abreast of developments
within the Harvard administration.[15]

   Throughout 1942 and 1943, Aiken continued to expand his
contacts within the Navy, informing both civilian and military
leaders of the potential utility of his calculating machine for
the war effort. As the machine neared completion, Aiken urged
his superiors that it would be more beneficial for the Navy,
rather than Harvard, to assume responsibility for the machine,
and that he should be named the project's acting commander.
According to Robert Campbell, "he started a sales campaign to
get the Navy interested in taking over the system some time
before the equipment was actually delivered [to Harvard]."[16]
Eventually, Aiken convinced Admiral A. T. Solberg and Commander David Ferrier of the Naval Research Laboratory, and the
two officers recommended that the Bureau of Ships take over
the operation of the calculator, pay Harvard rental fees for the

Official portrait of Commander Howard Hathaway Aiken, officer in charge of the Harvard Computation Laboratory. Courtesy of Archives Center, National Museum of American History, Smithsonian Institution.

machine, and staff the project with Navy personnel instead of Harvard employees.[17]

AIKEN TAKES COMMAND

On 27 April 1944, Lieutenant Commander Howard Aiken received orders to report to Cambridge as the officer in charge of the Automatic Sequence Controlled Calculator. He had successfully bypassed President Conant and the Harvard administration by employing the political and financial clout of the Navy in order to gain control of what he considered *his* project. But since the source of his authority lay with the military and not with the university, Aiken would run the Harvard Computation Laboratory like a military installation, not a university laboratory.

From the start Aiken adopted and enforced formal Navy protocol. He was not a research "director" but rather a "commander," and Mark I was his ship. According to Grace Hopper, he called the Computation Laboratory staff his "crew," and, like any Navy crew, they wore the proper uniform of the day, addressed Aiken as "commander" or "sir," followed a strict, hierarchical chain of command, and were on call seven days a week. "You were in the Navy," asserted Hopper. "You were on duty 24 hours a day. You were lucky if you went home to sleep."[18]

Seaman Robert Burns, one of the four original enlisted crewmembers, remembered that the laboratory even used the operational protocol found aboard ship. Hopper was in charge of creating a monthly "watch list" that assigned personnel to eight-hour shifts. The officers took turns at 24-hour "Officer of the Day" shifts. The Officer of the Day spoke with the authority of Commander Aiken, but was held directly accountable for mishaps or problems during his or her watch. Burns recalled that discipline was so rigid that the Officer of the Day had to relieve operators for lunch, and that "even then when you relieved the operator you had to say 'so and so properly relieved by Burns.'"[19]

Commander Aiken's understanding of Navy mores and his early life experiences forged his work ethic. Years spent in school during the day and working at night trained him to function effectively with little rest. Hopper, Bloch, and Campbell all remembered his seemingly unending stamina. It was not uncommon to see Aiken work a 12-hour day, leave for a late dinner, and show up again at his office from midnight to 4 a.m. Aiken's nocturnal habits could have detrimental consequences for the unprepared. Robert Burns recalled an incident when Aiken decided to show up unexpectedly at dawn one Sunday morning. Having forgotten his key, he pounded on the door, but there was no response from the night operator. "He finally got in and found the fellow was asleep," Burns recalled. "There's an entry in the log book that he was going to court-martial him. The fellow signed his own name as a witness." Word quickly got to the other enlisted operators that, if found asleep on duty, one would be shot at dawn.[20]

Just as there was little empathy for those who did not display Aiken's work ethic, he was loyal to those who did. "He was one of these individuals that you are either with him or against him," crew member Frederick Miller recalled. "If you were with him, why, there was nothing he wouldn't do for you. If you were against him, why, there was nothing good that you could do." Hopper remembered many nights spent sleeping on her desk in her attempt to keep up with the never-ending workload. Aiken came in early one morning, surprised to see his loyal lieutenant. "She'd been there most of the night struggling with Mark I," Aiken recalled. "I said, 'What have you been doing here all night?' And she said, 'Chaperoning these two damn computers!' "[21]

Hopper even braved a hurricane in the fall of 1944 to get to her post. "We held hands and one would hold on to the lamp post or a tree while the other two would string out and get to the next one and hang on," she recalled.[22] Richard Bloch kept up with the boss by drinking an unseemly amount of Coca-Cola each day. At one point during the war Bloch worked through the night two days in a row in order to meet a deadline. Recognizing that his subordinate was approaching physical exhaustion, Aiken escorted Bloch to his room on the other side of campus and would not leave him until Bloch had put on his pajamas and was safely tucked in bed.[23]

During his years as a plant operator, Aiken had developed an unbending ethic of efficiency, accuracy, and orderliness, which he later transferred to the Harvard Laboratory. Operators had to meticulously account for every minute of machine run time. Each day's (and night's) events were recorded in an operational logbook and on a publicly displayed operational chart. Aiken spent the first part of each morning reviewing the logbook and the operational chart and interrogating those responsible for any discrepancies. "He is probably one of the toughest bosses and also one of the best," Hopper recalled. "You could always make the mistake the first time and nothing happened to you. You might get bawled out and you got told not to make it again but nothing happened to you until you did the same dumb thing over again."[24]

Aiken's emphasis on efficiency permeated his approach to technical invention and innovation. Despite his doctorate in physics, Aiken was at heart a hard-nosed industrial engineer. Deadlines were written in stone, and no matter what, Miller recalled, "he was going to run it and get it done." Miller was impressed by Aiken's discipline to stick with a given design plan. Engineers, according to Miller, usually pay lip service to simplicity and elegance, but often add complexity with multitude variations that often sabotage the coherence of the final product. According to Miller, Aiken would say "I'm going to have one kind of relay that has six double throw contacts that will make it easy to test them and fix them."[25]

Aiken's efficiency in matters of hardware design went hand in hand with his autocratic style of decision making. He kept the overall vision of the project in his head and more often then not just assigned the tasks to be accomplished. "We each had different problems that we worked on," Hopper recalled. "Problems were assigned to us to solve." This did not mean that Aiken did not

Members of the Harvard Computation Laboratory staff working on the backboard wiring for Mark II, 5 June 1946. Courtesy of Archives Center, National Museum of American History, Smithsonian Institution.

consider other people's ideas; they just had to be prepared to defend their position. "I am a simple man and I want simple answers!" would be his typical response when one of the crew did not explain an idea clearly or concisely. Further opaqueness usually resulted in a barrage of expletives.[26]

The British mathematician Maurice Wilkes remembered visiting Harvard in the summer of 1946 and recalled the difficulty he had discussing design ideas that differed from Aiken's own. Once, when Wilkes asked about the potential of mercury delay lines, Aiken snapped back: "You are not committed to the mercury memory, are you?" Instead of defending himself, Wilkes avoided confrontation. "I was a little afraid of Aiken," admitted Wilkes, "and I made the defensive reply that I was not committed to anything."[27] Paradoxically, the members of the original Harvard crew who developed an effective working relationship with Aiken learned quickly that the best way to earn his respect was to match fire with fire. "I remember one time telling him that I thought he was a son of a bitch," Fred Miller recalled. "He considered that a real compliment."[28] Those who forged close bonds with the commander during those first years all had similar stories. One time when Burns and Aiken were in a heated discussion, Aiken yelled "Don't I scare you?" "Hell no," Burns replied. "You put your pants on the same way I do, one leg at a time." Instead of retribution, Burns's defiance generated a laugh and a pat on the back.[29]

Humor was Hopper's preferred technique for dealing with her domineering boss. If Aiken began pushing the crew too hard, a strategically placed practical joke served to relieve the tension and to indirectly remind the boss of his transgressions. During a week when Aiken was pressuring the crew exceptionally hard to meet deadlines, Hopper and the crew decided to revise the operational charts to show that the machine had been "down" all night when in fact it had been operating fine. When Aiken arrived in the morning and went through his ritual review of the operating chart, he became infuriated when he saw the continuous line of red indicating that the machine had been down all night. Aiken stormed from one person to the next, demanding why he had not been notified during the night. No one had a clue what he was so angry about. By the time he had returned to the operating chart, the chart's red lines had been replaced with blue. Aiken just stood there smirking, knowing that he had been had. Hopper, to the delight of the crew, then presented him with a medal she had made out of the chart's red line material. Aiken wore the medal on his uniform proudly for two days thereafter.[30]

Humor and practical jokes became a central part of the Computation Laboratory's culture, not only for the cathartic value of humor but also for its bonding power. "Any time off was very brief and usually it turned into pranks of one sort or another," Hopper recalled. "Comic relief almost."[31] Burns remembered that Hopper was always playing jokes on people in the name of "morale building."[32] Besides pranks, the artistic lieutenant became famous for her cartoon collection that captured the idiosyncrasies of the machine and the people who ran it in the difficult wartime environment. Her assortment of "gremlins" and "bugs" were blamed when programs did not run or the machine acted up, thus adding lightheartedness to tense, frustrating situations.

As might be expected, not everyone thrived under Aiken. Robert Seeber, for instance, held ill feelings toward Aiken long after the war. Seeber was an expert on IBM punch-card equipment who worked as a civilian for the Navy during the war. After reading about Mark I in August 1944, he requested a transfer to the Harvard Computation Laboratory. Seeber's wish was granted, but the unsuspecting technician immediately got on Aiken's bad side by requesting vacation time before joining the laboratory. Seeber survived at Harvard until the end of the war, enduring 90-hour weeks as a coder in addition to Aiken's constant pestering. He recalled trying to participate in the planning for Mark II during the spring of 1945, but Aiken ignored his ideas. The moment the war was over, Seeber quit and took his ideas to IBM. His experience under Aiken made him believe that "his aim in life must be to work for IBM and help them build a bigger and better computer than the Mark I."[33] That computer would be the IBM Selective Sequence Electronic Calculator, a 120-foot-long colossus completed in 1948 and displayed in full view on the ground floor of IBM's world headquarters in Manhattan.[34]

Problems with "fitting in" were not limited to civilian employees. Both officers and enlisted crewmembers had difficulty with
Aiken's heavy-handedness at times. "He was totally involved in
getting a job done for the Navy," Hopper recalled, "and if one
of the enlisted men made a mistake during the night on the
computer or went to sleep or something, he bawled the hell out
of him. Well, Dick [Bloch] would say you shouldn't treat a human
being that way, and as far as the Commander was concerned he
was supposed to be on duty and doing a job."[35]

Among the officers, it was Bloch who had the most volatile
relationship with Aiken, and Hopper usually found herself medi-
ating between the two. "I used to argue with Dick Bloch because
he was always getting in trouble," she said. "I would try to explain
to Dick that [Aiken] is just exactly like a computer, he's wired a
certain way [and] if you are going to work with him you must
realize how he is wired."[36]

Hopper believed that the root of the tension between Aiken
and Bloch was their similar disposition. Their similarities resulted
in a fiery working relationship, but also generated some creative
technical solutions, for Aiken respected the ideas of his young
protégé. When tempers boiled over, Hopper would remind the
youthful Bloch that all of them were doing a job for the Navy
and that their individual differences had to be suppressed in order
to fulfill the mission. "I don't think [Aiken] ever demanded any
more of anybody, anything more of anyone then he would have
aboard ship," she asserted. "It's true we were on dry land, but we
needed this and required this same discipline. Once you realized
that and realized what was going on and understood it, there was
no difficulty."[37]

Despite Aiken's and Bloch's differences, Hopper was able to
keep the peace. This was not the case with the Computation
Laboratory's executive officer, Lieutenant Commander Hubert

Arnold. Rather than play intermediary, Hopper's actions appeared to have heightened the tension between Aiken and his second in command during the war. "Arnold never should well, I can't say it that way. He wasn't really a naval officer; he was still a college professor," admitted Hopper. The challenge during wartime, according to Hopper, was finding mathematically qualified people who were also naval personnel. Arnold had a difficult time performing under pressure, and though he was a talented mathematician his limited aptitude for coding put a strain on the rest of the crew. "Every time his programs didn't run," Hopper recalled, "the Commander would come storming into my office and say 'Find out what's wrong with Arnold's routine!'"[38]

To make matters worse, Arnold lacked the leadership skill to manage the crew in Aiken's absence. Once, when Aiken was in Washington, tensions ran so high between Arnold and the crew that upon Aiken's return the executive officer complained to Aiken that the crew had been insubordinate in his absence. "Aiken went up to the ceiling and said, if you can't run the crew you shouldn't be a lieutenant commander," Hopper recalled. "You should be able to run, manage, your crew and discipline your crew, I'm not going to do anything about it for you."[39] Arnold was "reassigned" for the remainder of the war to the Widener Library, where he produced a bibliography for applied mathematics and numerical analysis that was included in Hopper's *Manual of Operation* for Mark I. "I think the Commander wanted him out of the Laboratory because the crew was insubordinate to the executive officer," Hopper recalled. "I'll admit it, we were. We played all kinds of tricks on him. We were insubordinate I guess, except he just asked for it, I swear he did."[40]

With Arnold physically removed from the Computation Laboratory, Aiken turned to Hopper to be in charge of Mark I. By the spring of 1945, Hopper had proved herself to be a talented coder, a dedicated member of the crew, and an enforcer of Aiken's system. "I think we were more scared of Grace than we were of the old man," the operator Robert Burns recalled. "They really didn't pull any practical jokes on Grace."[41] Not only had Hopper overcome the technical challenges presented by Mark I; she had demonstrated her leadership skills in an antagonistic environment. Being placed in charge of Mark I "was a victory on my side because when I walked in there [Aiken] had not wanted a woman officer and I had said he was going to want a woman officer," Hopper recalled.[42] Years later, reflecting on his female lieutenant's dedicated service during the war, Aiken said "Grace was a good man!"[43]

Aiken's crew taking a break from the wartime pressures. From left to right: Ensign Bloch on piano, Commander Aiken, Lieutenant (j.g.) Hopper, Ensign Brendel, Ensign Campbell. Courtesy of Archives Center, National Museum of American History, Smithsonian Institution.

LABORATORY CULTURE AND THE REALITIES OF WAR

The war shattered life's normal rhythms, and most Americans had to adjust to a variety of inconveniences. Restrictions on travel, rationing of food, and shortages of materials became the norm. If the pressures placed on the Harvard crew by Commander Aiken weren't enough, they were also faced with the stresses of the wartime environment. "Getting food was a difficult proposition," Hopper recalled. "We didn't have ration stamps because we were supposed to eat at the main mess that we could never get to. We only got ration stamps when we were on leave, and it was rough rounding up food."[44] Once a week Hopper would send one of the enlisted men across town to the Navy Supply Building to get food, Coca-Cola, and cigarettes for the crew.

Locating supplies for the Computation Laboratory was difficult too. Furniture was "borrowed" from other buildings on campus, and items as basic as paper were held at a premium. "We discovered the backyard of the Army store room which was next to the area the computer was in, and they had lots of nice paper and stuff," Hopper recalled. Periodically Hopper and Seaman Frank Verdonck would augment the Computation Laboratory's supplies by siphoning off Army supplies. Hopper remembered that Commander Aiken caught the two when they were removing an entire carton of graph paper. "I can remember what he said," Hopper recalled. "He said, 'Well you better leave one pack. The Army may not be able to count but they can tell the difference between none and some.'"[45]

More stressful for the crew were the pressures associated with the operational aspects of the war. Even though things looked better by the summer of 1944, there was no end in sight to the conflict. "The entire nation," Hopper recalled, "was operating on one idea. The whole drive was on, just one thing, just win that war."[46] Hopper and the rest of the crew believed that their work was instrumental to a successful conclusion of the conflict, yet that burden hung heavily on them. "There was one special phone," Hopper recalled, "which was connected directly to the Bureau of Ordnance in Washington. Well, we used to shake every time that darn thing rang."[47] Usually the Bureau was asking to have certain firing tables of calculations ahead of schedule, which put further strain on the laboratory. For the entirety of the war, Mark I was operating 24 hours a day, 7 days a week, with the staff working three 8-hour shifts. Free time and holidays were almost non-existent, and even Christmas leave was limited to 24 hours.[48]

The need for immediate results affected the technical choices Aiken and the crew made when designing Mark I and Mark II. Aiken was constrained by available materials and tended to choose standard components. "He had to build things out of what worked at the time," Hopper recalled. "He couldn't afford to fiddle around with circuits yet."[49] According to Hopper, the decision to use relay technology and not vacuum tubes in both Mark I and Mark II could be directly attributed to the pressures of the war. Aiken felt it was better to apply a tested and proven technology, such as switches. Vacuum tubes, though used in radios for years, had not yet been successfully applied to computation machines.

Early programming innovations also grew out of the intense pressure generated by the war. Hopper compared the experience to working in a long tunnel with only the problems to solve ahead of her. She and Bloch were constantly searching for ways to increase the speed of the coding process, and their solutions evolved out of expediency rather than intellectual curiosity.

"There was," Hopper recalled, "no theorizing, there was no higher mathematics. There was no future of computers, there was nothing but get those problems going, and what the computer was doing. The future in a sense did not exist."[50]

Hopper and crew usually were too busy solving problems for the war effort to speculate about the calculating machine's commercial potential. This was the case even after the laboratory received several inquiries from interested industry leaders through the summer and fall of 1944. A series of articles was published after the machine's official dedication on 7 August 1944, and companies such as Eastman Kodak and Goodyear Aircraft Corporation made inquiries about the possibility of running engineering problems. Each inquiry was met with a form letter from Commander Aiken regretting that the laboratory could not accommodate the request because Mark I was engaged in the solution of problems strictly for the war effort. In the final sentence, the letter said "perhaps, at some future date, after the war, we may be of service to you."[51]

The only discussion Hopper recalled during the war concerning the commercial potential of Mark I occurred while visiting her parents on Christmas leave in 1944. Hopper's father was a prominent figure within the insurance industry, with more than 50 years' experience, and her grandfather had been president of the Great American Insurance Company. When Hopper told her father about her work at Harvard, he immediately understood Mark I's commercial potential for keeping records, calculating premium tables, and generating premium and billing statements. "Now whether he had gone to New York and mentioned that to any of the insurance companies, I'll never know, but that was the first mention that I ever heard of using the computer in industry," Hopper recalled. "It was from my own father."[52]

THE POSTWAR ENVIRONMENT

With the conclusion of the war, the Harvard Computation Laboratory's future was in question. The Bureau of Ships contract was to run out, and Aiken had to find a new patron for his machine. Though the Harvard administration's attitude toward Aiken and the Computation Laboratory had softened with the success of the project, Aiken felt limited allegiance to those who had not supported him earlier. "We entered into a phase in which 'Howard Aiken had a computing machine and nobody in the University could get near it', which, in part, was true," recalled Aiken. "However, since we had paid for it ourselves or raised the money to pay for it, it did not disturb me very much."[53]

Since Aiken was not motivated by financial gain, he did not consider exploring his invention's business potential.[54] Instead, he renegotiated with the Navy and signed a new contract with the Bureau of Ordnance in the fall of 1945. The contract transferred control of Mark I to Ordnance from the Bureau of Ships, which dedicated the machine to engineering and scientific problems pertaining to national security. The contract also extended funding of the proposed Mark II and made provisions for research and development of Mark III.[55]

In order to preserve the Computation Laboratory's organizational continuity, the contract recommended that the indispensable members of the crew be removed from active duty and employed as civilians. This included Aiken, Hopper, Campbell, and Bloch in particular. Harvard agreed to assign Aiken and his staff to the newly created Department of Engineering Sciences and Applied Physics, naming Aiken an associate professor and Hopper, Campbell, and Bloch research associates.[56]

The original members of the crew served as the nucleus for the laboratory's postwar expansion. To maximize their investment, the Navy still wanted to operate the machine 24 hours a day and seven days a week. But since the staff was now civilian, the Navy had to abide by the peacetime directive of a 40-hour workweek. For this reason, it hired a second shift of operators and programmers. Numbers also increased because of the need to design and build the Mark II and Mark III. Because Aiken would not receive direct assistance from IBM or any other commercial manufacturer, the appropriate number of engineers and technicians had to be hired to meet the terms of the contract.

One of the first hires after the war was Harry Goheen, who had received his doctorate in mathematics from Stanford in 1940 and had enlisted in the Navy after Pearl Harbor because, he recalled, "it seemed that I might possibly be of greater assistance as an active duty officer at sea." But instead of finding glory and adventure on the bridge of a battleship, Goheen had a "terribly boring experience" as an armed guard in the Philippines.[57]

Goheen left Manila in July 1945 and arrived at the Computation Laboratory in August. Hired as a coder, on the side he helped Hopper prepare the *Manual of Operation*. "I never did learn to program, but that was what I was supposed to be doing," said Goheen. He was immediately struck by the intense, almost repressive nature of the laboratory's environment. In particular, he saw Aiken and Hopper as zealots who were completely dedicated to this strange new computing discipline. Even though the laboratory was transitioning to a peacetime environment, Goheen noted how martial the atmosphere remained.[58]

Goheen was very empathetic to those who were not enthusiastic about the laboratory culture. "There were a couple of people who, for one reason or another, had felt very badly put upon. I won't mention any names, but they left," he recalled. "And I don't blame them because from their own point of view they got a very raw deal at Harvard."[59] A confidential memorandum from

Lieutenant Commander Edmund Berkeley, dated 27 May 1946 corroborates Goheen's unsettling assessment. Berkeley, assigned by the U.S. Naval Proving Ground to the Harvard Computation Laboratory to aid with the design and construction of Mark II, reported to his superiors on the deteriorating conditions at Harvard after the end of hostilities. Berkeley placed ultimate responsibility and blame for the high rate of personnel turnover on the project's director, Howard Aiken.[60]

In his report, Berkeley systematically detailed the unfavorable conditions at the Computation Laboratory, including the length of the work day and the isolation of the staff from similar projects at MIT and the University of Pennsylvania. He named eleven talented people who had left or been dismissed by Aiken between August 1945 and May 1946, noting that all were "very bitter over the conditions on the project." The root of the problem, according to Berkeley, was that "in the Computation Laboratory there is no provision for appealing any decision or ruling what-soever made by the project manager." He was amazed that no one at Harvard and no one in the Navy seemed to have jurisdic-tion over the rogue director, so that Aiken was able to rule with near absolute authority. Paradoxically, Berkeley concluded, "It seems definitively undesirable that there should be a change in the project manager. The vigor, energy, directness, and intolerance of obstacles which make the problem of dealing with personnel difficult, are in many respects virtues in the struggle to wrest information out of the scientific unknown." Such was the con-tradiction of Howard Hathaway Aiken.[61]

With so many members of the crew leaving, their replacements had difficulty integrating into the Computation Laboratory's culture. The members of the original crew had forged a powerful bond during the hardship of the war years, and it became very difficult for new recruits to prove their worthiness. Harry Goheen got along with Grace Hopper, his immediate boss, but he was well aware that they were on two different levels in Aiken's caste system. "She was on the inside, you see. The difference between Grace and us was that she was the Commander's right-hand girl," stated Goheen. "And he was lucky to have her for a right-hand girl, because she was most skillful in writing and she worked hard, and she was a clever mathematician, and completely dedicated both to computing machinery and to Howard Aiken."[62]

Hopper's special relationship with Aiken afforded her freedom of thought and action that others did not possess. Fred Miller remembered that her opinions, both technical and organizational, carried more weight than those of other staff members. She entertained important visitors to the Computation Laboratory in Aiken's absence, and she was the only one permitted to travel to other computing projects. Hopper, Goheen recalled, "was the only one who had that freedom, not only of movement but of moving at [Aiken's] level."[63]

POSTWAR INNOVATIONS AND THE DEVELOPMENT OF SUBROUTINES

For Harry Goheen and for others who had joined the postwar Computation Laboratory, the laboratory's culture did not encourage experimentation and innovation. Aiken's hierarchical system left technical decision making to a chosen few. Campbell, Bloch, and Hopper, as members of the original crew, were given special license to innovate, though not at the expense of their primary duties. Despite the marginalization of the inventive spirit at the Computation Laboratory, Bloch and Hopper consolidated the programming insights gained during the war and developed a sophisticated system of subroutines for Mark I in their spare time.

A subroutine was a segment of code representing algebraic functions that could be recorded into and accessed from the internal memory of a computer. A collection of subroutines was known as a subroutine library. During her keynote address at the first History of Programming Languages Conference in 1978, Captain Grace Hopper held up a piece of paper and claimed that it was a subroutine that she had written back in 1944.[64] That audacious claim seems questionable on two accounts. First, subroutines are generally associated with stored-program computer architecture, and the Harvard Mark I did not have such an architecture. Second, the majority of the Hopper's audience, made up primarily of computer pioneers and historians, believed Maurice Wilkes to have been the originator of subroutines and subroutine libraries.[65]

Wilkes, a British mathematician who made important contributions to the wartime development of radar, was named the director of the Mathematical Laboratory at Cambridge University in 1945. In May 1946, Wilkes was visited by Leslie Comrie, who handed him an unpublished document, written by John von Neumann, titled "First Draft of a Report on the EDVAC."[66] The paper described the architecture of a modern computer: binary logic gates, stored instructions and data, and the serial execution of instructions.

Wilkes spent the summer of 1946 touring the United States in order to learn more about large-scale calculating machines. He attended the Moore School lectures on large-scale calculating machines at the University of Pennsylvania, where he met John Mauchly and Howard Aiken. Mauchly gave Wilkes a tour of the ENIAC, and Aiken invited the British mathematician to the Harvard Computation Laboratory.[67]

Inspired by the unique calculating machines he saw in Philadelphia and Boston, Wilkes returned to Cambridge determined to construct a machine of his own. The Mathematical Laboratory sponsored a series of colloquia on Thursday afternoons in which issues concerning the proposed computing machine were discussed, oftentimes over a few beers. The Cambridge colloquia attracted researchers and students alike, and it soon evolved into the team that would try to turn the stored-program machine into reality. On 6 May 1949, the EDSAC read its first program into memory and successfully printed the results.[68]

That same summer, Wilkes established a committee to design a library of coded subroutines. The idea was to generate code for the most widely used elementary functions and standard operations so that future users would not have to program from scratch. The main force behind the programming effort was a recent Cambridge graduate named David Wheeler. Wheeler's work, which included developing the protocol for the nesting of multiple subroutines, was published in July 1951 under the names of Wilkes, Wheeler, and Stanley Gill. (Gill was a research student.) One thousand copies were sold within the year, including one bought by the senior mathematician at the Eckert-Mauchly division of Remington Rand: Grace Hopper.[69]

Hopper recalled being impressed by the work of Wilkes, Wheeler, and Gill,[70] but found most of the concepts within the book quite recognizable. Seven years before the book's publication, Hopper and Bloch had stumbled across the subroutine concept while programming Mark I. During the war, they had developed the habit of saving snippets of code as reference material for future coding. "Gradually we built up quite a lot of these little pieces of code in our notebooks," Hopper recalled.[71] Soon it became apparent that different problems could apply the same

segments of code. By reapplying pre-written code to new problems, programming time could be reduced.

By the spring of 1945, it was common practice for Harvard
coders to share each other's notebooks in order to copy segments
of code. "We would borrow from each other and copy them,"
Hopper said. "When we copied them of course we had to
change the address. They all started from zero and we had to
add those addresses and then we also had to copy them into
another program."[72]

To facilitate the transfer of code segments into subsequent
programs, Hopper and Bloch developed a system they called
"relative coding." The codes were relative because they were
written in a general, abstract fashion that allowed them to be
entered anywhere in a given program. "I put the A's and B's in
instead of the specific storage locations," Hopper recalled, "and
what you had to do if you wanted to use it over again, was you
put your argument in A, and so on in B."[73] Hopper's relative
codes provided the framework for a given mathematical function.
All the user had to supply was the specific parameters of the
operation. For example, if the relative code was a general segment
for sine, the coder may specify solutions for a range of angles.

Even though Hopper and Bloch's system of relative coding
made it easier to write more accurate codes in less time, the
system itself was haphazard. It was up to the coder to remember
the contents of the notebooks. When a useful code segment was
located, it was copied by hand into the subsequent program.
Furthermore, the data and parameters unique to the problem
were hand-punched and manually fed into a set of mechanical
inputs called interpolators. Human intervention in the copying
process increased the probability of mistakes.

With the conclusion of the war, Hopper and Bloch had
more time to systematize the relative coding process. The rigid

sequential nature of Mark I design proved to be a considerable hindrance. The main sequence mechanism was unidirectional, meaning that reversing or back-stepping the mechanism was impossible. If a segment of code was to be repeated in a given problem, the entire sequence had to be punched into the tape multiple times, since each line of code could be executed only once. "No matter how clever the coding," Bloch recalled, "it was not possible (without manual intervention) to arrange for embedded subroutines, or to skip certain lines of code, or to branch to another segment of the program."[74]

Branching permits a computer to make a decision based on the result of intermediate output. That is, intermediate output A would initiate coding instruction X, whereas output B would precipitate instruction Y. During the war, branching was achieved by having the enlisted operators monitor intermediate results and manually switch or advance main sequence tapes when desired outputs appeared. "The operator would twirl the drum that held the tape over to an indicated branch line and proceed from there," Bloch recalled. "You had instructions that would say 'if the machine stops here, move it over to the red line next. If it stops somewhere else, ship it over to the blue line.'"[75] This crude and time-consuming procedure was painfully evident when trying to calculate John von Neumann's implosion problem for the first atomic bomb in the fall of 1944. The complex partial differential equations associated with the implosion problem required hundreds of manual manipulations, much to the dismay of Mark I operators.[76]

In the summer of 1946, shortly after his decommission from the Navy, Bloch took on the challenge and produced a subsidiary sequence unit that permitted full branching capability. The unit could call in up to ten different sub-sequences of code, each with up to 50 lines of instruction. The sub-sequences of code were in fact the relative codes from the notebooks, pre-punched and devoid of bugs. In essence, Bloch and Hopper had created a fully functioning subroutine system, albeit saved on paper tape instead of stored in the machine's memory. "This was," Bloch recalled, "the first instance that I know of subroutines in any computer and branching of that nature, being able to go to any of ten subroutines based upon the results that might occur."[77]

Combining the subsidiary sequence unit with relative codes provided Harvard coders with a powerful programming tool. "You avoided errors because you used previously checked out valid pieces of code that you knew worked which meant you could write the program much faster and much easier," Hopper recalled.[78] Once a clean code was created, it could be plugged into any number of problems. This eliminated several steps, including translating the mathematical problem into code, punching the code, debugging the code, and testing the code. With blocks of relative codes controlled by the subsidiary sequence unit, new problems no longer had to be solved from scratch.

Hopper's and Bloch's coding innovations were captured by Aiken in the design of his third calculating machine, the Harvard Mark III. Mark III was assembled at Harvard on contract for the Dahlgren [Virginia] Naval Proving Ground between 1946 and 1948 and was delivered to Dahlgren in January 1950. The machine was unique in utilizing magnetic tape for the input and output of data, vacuum-tube circuitry for registers, and separate magnetic drums for data and instructions storage.[79]

The magnetic drums were Aiken's attempt to solve the problem of effective, high-speed internal memory.[80] Each was 8 inches in diameter, 40 inches long, and covered with a thin plastic layer with embedded ferrous oxide. As the drum rotated, the read/write heads magnetized spots that represented data along the drum's surface, which could be re-read at a later date. In this respect magnetic drums operated in a similar fashion to audiocassette tapes, but the information could be accessed randomly and not just in sequential fashion as with tapes. Hopper recalled the difficulty the crew had finding a manufacturer who could produce a drum that did not bulge in the middle when rotated at high speeds.[81] Eventually the horizontally mounted drums achieved an operating speed of 6,900 rpm and could store up to 4,000 instructions, making them the most robust storage medium to date.

The expanded memory permitted programs to be stored internally,[82] which allowed instructions to be accessed at the speed of the arithmetic unit. Now all that was necessary was to speed up the coding process itself. Aiken's solution was to mechanize Hopper and Bloch's relative code system. A library of pre-written relative codes was housed within a mechanical coding device (later referred to as the Instructional Tape Preparation Table). That device permitted the coder to introduce complete, multi-instruction subroutines at the push of a button. For instance, the "cosine" button placed the proper code sequence onto the magnetic instruction tape, set parameters for the position of the decimal point, and managed address storage information for instructions after completion of the cosine routine.[83]

The Instructional Tape Preparation Table was split into lower and upper sections, the lower section holding the more commonly used routines. The Table could print the content of an instructional tape in order to facilitate debugging before uploading the tape into Mark III's internal memory. If a change had to be made, the coding machine could overwrite previously entered instructions.[84]

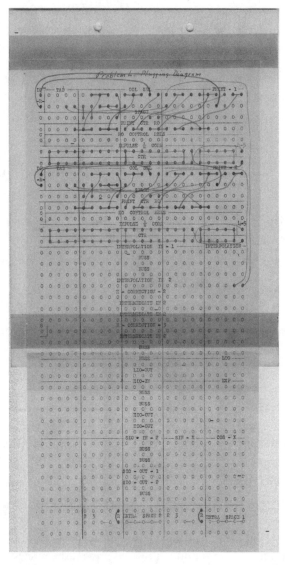

Example of operating instructions for Mark I. Courtesy of Archives Center, National Museum of American History, Smithsonian Institution.

Mark III's Instructional Tape Preparation Table was a mechanized version of many of the concepts discussed in Wilkes, Wheeler, and Gill's 1951 book on subroutines. The coding machine embodied programming innovations that Hopper and Bloch had developed between 1944 and 1946 while programming Mark I and Mark II. The question arises: Did programmers in the Harvard University Computation Laboratory and the Cambridge University Mathematical Laboratory have any contact between 1944 and 1951?

SUBROUTINES: AN EXAMPLE OF SIMULTANEOUS INVENTION

When historians consider the path of a technical innovation, they come across a strange and unexpected phenomenon: Often, different inventors invent a technology simultaneously in different geographic locations. Further investigation uncovers no other connections between these disparate groups, as is the case of such well-documented examples as the telegraph, the light bulb, and the turbojet.[85] Without any formal communications between the different inventors, it is tempting to write off the occurrence as chance or coincidence.

But the frequency of simultaneous invention dismisses serendipity on statistical grounds. Why simultaneous inventions occur appears to be contingent on a variety of factors, including the society's overall scientific and technical acumen and the process of how technological problems are defined and chosen. In the case of subroutines, the problems associated with programming were similar on the two sides of the Atlantic because the hardware was similar. Early pioneers in large-scale computing machines criss-crossed the Atlantic, attended joint conferences, and shared published and unpublished documents, the most famous being John von Neumann's "First Draft." Because of the similar hardware solutions, comparable programming problems arose as these machines became operational.

The more difficult question that arises is why members of the Harvard crew and the Cambridge staff came to such similar solutions. Since the concept of technological determinism carries little weight with most historians, it is not wise to conclude that subroutines were the best or the most logical solution to the problem. Yet why "closure" occurs for one expression of technology but not for another is far from transparent.[86] Technical "closure" has its roots in the concept of scientific certainty. During the process of scientific inquiry, consensus within the scientific community tends to form around a certain interpretation or theory. A similar process occurs when consensus emerges around a particular technology design. Communities of engineers, designers, and consumers interact until a technology design stabilizes and reaches closure. The closure process has produced rear-chain bicycles, QWERTY keyboards, and gasoline-powered automobiles. It is important to remember that these technologies and others could have stabilized with other design attributes.[87]

In the case of subroutines, closure may have occurred because there was much more sharing of information between Harvard and Cambridge than first meets the eye. During the summer of 1946, Wilkes accepted an invitation by Howard Aiken to visit Harvard after the completion of the Moore School lectures.[88] Wilkes arrived in Boston on 11 September and remained there for a week. The young Brit recalled observing Mark I in full operation as well as having a variety of conversations with Harvard staff.[89] Hopper remembered his visit years later: "We had gotten to concepts of subroutines [by 1946] and I think a little bit had influenced Wilkes, who had been there from England."[90]

Another connection to Wilkes runs through British mathematician Leslie Comrie. Comrie managed the British Nautical Almanac Office from 1930 to 1936 and founded the Scientific Computing Services Ltd. in 1937. As a leading proponent of calculating technology in Britain, Comrie kept abreast of developments in America and passed them on to Maurice Wilkes. It was Comrie who provided Wilkes with a copy of John von Neumann's report on the stored-program concept, which heavily influenced the design of the British EDSAC.[91] As the historian James Cortada observes, "his help to Wilkes was typical, and that of the EDVAC report was only one in a long series of favors to Wilkes."[92]

In a review of Hopper's *Manual of Operation* in the 26 October 1946 issue of *Nature*, Comrie noted that he was extremely impressed with the "brains of the machine" (that is, the sequence-control tapes). What struck him was the fact that these tapes represented a sequence of processes that were independent of the actual figures used, thus allowing the same tape to be used multiple times. He explicitly mentioned the Computation Laboratory's "tape library," which significantly lessened the coding burden and made Mark I more efficient than a well-equipped manual computer.[93] Though it cannot be confirmed that Comrie passed knowledge of the Harvard tape library to Wilkes, we do know that Comrie was aware of Hopper's and Bloch's coding innovations and that he kept Wilkes informed of developments in the United States.

Wilkes returned to the United States in the summer of 1950 in order to learn more about a new machine being constructed by the Eckert-Mauchly Computer Corporation: the UNIVAC I. By that time, Wilkes's Cambridge colloquium on programming had been meeting for a year. In Philadelphia, Wilkes got to spend some time with Grace Hopper and her programming staff. Hopper had left Harvard in 1949 to join the EMCC as a senior mathematician. Wilkes remembered particularly stimulating conversations with Hopper and her group: "I found that they had a full appreciation of the importance of programming and of the need to develop organized and disciplined methods. I felt that I was among people who looked at things in the same way that I did myself."[94]

Whether or not Hopper and Bloch influenced Wilkes's development of subroutines and subroutine libraries for stored-program computers, Wilkes was the first to publish on the topic. Though Hopper discussed subroutines in her 1949 *Description of a Relay Calculator*,[95] she admitted that Wilkes, Wheeler, and Gill systematically defined the programming concept and disseminated it to a wide audience.

Ten years before her bold proclamation that she had written the first subroutine in 1944, Hopper candidly admitted in an interview that innovation at Harvard did not follow a smooth, logical path, and that at times Hopper and her Harvard colleagues were not fully conscious of the significance of their creations: "Those were essentially relative subroutines, though we did not know it [in 1945]; we didn't realize it. In fact, I wasn't aware of it fully until I got down to UNIVAC, when I had input-output under my control, and could store those on tape and call them back into a program without having to copy them."[96] Her confession does not take away from the accomplishments of the Harvard crew, but it reminds us that sometimes inventors do not understand the significance of their creations until well after the fact.

During World War II, the crew of the Harvard Computation Laboratory constituted a significant portion of the emerging computer community. The members of the crew were bound together by shared ideas and knowledge, but being a member of the crew went beyond the sharing of technical information. The group cultivated its own style of being and sense of purpose. Howard Aiken, Grace Hopper, and the external influence of the Navy were all instrumental in developing this disposition, demeanor, and outlook. Ultimately the Harvard Computation Laboratory became more than just a place to house a large calculating machine. It was a community of practitioners capable of generating, capturing, and disseminating highly esoteric technical knowledge.[1]

WARTIME ISOLATION

During the war, the Harvard Computation Laboratory functioned in near isolation. One obvious reason was the fact that there were only a few other programs. In England, Alan Turing's work at Bletchley Park on the code-breaking machine Colossus was shrouded in secrecy. In the United States, Eckert and Mauchly's ENIAC project at the University of Pennsylvania was in its infancy at the time of Mark I's dedication. "To a considerable extent," Robert Campbell recalled, "the Harvard project was sort of self-contained. It pretty much went its own way, and there was not an awful lot of interchange."[2]

Hopper recalled hearing about a computing program at MIT during the war, but admitted that none of the Harvard crew ever interacted with their MIT counterparts. It seems strange that two programs so close geographically to one another would not share information, but a confidential memorandum to Harvard president James Bryant Conant from MIT president Karl Taylor Compton (dated 7 February 1940) sheds light on the matter. Compton wanted to make sure that Conant was mindful of two facts. First, for several years there had been a undisclosed program at MIT that had developed numerical computing devices. Second, the MIT program and its members were interested in obtaining patents for their work. As a result, according to Compton, "there could be no cooperation between Dr. Aiken and the MIT group as concerns the methods involved."[3] Compton goes on to question the wisdom of developing a computing program at Harvard: "The lack of a practical engineering viewpoint permeating the institution" looked like a significant handicap to the MIT president, both in the development and utilization of such computing machines. Dependence on IBM was believed by Compton to be another notable shortcoming, for "the utility of such a machine, born fully developed, would be impaired by the fact that the necessary personnel would not have passed through the evolutionary stages with the machine." In contrast, the growth of the computing center at MIT had been an evolutionary process. It had started with Vannevar Bush's analog differential analyzer. As of February 1940, the center had a variety of calculating machines and a seasoned staff, all housed in a 5,600-square-foot space. The tone of the memorandum forcefully suggested that the development of computing devices should be left to MIT, though that wasn't stated explicitly.[4]

Compton's implied advice went unheeded, largely because Howard Aiken persevered and because IBM and the Navy backed him. On 7 August 1944, Aiken celebrated his triumph with a formal ceremony marking the transfer of the Automatic Sequence Controlled Calculator (Mark I) from IBM to Harvard University and the founding of the Harvard Computation Laboratory. Aiken captured the event in pictures , and the Computation Laboratory worked closely with the Harvard News Bureau to prepare a news release.

The release was picked up by Boston's newspapers (the *Herald,* the *Globe,* the *Daily Record,* and the *Post*), and also by the *New York Times*, the *Christian Science Monitor,* and the New York *Herald Tribune.* Headlines such as "Navy Man Inventor of World's Greatest Calculator" and "Aiken's Calculator" infuriated IBM's president Thomas Watson and began a well-documented feud between Aiken and IBM that would last through Watson's lifetime.[5] Despite Watson's accusations and objections, Aiken's crew rallied around their leader. When questioned about the feud in the years to follow, Hopper maintained her staunch support of Aiken, insisting that the overall concept of the machine, as well as the design of the sequence mechanism and interpolators were his, not IBM's. "IBM never gave the credit they should have to Aiken," she stated.[6]

Aside from the tensions between Aiken and IBM, the formal dedication on 7 August 1944 marked the start of a new era in mechanical information processing. Harvard faculty members and administrators and high-ranking Navy officers attended the

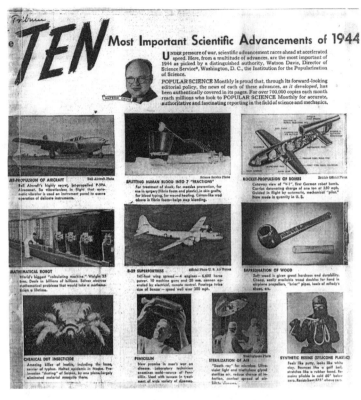

Mark I listed as one of the ten most important scientific advancements of 1944 in *Popular Science*. Courtesy of Archives Center, National Museum of American History, Smithsonian Institution.

event. Most notable among the latter were Rear Admiral Edward L. Cochrane (chief of the Bureau of Ships), Rear Admiral A. H. Van Keuran (director of the Naval Research Laboratory), and Rear Admiral Julius Furer of the Office of Naval Research. Those three naval organizations would play particularly important roles in the future development of the computing industry.

JOHN VON NEUMANN AND MARK I

Also present at the dedication of Mark I was the mathematician John von Neumann. Von Neumann played a pivotal role in the early history of computing, for he authored one of the most influential papers in the field, "First Draft of a Report on the EDVAC."[7] The "First Draft," dated 30 June 1945, outlined the architecture of a stored-program, general-purpose machine (the basic architectural framework on which present-day computers are based). Von Neumann's paper quickly became the working blueprint for the next generation of computers, including EDSAC and ACE in England and UNIVAC and the IAS computer in the United States.

The "First Draft" was also the center of a considerable controversy involving J. Presper Eckert Jr., John Mauchly, and John von Neumann. Herman Goldstine, the US Army's liaison officer to the ENIAC project in 1944–45, holds von Neumann most responsible for the ideas presented in the document: "This report represents a masterful analysis and synthesis by [von Neumann] of all the thinking that had gone into the EDVAC from the fall of 1944 through the spring of 1945. Not everything in there is his, but the crucial parts are."[8] Through the years Eckert and Mauchly disagreed adamantly about Goldstine's interpretation. The inventors of the ENIAC claimed that they had developed many of the concepts found in the "First Draft" during the spring of 1944, months before they even met von Neumann. Despite their claims, it was not until 3 months after the release of the "First Draft" that Eckert and Mauchly recorded their ideas (in a paper titled "Progress Report on EDVAC").[9]

If Goldstine's interpretation is correct and von Neumann was responsible for the architecture concepts in the "First Draft," the question remains: what was the source of von Neumann's inspira-

John von Neumann. Courtesy of Los Alamos National Laboratory Archives.

tion? Goldstine identified the source as the famous mathematician's "genius." Further historical inspection, however, shows that the time frame in which von Neumann developed the ideas for the famous paper coincides with his four-month stay at the Harvard Computation Laboratory. Though it is too strong to assert that the work at the Harvard Computation Laboratory served as his inspiration, there is no denying that von Neumann served as a bridge between the Mark I and ENIAC computer projects during the fall of 1944, or that his vision of a general-purpose stored-program computer grew out of his conversations and observations in Cambridge and Philadelphia.

Identified during his youth as a gifted mathematician, John von Neumann received his doctorate in mathematics from the University of Budapest at the age of 22. After a three-year stint as a Privatdozent in mathematics at the University of Berlin, von Neumann became a visiting professor at Princeton University. As a result of Adolf Hitler's ascendance to power in 1933, von Neumann decided to remain in the United States and accepted a position as a professor of mathematics at Princeton's Institute for Advanced Study. While at the IAS, von Neumann became increasingly interested in applied mathematics, and particularly in problems concerning supersonic and turbulent fluid flows. Mathematical representations of dynamic fluids required knowledge of non-linear partial differential equations, and by the commencement of World War II von Neumann was one of the leading experts in that field. Since shock and detonation waves fell under his expertise, von Neumann was vigorously sought after by the Army's Ballistic Research Laboratory and the Navy's Bureau of Ordnance.

His growing reputation gave von Neumann unparalleled access to classified projects, including the top-secret Manhattan Project.

For the Manhattan Project's scientists and engineers working in secrecy in the New Mexico desert, von Neumann's knowledge of fluid dynamics was highly valued, and he joined the group as a consultant in late 1943. The Los Alamos team was considering various ways to transform a non-critical mass of fissionable material, such as uranium or plutonium, into a critical mass as rapidly as possible. Once critical mass was achieved, the scientists theorized, an atomic chain reaction should release tremendous amounts of energy. One theory (proposed by Seth Neddermeyer) was to forcefully implode a sub-critical sphere by means of conventional explosives in order to compress it into a critical state. Von Neumann was called in to help develop a mathematical model for Neddermeyer's implosion process. The resulting partial differential equations were extremely difficult to solve for the Los Alamos human computers, with their desk calculators. In March 1944, in an attempt to speed up the process, von Neumann asked his friend Emory L. Chaffee about the possibility of using the new Harvard machine. Chaffee was the head of Harvard's physics laboratory and Howard Aiken's former graduate advisor. With time of the essence, von Neumann replied: "The possibility of making these calculations on your new device was an exceedingly tempting one."[10]

Aiken agreed to allocate machine time to von Neumann's problem, and von Neumann arrived at Harvard for the dedication ceremony on 7 August 1944. It was, Aiken recalled, von Neumann's first exposure to large-scale calculating machines. "He wanted to see the machine and I told him how it worked and what it did."[11] Impressed with the machine's potential, von Neumann decided to work with the Harvard crew and attempt to solve the implosion problem on the experimental machine.

Hopper remembered von Neumann's arrival and recalled his immediate dependence on the crew "because that was the first computer he had his hands on."[12] Bloch was impressed how rapidly the computer neophyte picked up both the design concepts and coding procedures. "He had a mind that moved in rapid fashion on any subject relating to mathematics or physics," Bloch recalled.[13] Hopper and Bloch helped him "set up shop" in the conference room off the main computer room with a large table and a blackboard. Von Neumann quickly became a semipermanent fixture in the conference room.[14]

Since Hopper had arrived only 2 months before von Neumann, Bloch headed up the programming of the problem while Hopper assisted. For security reasons, the two coders were told the specifics of the problem, a partial differential equation of the second order, but not its context. In fact, not until the destruction of Hiroshima and Nagasaki almost a year later did Aiken, Bloch, and Hopper become aware of the magnitude of their work. But in the fall of 1944, von Neumann's problem was nothing more than an interesting mathematical challenge. "The attack itself," Bloch recalled, "was relatively new. Such equations had not been attempted numerically before."[15] Luckily for Hopper, she was well versed in partial differential equations, for they were the focus of her study with Richard Courant at New York University during the fall and spring of 1941.

Though the problem setup and the coding went relatively smoothly, the speed limitation of Mark I hardware became a significant issue. The numerous intermediate calculations needed to solve the equation, coupled with Mark I's 300 millisecond processing speed, stretched the time of computation to the point of impracticality. "Out of expediency, we had to stop at a certain level [of accuracy] because it was just going to be too long," Bloch recalled. I guess the war would have been over by the time the machine would tackle it at a higher degree [of accuracy]."[16]

As the Harvard team stumbled through the difficulties of such a complex problem, von Neumann provided feedback concerning the accuracy of intermediate results. Hopper recalled that the prominent mathematician had an uncanny ability to "predict accurately what the numbers would turn out to be."[17] She aided him in retrieving and interpreting data from the print-outs, data that he would peer at intensely and then make suggestions concerning future runs. By December, Bloch had presented the results in a final report to be taken back to Los Alamos and compared with the progress of the human computer team. "Von Neumann insisted that my name be put in front of his as the author, which embarrassed me a little bit because he was the great mathematician and mathematical physicist of the day," Bloch recalled.[18]

By the end of von Neumann's stay, the Harvard crew had gained valuable experience operating Mark I and was markedly closer to developing a fast and efficient system of programming. Not only did von Neumann have a mathematical answer to the implosion problem, but also he was one of the first people outside the Harvard team to have a hands-on education on how to program and operate a large-scale digital calculating machine. That newfound knowledge would have a significant impact on the future direction of the computing developments at the University of Pennsylvania.

VON NEUMANN'S "FIRST DRAFT"

About the time that von Neumann arrived at Harvard to program his problem on Mark I, the famous mathematician had a chance encounter on a railroad platform in Aberdeen, Maryland. A young Army officer named Herman Goldstine introduced himself and the two struck up a conversation. Lieutenant Goldstine was not a typical young officer, for he had obtained a doctorate in mathematics from the University of Chicago in 1936. Upon entering the service in July 1942, the mathematically talented officer was assigned to the US Army Ballistics Research Laboratory (BRL) at Aberdeen.[19]

The BRL was the army's primary test site for artillery and other weapons. One of Goldstine's jobs was to manage the group of human computers assigned to produce ballistic firing tables. Gunners and bombardiers used firing tables to adjust their weapons in order to hit targets that were beyond the horizon. A multiplicity of variables, including horizontal distance to target, wind direction and velocity, humidity and temperature, and elevation above sea level, had to be taken into account in order to achieve accuracy. The BRL's human computers created ballistic tables that accounted for these variables and informed the gunner to which azimuth to set his weapon.

In general the mathematics behind ballistics tables were not complex, but rather time consuming to produce with a paper, pencil, and a desk calculator. A typical trajectory required about 750 separate calculations, or about 12 hours for a human computer.[20] As the war progressed the backlog of firing tables grew as the BRL struggled to keep up with demand. Goldstine first attempted to alleviate the situation by teaming up with the University of Pennsylvania to create a training program for mathematically inclined young women. The faculty, consisting of Goldstine's wife Adele, Mildred Kramer, and Mary Mauchly, worked diligently to identify and train smart, young women from the Philadelphia area. Their efforts quickly turned the BRL into one of the largest information processing centers, staffed by more than 200 human computers.

Mary Mauchly's husband John, an instructor at the Moore School of Electrical Engineering, offered a second way to deal with the growing demand. In August 1942, Mauchly produced a memorandum describing an electronic calculating machine, which caught the eye of both Goldstine and a young graduate student at the Moore School, J. Presper Eckert Jr. On 9 April 1943, Eckert and Mauchly presented a more advanced proposal to Colonel Leslie Simon, director of the BRL, and Colonel Paul Gillon, assistant director. Simon signed the order to fund Project PX, Gillon named the proposed machine ENIAC (standing, as has already been noted, for Electronic Numerical Integrator and Computer), and Goldstine became the BRL's official liaison to the ENIAC project.[21]

By the time Goldstine had met von Neumann on the railroad platform, the design of the ENIAC was complete and construction just underway. Goldstine was very active in his role as liaison and had participated in many of the theoretical discussions concerning design. "When it became clear to von Neumann that I was concerned with the development of an electronic computer capable of 333 multiplications per second, the whole atmosphere of our conversation changed from one of relaxed good humor to one more like the oral examination for the doctor's degree in mathematics," Goldstine recalled.[22]

Excited by an electronic machine thousands of times faster than the Harvard Mark I, von Neumann soon accompanied Goldstine to Philadelphia to see if the machine could potentially handle partial differential equations. "He grasped what we were doing quite quickly," said Eckert.[23] But to von Neumann's disappointment, the ENIAC, though potentially a great deal faster than the Harvard machine, was limited in its mathematical versatility. Much like the differential analyzer developed by Vannevar Bush, the machine was "programmed" by the interconnection of its physical units. Such a design was not an accident, considering that the Moore School operated a differential analyzer, and both John Mauchly and Presper Eckert (as he was usually called) had worked with it. The ENIAC, then, was a hardware-specific machine designed to create ballistic tables, but not equipped to handle partial differential equations.

Von Neumann did, however, see the potential of electronics when applied to automated computing and remained engaged with the ENIAC group while working with Harvard. On 21 August, Goldstine wrote to the executive officer of the BRL, Colonel Gillon, and informed him that the prominent mathematician was "displaying great interest in the ENIAC and is conferring with me weekly on the use of the machine."[24] According to Goldstine, von Neumann quickly became a powerful influence on the project, stimulating discussion about computer theory and practice, and pushing forward ideas for the second machine.

Some of those ideas were already evident in Goldstine's letters to Colonel Gillon in August and September 1944. In the letter dated 21 August, Goldstine suggests that "switches and controls of the ENIAC now arranged to be operated manually, can easily be positioned by mechanical relays and electromagnetic telephone switches which are instructed by a teletype tape." He goes on to point out that "we would not have to spend valuable minutes resetting switches when shifting from one phase of a problem to the next."[25]

From a letter written by Goldstine 12 days later, it is evident that von Neumann had been updating the Philadelphia group about developments at Harvard. "To illustrate the improvements

I wish to realize," Goldstine wrote, "let me say that to solve a quite complex partial differential equation of von Neumann's the new Harvard IBM will require about 80 hours as against 1/2 hour on ENIAC." But where the ENIAC's theoretical processing superiority was obvious, the reality was that its programming deficiencies erased any processing gains. Even a less complex problem demonstrated that the two systems were relatively equal in performance, despite the ENIAC's overwhelming advantage in computational speed. "To evaluate seven terms of a power series took 15 minutes on the Harvard device of which 3 minutes was set-up time, whereas it will take at least 15 minutes to set up ENIAC and about 1 second to do the computing."[26]

According to Goldstine, the 2 September letter represents the first example of the stored-program concept in writing:

To remedy this disparity we propose a centralized programming device in which the program routine is stored in coded form in the same type storage devices suggested above. The other crucial advantage of central programming is that any routine, however complex, can be carried out whereas in the present ENIAC we are limited now that we seem to be on the fairway as far as development goes, I feel it most important to make plans for further improvements to realize in a second machine the highly important features that seemed too difficult in the first model.[27]

According to Goldstine, von Neumann had derived the essential concept of the stored-program architecture "in the fortnight between the two letters." The concept would be fleshed out through the fall of 1944 and captured in June 1945 in "First Draft of a Report on the EDVAC."

What Goldstine failed to mention in his recollections was that the period he referred to as "the most eventful time in the intellectual history of the computer" was the same time frame that von Neumann worked regularly with the Harvard crew. Ideas concerning how to redesign the ENIAC generated in conversations with Eckert, Mauchly, and Goldstine coincided with the practical learning gained from programming Mark I with Bloch and Hopper. Von Neumann served as a living conduit between two isolated, top-secret computer projects.

From the Harvard project it appears that von Neumann was influenced by the concept of automatic sequential control. Unlike the ENIAC, the projected EDVAC would be programmed to process commands in sequence similar to Mark I.[28] "The instructions which govern this operation must be given to the device in absolutely exhaustive detail," wrote von Neumann. "Once these instructions are given to the device, it must be able to carry them out completely and without any need for further intelligent human intervention."[29] Though in practice Mark I depended on operator intervention, in theory Aiken had designed a machine that was fully automated.

Von Neumann also noted that fully automatic-computing devices such as Harvard's Automatic Sequence Controlled Calculator used teletype tape and punch cards as the means to input the instruction and data sequence, but concluded that "a really high speed device would be very limited in its usefulness, unless it can rely on M (internal memory)."[30] Internal memory was the key ingredient to allow long and complicated sequences of operations to be executed at an electronic rather than a mechanical speed. This single point was the great insight of the stored-program architecture, and married the electronic speed of the ENIAC with the automatic sequence control and programming capability of Mark I.

Von Neumann's proposed architecture broke from the Harvard machine on a number of levels other than the use of vacuum tubes. The most important distinction concerned the separation of instructions from data. The Harvard machine isolated the two, which aided the programmer during the debugging process. "First Draft" recommended that instructions and numerical quantities be stored together within the internal memory. This permitted both data and instructions to be modified, and created the flexibility to generate an unlimited number of subsequent instructions and data in memory. Non-linear partial differential equations could then be solved with far fewer original instructions and operator interventions. Hence, the burden of writing out the sequential variations of instructions, as prepared by the Harvard crew during the implosion problem, was shifted from the coder to the machine.

On balance, this does not mean that all credit should be given to the Harvard crew for the logical control and programming concepts included in "First Draft," nor does it discount von Neumann's intellectual capacity to generate original ideas. Creative concepts do not appear out of a vacuum, and during the fall of 1944 von Neumann had a privileged perspective of the nascent computing field. He could identify the strengths and weaknesses of both projects and fashion a new technical variation with shared elements. "He obviously had a very very loud voice in the sense that he was very influential," Aiken recalled. "The result was that things that he proposed, good, bad, or indifferent, were in some cases followed."[31] Interestingly, von Neumann cites Aiken in the "First Draft" but does not cite Eckert or Mauchly.

THE MAKING OF ORTHODOX COMPUTER HISTORY

"First Draft of a Report on the EDVAC," though never officially published, was one of the first documents distributed among the emerging computing community. In the fall of 1944 Aiken also set out to record the technical developments at the Harvard Computation Laboratory, and he chose Grace Hopper as his author. As the story goes, Hopper was sitting at her desk busy with a coding task when Commander Aiken interrupted her work. He stated with his typical tone of urgency, "You are going to write a book!" Both the abrupt statement and the nature of Aiken's request caught Hopper off guard. "I can't write a book," she retorted; "I've never written a book." With the war on and the machine operating around the clock, seven days a week, there was no way that she would be able to take on such a monumental task and keep up with her other coding and managerial duties. Aiken acknowledged his new Lieutenant's concerns, but still insisted that she would somehow find the time to write the book. "You're in the Navy now!" he reminded her.[32]

Whatever the veracity of the story's details, Aiken did in fact order Hopper to write the first manual of operation for Mark I. And somehow between her other duties and responsibilities, Hopper completed the 561-page manuscript in time to be published by the Harvard University Press for its 1946 fall books release.[33] "I wrote about five pages a day," Hopper recalled, "which I had to read to [Aiken] at the end of the day. If he rejected them, I had to start them over again."[34]

In view of Aiken's hands-on editorial approach, the fact that he trusted Hopper to write the manual for his prized machine is significant. It would have made more sense for Robert Campbell to do the job. Campbell had been with Aiken since 1942. He participated to some extent in the design process, oversaw the construction of the machine while Aiken was serving the Navy in Norfolk, and programmed the first test problems for the machine. His intricate knowledge of the hardware and the coding process made him the ideal candidate. But by the fall of 1944, Aiken and Campbell were already making plans for an improved follow-on machine, so Aiken entrusted Hopper with the task of creating the first computer manual.

Hopper believed that Aiken had picked her because her reports during her first months at Harvard had demonstrated a talent for clear, fluid prose. Hopper had been encouraged as a child to write, a habit she had kept up during her 13 years teaching mathematics at Vassar. "When they [meaning her Vassar students] came into my probability course," Hopper recalled, "the first thing I did was give them a lecture on Sterling's formula and then asked them to write it up as an essay. I'd cover it with ink and I would get a rebellion because they were taking a math course, not an English course. Then I would explain: it was no use trying to learn math unless they could communicate with other people."[35]

The ability to communicate ideas clearly in writing is not usually viewed as a crucial skill for an engineer or an inventor. An emphasis on technical knowledge and a strong mathematical foundation at the expense of non-technical disciplines is even codified in most engineering school curriculums. Both Aiken and Hopper understood that inventions are not self-evident, especially one so unique and complicated as the Harvard Mark I. Mark I would have to be described not only to other scientists and mathematicians but also to university administrators, Navy officers, business leaders, and government civil servants. Writing in such a way that this disparate audience could grasp what Aiken and his team had accomplished was crucial to the ultimate success of the invention.

Hopper completed the manuscript in the spring of 1946. Remarkably, she was not listed as the author. Like all published documents written by Aiken's staff, *A Manual of Operation for the Automatic Sequence Controlled Calculator* was "Dedicated to the Staff of the Computation Laboratory." At the Computation Laboratory, credit was distributed hierarchically, starting with Comdr. Howard H. Aiken, USNR, Officer in Charge, followed by staff members in order of their Navy rank: officers, enlisted, and civilians last. Because of her rank, Hopper's name appeared third on the inside cover. Though such a hierarchical ranking may not appeal to a modern sense of fairness, in certain respects such a system benefited Lieutenant Hopper. Aiken's constructed caste system was based on the quality of ideas and on military rank, both of which, for the most part, superseded gender. In the same way, Aiken's insistence on military protocol, including military dress and titles, further dissolved societal gender roles. Such an environment permitted Hopper to compete on a more equal footing with her male colleagues, so long as she played within the boundaries of the Aiken system.

THE CONTENTS OF HOPPER'S MANUAL

The manual began with a historical summary of the development of mechanical aids from the abacus up to Aiken's idea for Mark I. Hopper's history outlined the trajectory of technological progress and created a sense of connection between the handful of talented individuals who advanced the computing art. Hopper's history is interesting on a variety of levels. First, it is one of the earliest attempts to document the historical progression of the field. Second, and more importantly, it provides insight into Hopper's view of technological change.

Because of travel limitations during the war, Hopper's historical research was limited to resources found in Harvard University's

Widener Library.[36] The first significant figure introduced to the reader by Hopper is Blaise Pascal. Pascal (1623–1662) is highly regarded as a Christian thinker and as a scientist-mathematician, but few acknowledge his skills as an engineer. Pascal the engineer was responsible for inventions as diverse as the medical syringe, the hydraulic press, the wheelbarrow, and a horse-drawn public transportation system used in Paris during the 1660s. Pascal's father, Etienne, served as the chief tax collector for the Rouen district in France during the 1640s, a job that required a vast amount of tedious calculations. To escape the drudgery of his father's work, the clever youth devised plans for a machine that would automate the process and produce error-free results. The basic machine was a metal box containing a system of wheels and cylinders that could add, subtract, and carry over numbers. The most difficult problem Pascal faced was how to carry over numbers automatically. Teaching a child to add 14 plus 8 and carry over a 1 to the tens column to arrive at 22 is simple, but to teach a machine to do the same is another matter. Pascal invented an ingenious weighted ratchet system connected to the counters in each wheel. With each turn of the dial to the next notch, the ratchet was raised. When the respective wheel passed 9, the ratchet sprung and tripped a weight that turned the next wheel to the left one space and the original wheel back to 0. The direct actuation of a numbered wheel and its carrying method, Hopper wrote, "are the foundation on which nearly all mechanical calculating machines since have been constructed."[37]

The next significant individual on Hopper's historical path leading to Aiken and Mark I was Gottfried Wilhelm von Leibniz (1646–1716). Leibniz, the consummate genius of his day, excelled as a mathematician, a diplomat, a lawyer, a historian, and a philosopher. Apart from his more celebrated accomplishments, Leibniz was also responsible for an extraordinary automated calculating machine, which he completed in 1694. Hopper commended Leibniz for achieving multiplication and division through an ingenious system of stepped wheels. These wheels, similar to the inner workings of a mechanical clock, were interconnected in such a way that mathematical solutions rather than the time of day were their output. According to Hopper, the device's "stepped reckoner" design was so mechanically eloquent that it would be included in most calculating machines thereafter and serve as an important link to Mark I.[38]

The most significant section of the manual is dedicated to the English philosopher-mathematician Charles Babbage. The story of Babbage's computing engines begins with his honeymoon in 1819. While touring Europe, Charles and his new wife met the prominent French civil engineer Gaspard Francois de Prony. Years earlier, while making tables for the fledgling French Republic, de Prony had applied an idea he had encountered while reading Adam Smith's *Wealth of Nations* (1776). Inspired by Smith's concept of the division of labor, de Prony applied it to his teams of mathematicians. One group considered formulas, another applied them numerically, and the third did the computations. The efficiencies created by such a division produced more accurate tables in less time. Babbage borrowed this concept and made it a part of his machine designs.

Between 1820 and 1822, Babbage developed the plans for his first computing machine, which he named the Difference Engine. The Difference Engine would calculate a table for any linear mathematical function by using Newton's method of differences, which allowed complex polynomial equations to be solved without any need to multiply or divide. The first prototype of the Difference Engine required a variety of precise manufacturing processes and quickly evolved into the most expensive government-funded research project of its day. But by the mid 1830s the expensive project began to unravel for lack of concrete results. To make matters worse, Babbage began championing a completely new design concept. His novel idea developed into the blueprints for his Analytical Engine, a device that broke from earlier calculating machines. But his change of course cost Babbage his supporters in government and scuttled any chance of his finishing the Difference Engine.

The Analytical Engine was not just an extension of the Difference Engine; it was a new concept in automated information processing. Information would be continuously fed into the "mill" of the machine by means of the ingenious punchcard system that Joseph Jacquard used to automate his textile looms. Hopper emphasized that two distinct decks of cards fed the machine: "The first set was designed to select the particular numbers to be operated upon from the store; the second set, to select the operation to be performed by the mill. Since the deck of operational cards represented mathematical solutions independent of the variables involved, the analytical engine was general in regard to algebraic operations."[39]

The one person who truly understood the ramifications of Babbage's new machine was a beautiful and eccentric woman 23 years his junior. Ada Byron King, Countess of Lovelace and daughter of the renowned poet Lord Byron, was a mathematician who had become interested in Babbage's work. In 1834 she began to write regularly to the older mathematician, and the two became close friends and colleagues. By 1840, Babbage had completed the basic blueprints for the Analytical Engine. Ada Lovelace wrote seven technical essays that provided powerful explanations for what the machine could do and how it could do it, including what today would be called a computer program.

Lovelace's work, published in 1843, did not aid Babbage in successfully securing the vast amounts of funding needed to construct the Analytical Engine. The aging mathematician had used up his goodwill with the government on the uncompleted Difference Engine. Babbage would not be able to turn his idea into reality during his lifetime. According to Hopper, the world had to wait until 1943 before Babbage's dream would materialize in the laboratory of Howard Hathaway Aiken.

THE HOPPER VERSION OF HISTORY

Grace Hopper's account of computing's early history is interesting on a variety of levels. It is the story of a series of brilliant men separated by vast expanses of time but connected by the dream of automating the drudgery of mathematical calculations. Each one was personally responsible for introducing radical and potent conceptual ideas, which were then constrained by the technologies of the day. Their advances were discontinuous and independent from the work of others. Such a historical interpretation sheds light on the name Aiken gave to his creation: Mark I. Mark I was a one-of-a-kind, discontinuous invention.

The historical account also provides the reader a sense that with the publication of the Mark I manual the computational torch had been officially passed to Howard Aiken and his team.

The epigraph to chapter 1 of the manual includes this passage from Babbage's autobiography:

If, unwarned by my example, any man shall undertake and shall succeed in really constructing an engine embodying in itself the whole of the executive department of mathematical analysis upon different principles or by simpler mechanical means, I have no fear of leaving my reputation in his charge, for he alone will be fully able to appreciate the nature of my efforts and the value of their results.[40]

In a very real sense, Aiken believed that Babbage was speaking directly to him through the years. Shortly after the publication of the *Manual*, Aiken developed a personal relationship with Babbage's great-grandson and decorated his office with Babbage memorabilia, including books once owned by Babbage with marginal notes in Babbage's own hand. He even acquired (through the Harvard library) original parts of the partially constructed Difference Engine.[41]

When the Harvard crew moved into the new Computation Laboratory facilities in 1946, the Babbage memorabilia were gallantly exhibited in the vestibule. For members of the laboratory crew, Aiken's copy of Babbage's autobiography, *Passages from the Life of a Philosopher*,[42] became mandatory reading. Hopper recalled being handed a copy when arriving at Harvard in the summer of 1944. "The book [Babbage's Autobiography] gave you a feeling that the development was inevitable," she remembered. "It was bound to come." *Passages from the Life of a Philosopher* also exposed Hopper to Ada King for the first time: "She wrote the first loop. I will never forget; none of us ever will." Nor did people let Hopper forget the uncanny coincidence of history, casting Aiken in the role of Babbage and Hopper in the role of Lady Lovelace.[43]

Commander Aiken and Lieutenant (j.g.) Hopper posing with a piece of Charles Babbage's difference engine for the *Christian Science Monitor*, March 1946. Courtesy of Archives Center, National Museum of American History, Smithsonian Institution.

THE IBM AUTOMATIC SEQUENCE CONTROLLED CALCULATOR:
SAME MACHINE, DIFFERENT HISTORY

About 6 months after Hopper was assigned the task of writing
the Mark I Manual, an anonymous technical writer at IBM
produced a pamphlet aptly named "IBM Automatic Sequence
Controlled Calculator." This competing document provided a
general description of the same machine, yet its differences speak
volumes about underlying conceptions. Like Hopper's manual,
the first section of the pamphlet summarized the history leading
up to the machine and its creation:

The IBM Automatic Sequence Controlled Calculator dedicated at
Harvard University on Aug. 7, 1944 marked the latest advance in
International Business Machines Corporation's program of adapting its
equipment to use in the field of scientific computation, in which for
many years it has been collaborating with leading universities and
research organizations.[44]

One can quickly glean the direction of the IBM narrative from
the opening sentence of the document. First, the assertion that
the dedication marked the "latest advance" suggests a continuous
process in which the Automatic Sequence Controlled Calculator
was just the newest iteration. The "corporation's program of
adapting its equipment" further emphasizes continuity of process,
and reminds the reader that the technology used in this machine
was no different than that already employed in other IBM business
calculating machines. Finally, the very idea of applying business
machines for scientific computation is not novel, as IBM "has
been collaborating with leading universities and research organizations" for many years. That collaboration, according to the IBM
narrative, began in 1928 with the founding of the Columbia
University Statistical Bureau. The Bureau was established solely

"for the purpose of assisting other educational institutions and scientific and research organizations in adapting IBM mechanisms to their computing requirements."[45] It was here that machines such as the IBM Difference Tabulator and the IBM Summary Card Punch were developed. In 1934 a separate laboratory was established in the Columbia Department of Astronomy, and since 1937 the Thomas J. Watson Astronomical Computing Bureau, a joint enterprise of IBM with the American Astronomical Society and Columbia University, operated the laboratory.

Because IBM had been applying standard machinery to scientific calculations since the 1920s, it was no wonder that "Harvard University's need for a machine such as the IBM Automatic Sequence Controlled Calculator had long been a topic of discussion among members of the Harvard Faculty."[46] Howard Aiken's inquiry had been but "one of these discussions." Moreover, it was Professor Harlow Shapley (director of the Harvard Observatory) and T. H. Brown (Professor of Business Statistics) who pointed out to Howard Aiken that "IBM standard equipment for some time had been successfully used for scientific calculation purposes."[47]

The IBM narrative squarely attempts to marginalize Aiken and his role in the development of the machine. It was Professor Brown "who brought the subject to the attention of Mr. J. W. Bryce, dean of IBM's scientists and inventors," and it was Bryce who determined "the company's ability and willingness to build the machine."[48] Acting on Brown's and Bryce's recommendations, Aiken met with IBM engineers and "outlined the University's requirements."[49] The IBM history does not acknowledge Aiken as the initiator of the project or as the inventor of the machine. Furthermore, it reminds the reader that Aiken was called to active duty in the Navy and thus spent a significant time away from the project.

In fact, the IBM document shrewdly underlines Aiken's limited role with Aiken's own words, quoting strategically from his laudatory speech at the machine's dedication ceremony on 7 August 1944[50]:

We approached the International Business Machines Corporation and asked their support to build such a machine and construct it and put it into operation Our first contact with that company was with Mr. J.W. Bryce. Mr. Bryce for more than thirty years has been an inventor of calculating machine parts, and when I first met him he had to his credit over 400 fundamental inventions—something more than one a month. They involved counters, multiplying and dividing apparatus, and all of the other machines and parts which I have not the time to mention, which have become components of the Automatic Sequence Controlled Calculator that you are to see this afternoon.[51]

With this vast experience in the field of calculating machinery, our suggestion for a scientific machine was quickly taken and quickly developed. Mr. Bryce at once recognized the possibilities. He at once fostered and encouraged this project, and the multiplying and dividing unit included in the machine is designed by him.

On Mr. Bryce's recommendation, the construction and design of the machine were placed in the hands of Mr. C.D. Lake, at Endicott, and Mr. Lake called into the job Mr. Frank E. Hamilton and Mr. Benjamin M. Durfee, two of his associates.[52]

Indeed, Aiken, in his own words, appears to give credit for the invention, design, construction, and operation of the machine to IBM engineers.

DIFFERENT HISTORIES, DIFFERENT AGENDAS

Why do the historical accounts written by Grace Hopper and IBM differ to such a great extent? One obvious explanation attributes the divergence to the well-documented animosity

between Thomas Watson Sr. and Howard Aiken.[53] On the surface this is reasonable, for evidence can be found that self-
importance drove each man to call the project his own. But in
this case, it seems that history is being employed as a tool for
ambitions greater than individual pride.

For Thomas Watson Sr., IBM interests were best served by
replacing individual history with organizational history. The
locus of technological innovation, according to IBM, was the
corporation. The myth of the lone radical inventor working in
the laboratory or basement was replaced by the reality of teams
of faceless organizational engineers contributing incremental
advancements in the name of the company.[54] To drive this point
home, the IBM narrative includes the following list:

Of the many basic units of the Calculator, invented or developed by
IBM engineers, the more important are:

- Multiplying Machine, invented by Bryce in 1934.
- Dividing Machine, invented by Bryce in 1936.
- Multiplying Dividing Machine invented by Bryce and Dickinson in
1937.
- Unit Counter invented by Carroll in 1925.
- Ratchet Type Plate Counter, invented by Lake and Pfaff in 1935.
- Pluggable Type Relay, invented by Lake and Pfaff in 1937.
- Double-Deck Card Feed, invented by Lake in 1921.
- Electromatic Typewriter developed for automatic operation by Lake
and Hamilton in 1936.
- Counter Readout and Emitter, invented by Bryce in 1928.
- Commutator Total-Taking Mechanism, invented by Daly in 1926.[55]

The majority of these technical advances predate Howard
Aiken's inspiration for Mark I, serving as further proof of his
marginal role. Not even Aiken's inspiration, Charles Babbage,
was safe from IBM's historical scrutiny. Again, applying Aiken's

own words , "I say Babbage failed but I would like to make it
especially clear that he failed because he lacked the machine
tools, electrical circuits, and metal alloys"[56] In other words,
Charles Babbage failed because he lacked the support of a corporation such as IBM.

IBM hoped to direct the future of calculating machines by
controlling the past. The Automatic Sequence Controlled Calculator was not a disruptive technology that would spawn a new
calculating industry separate from IBM's comparative advantage
in punch-card equipment.[57] Rather, innovation would be contained within the research facilities of Endicott and the patents
retained by the organization. Eventually, IBM planned to
dominate the scientific and mathematical markets, much as it
controlled the business market for punch card machines.

For Aiken and Hopper, on the other hand, the connection
with notable geniuses such as Babbage served practical agendas
both inside and outside the Computation Laboratory. Years
later, Hopper stated: "I'm quite sure that he [Aiken] discovered
Babbage well after he had the concept of the engine and that he
used it as a selling thing that made it more legitimate."[58] In fact,
I. Bernard Cohen has considered the question of how much
Babbage's machines influenced Aiken, precisely because Aiken
had equated himself with Babbage as far back as 1937.[59] It
appears however, that Aiken did not covet Babbage's ideas so
much as he coveted his prestige. To be associated with the man
who held the same chair of mathematics at Cambridge as Sir
Isaac Newton would help the rather undistiguished 37-year-old
graduate student turn diagrams and notes into an 81-foot machine
that weighed 9,445 pounds, contained 530 miles of wire, and
cost $750,000.[60]

With the completion of the Mark I manual, the need for legitimacy, as well as the benefits from it, had grown exponentially. The general demobilization at the end of World War II affected research projects at universities across the United States. Federal plans for a return to normalcy necessitated termination of wartime contracts, which meant that Commander Aiken and his machine would have to find sustainable sources of revenue to keep the operation afloat. This was particularly daunting since relations with IBM were in shambles. Moreover, Aiken's position at Harvard was somewhat precarious, given his lack of tenure, a volatile disposition, and the administration's tepid support for applied mathematics.

The Mark I manual served as a manifesto for automated computation after the war. Hopper produced an account in which the machine represented both a technical and a conceptual break from the past. This break is captured by the machine's official name, the Automated Sequence Controlled Calculator. A fully automated machine would free itself from the limitations of the human mind. As Aiken and his team proved during the war, a fully automated machine could operate 24 hours a day, seven days a week. The automation of mathematics and information processing would subject society to unprecedented technological forces. Just as the steam engine became the technological foundation of the industrial revolution, the Automated Sequence Controlled Calculator could become the technological foundation for a new type of revolution dealing with information.

From 1945 to 1947, the popular press embraced the Aiken-Hopper version of history and propagated it.[61] The successful spread of their account is best represented by the Boston *Sunday Post*'s cover story of 28 December 1947. Titled "Professor Aiken of Harvard Computation Laboratory Talks of Wonders / Says Era of Mechanical Calculators Lies Ahead of Us," the article includes a picture of Richard H. Babbage, great-grandson of Charles Babbage, talking with "Professor Howard Aiken, father of the modern calculating machine" while they inspect a piece of Babbage's Difference Engine. The article includes a condensed version of Hopper's history that recapitulates text found in the Mark I manual almost verbatim.

The academic press recognized Hopper's version of events just as quickly. In 1946, in the British scientific journal *Nature*, the British mathematician Leslie J. Comrie published a review of the Mark I manual titled "Babbage's Dream Comes True." Comrie concludes that Aiken's machine "is the realization of Babbage's project in principle," though he is "astonished" by the omission of IBM from the title and from Aiken's preface.[62] As a leading proponent of large-scale computational machines in Britain, Comrie openly lamented the fact that the British government had failed to bring Babbage's machines to their successful conclusions, which had "cost Britain the leading place in the art of mechanical computing."[63]

Aiken and Hopper also published three articles in *Electrical Engineering*, the primary journal of the American Institute of Electrical Engineers. Written once again by Hopper, the articles summarize the Mark I manual.[64] Their purpose was not only to educate a wider audience about computers but also to highlight the heroic achievement of Aiken and his crew deep in a basement at Harvard during the war. While some (at IBM and elsewhere) took issue with Aiken's depiction as a heroic inventor, Hopper— who believed that his forceful personality had helped to launch the computer age—defended her former boss. Reflecting years later on her time at Harvard, Hopper said:

If somebody has imagination and thinks up new concepts and new ideas, we are very apt to put a committee around them and cut them down to size. We don't tend to grow any giants anymore; we try to cut them back to the average to make them like everybody else. We are afraid of giants, so we are not growing any. We need a few giants.[65]

Hopper's public defense of Aiken and his achievements after the war enhanced her position at Harvard and her position in the nascent computing community. From the day she was assigned to Harvard, Hopper's instinct was to work hard and make her mathematical and writing skills indispensable to Aiken. Regardless of her military rank, Hopper was faced with the challenge of how to gain power from the margins, especially in view of Aiken's open distaste for being assigned a female officer. By embracing Aiken's embryonic vision and nurturing it with skill and care to maturity, Hopper endeared herself to her boss while creating a foundation for his postwar career as well as hers.

SPREADING THE WORD: HARVARD'S POSTWAR PR EFFORT

Hopper's *Manual of Operation* and her articles captured the technical achievements of the Harvard Computation Laboratory. These documents, combined with Aiken's library of photographs of the machine and its crew, were distributed to reporters, engineers, scientists, and businessmen who were interested in the field of large-scale computational machines. The documents outlined the technical aspects of the machine and placed Mark I, its inventor, and the Harvard Computation Laboratory at the dawn of the computer age.

With the conclusion of the war, Aiken encouraged dissemination of information concerning his machine. Though he had forfeited any patent rights to IBM in exchange for funding,

Aiken was never one to focus on the machine's commercial applications. Much like John von Neumann, Aiken believed that "essentially the primary object is to promote science."[66] In this light, the commander of Mark I believed the spread of computing technology to be a public good. His views were incorporated into the postwar contract with the Navy Bureau of Ordnance, which stated that no attempt would be made to restrict publication of results except in certain instances involving national security. This included information concerning the proposed Mark II and Mark III machines.[67]

To facilitate the flow of information, Aiken opened the doors of the Computation Laboratory to interested visitors. "It was 1946," Hopper recalled, "and we began to do more teaching. We had a little lecture room, and we began to have more visitors." With her academic experience, Hopper was the natural choice to lead private tours and give lectures. In the postwar environment, Hopper found herself spending a significant amount of time escorting important visitors and explaining to them how the new computing machines could be applied to a variety of fields. By the fall of 1946, Hopper was more concerned with public relations and the management than with writing code herself.[68]

By the beginning of 1947, Howard Aiken had taken his place among the elite of the budding computing community, and his staff, including Grace Hopper, basked in his glow. The newly minted Harvard Ph.D. who in 1940 had been informed by President James Conant that he would not be able to advance above faculty instructor was now a permanent fixture on the Harvard campus.[1] Aiken utilized the organizational and financial weight of the Navy to push a reluctant university to the forefront of mechanical computation and applied mathematics.

Harvard's heightened role within the computing community was physically represented by the construction of a modern two-story brick-and-glass building to house the new Computation Laboratory. The Laboratory was envisioned as the first of a number of new buildings that would make up Harvard's "Science City."[2] Given the emergence of science and the newfound relationship between universities and government in the postwar era, the Harvard administration hoped to improve the school's reputation in the sciences. In response to the new conditions, the Department of Engineering Sciences and Applied Physics was formed in 1946.

The Harvard Computation Laboratory featured on the cover of the *Journal of Applied Physics*, October 1946. Courtesy of Archives Center, National Museum of American History, Smithsonian Institution.

Aiken retired from active military duty on 1 January 1946, but retained his position as head of the Computation Project at the insistence of the Navy's Bureau of Ordnance. As a condition of Research and Development Contract 8555 between Harvard University and the Navy, Harvard agreed to make Aiken an associate professor of engineering mathematics within the new department. The contract also gave Aiken authorization to reassign wartime military staff members to the Harvard University research faculty. Aiken chose Grace Hopper, Richard Bloch, and Robert Campbell as the chief deputies of his growing Crimson fiefdom.[3]

SHARING KNOWLEDGE

In the years 1944–1947, the Harvard crew had demonstrated that a calculating machine could produce timely, accurate mathematical solutions on a continuous basis. Farther south, Presper Eckert, John Mauchly, and their team of female operators proved the feasibility of calculation at the speed of electricity. These early successes generated a wave of new projects including BINAC and UNIVAC (Electronic Control Company), Mark II and Mark III (Harvard Computation Laboratory), SSEC (IBM), Whirlwind (MIT), EDVAC (University of Pennsylvania), MANIAC (Institute for Advanced Study), and ERA (Engineering Research Associates). In England, the National Physical Laboratory's ACE and the University of Manchester's Mark I were under way, and at Cambridge University Maurice Wilkes was beginning his plans for the EDSAC.

With most of these programs in the early design phase, Aiken decided to magnanimously spread the knowledge gleaned at Harvard by hosting a conference on "large-scale digital calculating machinery" (computers) alongside the official opening of the Harvard Computation Laboratory. "Aiken felt it was time—there was enough development to get together," Hopper recalled. "We'd all been isolated during the war, you see, classified contracts and everything under the sun. It was time to get together and exchange information on the state of the art, so that we could all go on from there."[4]

Aside from getting together, Aiken saw the Symposium on Large-Scale Digital Calculating Machinery as a forum to highlight the superb work that was being done at Harvard. He believed himself and his loyal crew to be the founders of the field, and he wanted to continue the effort to educate fellow academics as well as industry and government officials about the lessons learned at Harvard. In the words of the January 1947 edition of the Harvard's alumni bulletin: "They came to see and hear what Professor Howard Hathaway Aiken and his staff had accomplished. To this giant in mathematics the pilgrims paid appropriate homage."[5]

Not only would the invitees be impressed with the new facility that housed Mark I, but they would experience a fully operational and automated data-processing center as well. By January 1947 the operation of Mark I had been fine-tuned by Hopper and her staff to the point where the machine ran flawlessly 23 hours in a given day. The machine's reliability and speed were unmatched by any mechanical or human computation facility, and a significant body of work—including multiple volumes of valuable engineering tables—had been completed. Much of the machine's output, however, was still couched in military secrecy, so few people were aware of the Computation Laboratory's accomplishments.[6]

In typical Aiken fashion, nothing during the symposium would be left to chance. He convened an organizing committee made up of Hopper, Benjamin Moore, and Joseph Harrison.[7] The committee identified experts in academia, business, and government who would be interested in the progress of calculating machinery. "Nobody realized it was an industry—it was a branch of research of some kind," Hopper recalled. "There was beginning to be more people; it was time to pull them together."[8]

The committee invited computing leaders from MIT, the University of Pennsylvania, and Princeton to mix with executives from General Electric, Prudential Insurance, National Cash Register, and IBM. The Navy Brass from the Bureau of Ordnance and the Office of Naval Research sat side by side with members of the National Research Council and the National Bureau of Standards. In true fashion, Aiken reserved final judgment on who attended and who spoke. "I made up my mind who was going to be on the program, and I called him up on the telephone and told him he was going to be on the program and what he was going to speak about," Aiken recalled. "Now I didn't put words in his mouth, but I told him the subject about which I wanted him to talk."[9]

BABBAGE IN THE FLESH

One of the initial people Aiken contacted was Richard Babbage, the great-grandson of the famed mathematician and failed computer-maker Charles Babbage. Aiken first contacted Babbage on 17 April 1946 to inform him about Hopper's completed book concerning Mark I: "We have recently delivered to the Harvard University Press a manuscript dealing with large-scale calculating machines. This is a book of some six hundred pages, of which the first chapter titled 'Historical Introduction' deals in large part with Babbage's work."[10]

In the ensuing correspondence, Aiken discussed Richard Babbage's great-grandfather's role in the evolution of calculating machines as described by Hopper; he also inquired about any memorabilia or other information of historical interest concerning his ancestor that Babbage might have in his possession. Aiken explained that the material would be included in an exhibit to be set up in the new Computation Laboratory. This material would be reunited with a piece of Babbage's Difference Engine that Richard's grandfather, Admiral H. P. Babbage, had donated to Harvard in 1886.

Richard Babbage was thrilled that a Harvard professor had taken such interest in his obscure and sometimes unappreciated ancestor, and was willing to help Aiken in any way he could. Although the Analytical Engine plans and other mathematical memoirs were part of a display in the Science Museum of London, Babbage did his best to track down other valuable memorabilia within the family. Over the next year, Aiken was supplied with a stream of Charles Babbage's books, papers, essays, treaties, and tables.

The donations culminated with a rare engraving of the famous mathematician made by Colghin of London in 1832 while Babbage was Lucasian Professor at Cambridge University, the same position held by Sir Isaac Newton. The younger Babbage offered the engraving to Aiken "with the thought that it might hang in your office in proximity to the other mementos and works which you already have." He believed Aiken to be the intellectual successor of Charles Babbage, and thanked the Harvard professor for providing him with the "unique opportunity to secure for my ancestor a measure of appreciation that did not come his way in life." The "unique opportunity" of which Richard Babbage spoke was his role as a guest speaker at the Harvard Symposium on Large-Scale Digital Calculating Machinery.[11] During his speech Babbage praised Aiken and his staff for persevering in their pursuit for automated computing. This was a quest in which his ancestor fell short, partly because, in his opinion, "all Englishmen [inherently] object to inventions."[12]

THE HARVARD SYMPOSIUM

On the morning of 7 January, the first day of the Symposium, the distinguished guests were treated to the first public demonstration of the Computation Laboratory's second creation, the Harvard Mark II. Unlike Mark I, Mark II was designed and constructed entirely by the Harvard crew. Aiken and Campbell were the chief designers, with periodic input from Hopper and Bloch. "The early thinking about Mark II," Campbell recalled, "was that it would have relay components, almost completely, both for control and for computations. This would be a departure then from the Mark I, which used electromechanical counters for simulation and for storage."[13]

Relays had proven reliable in Mark I, and Aiken decided to extend the technology as a solution for the problem of memory. The crew devised an ingenious latching relay that could stay in a given position without the continuous application of power. The more advanced relay system provided 200 words of memory, while an improved logical design made Mark II twelve times as fast as its ancestor. "The big step forward in Mark II," Hopper recalled, "was the tremendous development of the multi-processor and the multi-programmer."[14] Mark II was a dual processor, meaning the machine could be split into two halves that could run independently, or combined in parallel into one multiprocessor. The reason behind this innovation was that one half of the machine could be run against the other as a way to check output accuracy.[15]

Symposium guests were then escorted from the Gordon McKay Laboratory that housed Mark II to the new Computation Laboratory. Passing the exhibit dedicated to Charles Babbage, the visitors were led to a specially designed gallery with windows two stories high overlooking the Mark I operation. The efficient performance by the machine and its operators was the culmination of years of machine debugging, organizational design, and personnel training. Aiken liked to compare Mark I's performance to that of a power generating plant. Instead of generating electricity, Mark I and its crew of operators generated numbers.[16]

The Symposium formally commenced with opening remarks from the administrative vice president of Harvard University, Edward Reynolds. Harvard President James Conant had taken ill and could not attend, perhaps an indication of lingering animosity between Aiken and the Harvard administration. Along these same lines, Reynolds seemed to go out of his way to point out that the developments in computing at Harvard could not have been accomplished without help from IBM, and that the credit for the Automatic Sequence Controlled Calculator must be shared with IBM engineers Clair Lake, Frank Hamilton, and Benjamin Durfee.[17]

Conversely, Rear Admiral C. Turner Joy, Commanding Officer of the Naval Proving Grounds at Dahlgren, Virginia, highlighted Aiken's forceful leadership in the new field and applauded the novel relations between Harvard and the Navy. He noted that the modern tools of warfare were now the domain of scientists like Aiken, and was relieved that he personally was too old to have to learn about these new machines. More importantly to many in the audience, Joy pledged that Navy calculators would be made available to all scientists in the future after the backlog of work in guided missiles and aerodynamic supersonic problems had been disposed of. His most audacious statement, however, concerned the future impact of computing machines, for he believed that "the new interest in mathematics might appear more likely to usher in an age of reason than the new interest in atomic energy."[18]

Aiken's comments mirrored the many lectures and presentations he had given on automatic calculating machines since the end of the war. He began with Hopper's computing history, introducing the audience to "the names of some of the greatest mathematicians and physicists of all time associated with the development of calculating machinery,"[19] which led, of course, to his office doorstep at Harvard. These remarks were amplified by the words of Richard Babbage, who later admitted in a letter to Aiken, "I could not help thinking how pleased Charles Babbage would be if he could come alive now and meet the man who discovered how to build a machine that would produce accurate answers to questions which only a genius can put to it!"[20]

Aiken forcefully stated that the focus of the Symposium should be the transmission of ideas concerning the design of calculating machines for scientific applications. He outlined the growing demand for more powerful calculating methods in the mathematical and physical sciences, including the fact that many recent scientific and engineering developments were based on nonlinear effects. Since the only methods available to solve differential equations involved labor-intensive expansions of infinite series and numerical integration, it was imperative that scientists and engineers embrace the new field of calculating machinery in the name of progress.[21]

Aiken did admit, however, that there might be some room for applications in quantitative social sciences such as economics. He invited his Harvard colleague Wassily Leontief to comment on the applications of Mark I in the field of economics. In his paper titled "Computational Problems Arising in Connection with Economic Analysis of Inter-industrial Relationships," Leontief described "input-output" economics, an early example of econometrics in which segments of the economy are mathematically represented by large systems of simultaneous linear differential equations. These equations described the not so obvious connections between industries as diverse as steel, textiles, and paper.[22]

Mathematical models, brought to life by large calculating machines, would provide economists the ability to answer a variety of once inconceivable questions: When a steel mill closes in Pennsylvania, how is the output of textiles affected? When the price of steel goes up, how does the price of automobiles change? With the help of Mark I, Leontief demonstrated that a general wage rise of ten percent in the United States would increase the cost of living by four percent. Leontief's work was the first application of a calculating machine in the social sciences, and would eventually lead to a Nobel Prize in economics.[23]

The first technical papers presented on the afternoon of the first day were again focused on the Harvard Computation Laboratory. Richard Bloch described the hardware and operating principles behind Mark I, and Robert Campbell's discussion focused on Mark II. Grace Hopper was conspicuously absent from the list of speakers. Hopper suggested that she was passed over because the Symposium's focus was on hardware and engineering, not programming. "There was nothing on software, yet—nothing on programming. You'll find it was all hardware and engineering, and specific [engineering] problems—not on the programming techniques yet."[24]

For the most part, Hopper's observation was accurate; however, Bloch did manage to inform his audience about some of the Mark I coding practices and techniques developed by the duo. He explained the practice of coding in rudimentary terms, and then highlighted certain changes made in programming and hardware that augmented Mark I's processing speed. Finally, Bloch described the introduction of branching to the main sequence mechanism. Branching permitted Mark I to make decisions based on intermediate output and to follow any of several calculation paths without the need for human intervention. Branching was the first example of if-then conditional commands, and made Mark I far more flexible and time efficient.[25]

Aside from Bloch and Leontief, engineering problems dominated the rest of the Symposium, and computer memory was at the forefront of the technical talks. Though a lack of machine memory made Mark I tedious to code and operate, the machine's slow processing speed allowed both instructions and data to be mechanically fed into the machine in a synchronous fashion. Conversely, electronic machines (such as the ENIAC), which made calculations thousands of times as fast as Mark I or Mark II, could not be coded in such a fashion, and therefore had to be physically reconfigured for each problem. The reconfiguring process was so time consuming that the ENIAC had little utility other than running the same problem hundreds of times, such as in the creation of a specific ballistics table with incremental variable changes.

In order to overcome the ENIAC's limitations, Presper Eckert, John Mauchly, and John von Neumann concluded that one way to take full advantage of the computational speed of an electronic calculating machine was to hold both the instruction code and data in some form of internal memory. Information would be accessed at electronic speeds, and both data and instructions could be modified as a given problem progressed. The stored-program concept, as it was later named, was first described in the famous unpublished but highly circulated document von Neumann wrote in June 1945 titled "First Draft of a Report on EDVAC."[26]

For the attendees of the conference who were contemplating building an electronic computer with a stored-program capability, it was imperative to solve the engineering issues surrounding memory. During the four-day Symposium there were a variety of memory proposals discussed within the corridors of the Computation Laboratory. Harvard's Benjamin Moore presented on magnetic coated disks and drums, MIT's Jay Forrester spoke on high-speed electrostatic storage, and T. Kite Sharpless of the University of Pennsylvania lectured on mercury delay lines. Other options discussed included optical and photographic storage techniques, and a variety of high-speed transfer mechanisms between external and internal memory.[27]

The only apparent tarnish on a perfectly organized and executed Symposium was the noticeable absence of two of the early community's most notable members. Professor Norbert Wiener, the distinguished mathematician and founder of the field of cybernetics, decided not to attend for moral reasons. Even though Wiener had served during World War I as a human computer for Army Ordnance at Aberdeen Proving Ground and worked on antiaircraft defense systems during World War II, he refused to attend the Symposium on the grounds that the Navy had been a joint sponsor. Six months earlier, *The Atlantic* published a letter stating Wiener's new position: he "would no longer cooperate in scientific research that might result in improved guided missiles for bombing or poisoning of defenseless peoples or otherwise do damage in the hands of irresponsible militarists."[28]

Another noted mathematician, John von Neumann, had no such reservations, but decided instead to take a well-needed vacation during the Symposium. The famous mathematician was quite familiar with the Harvard Mark I, as stated earlier, having run the crucial Los Alamos nuclear implosion problem on the machine during the war. Furthermore, both von Neumann and Aiken were recently named to an elite Committee on High Speed Calculating Machines established by the National Research Council, and they would see each other during a committee meeting after the Symposium.[29]

Believing that he and Aiken represented the leadership of the budding computing community, von Neumann unabashedly offered his colleague some words of advice as they worked to construct the boundaries of the new profession:

We are concerned with developing a relatively new subject—at least new as far as its impact on a major sector of the mathematical community is concerned—and we should, therefore, be very jealous of our standards of publications. It is very probable that we have not yet found our proper level, nor the majority of the mathematical talent that will be ultimately interested in this subject (of this, I am quite particularly strongly convinced), nor the literary form and style and vehicles for the expression of our ideas. At this moment, we are going through a period of expansion and the unavoidable accompanying confusion. We should not permit a low literary standard being established in our field, and it seems to me that it would be a serious mistake to go too easy with neophytes.[30]

Von Neumann went on to recommend that the two of them should work to establish publishing standards and regulatory mechanisms as customary to more established fields in the exact sciences. Since he would not be in attendance, his final recommendation was that "the speakers should be encouraged to submit manuscripts but the full editorial and reviewing authority should be retained by you."[31]

AFTER HOURS

For all of Aiken's attempts to control the agenda of the conference, what he could not direct was what occurred between the Symposium's formalities. "I don't think that any [of us] ever stopped talking the whole time," Hopper recalled, "and everybody stayed up all night talking about things—it was just a steady run of conversation." The dearth of computing publications was a poor indication of the amount of knowledge already generated by the evolving community of practice. Instead of being physically located in books and journal articles, knowledge resided in the minds of the pioneers. The symposium's most unexpected outcome was that the majority of learning occurred in between and after the formalities of the day, aided by the lubricating flow of alcohol.

The informal learning, according to Hopper, diverged considerably from Aiken's planned program of events. Much of the discussion in the halls and during meals centered on the potential uses for the machine. Aiken's assertion that computers were primarily scientific instruments was obvious, but the potential was there for so much more, including automated command and control, aeronautical design, medicine, insurance, and a variety of statistical applications in the social sciences. Another concern centered on the need to attract more young people into the field in order to fuel the envisioned growth. This included not only machine designers, but also mathematically trained coders and operators. "The informal conversations are all lost," Hopper lamented, "but, I dare say, that it gave quite an impetus to the industry because everybody began getting ideas from everybody else; they'd been living in isolation, and this brought them all together."[32]

RAMIFICATIONS OF THE SYMPOSIUM

As the letters poured into the Harvard Computation Laboratory in the following months, it became evident that the conference had been an immense success. "I can't pinpoint any particular thing that occurred as a result of it," Hopper later recalled, "but I think a great deal that happened in the next few years were a result of it, because we began to get cross fertilization and communication."[33]

The most obvious effect was the creation of a forum for dispersed people to come together and exchange ideas concerning the new technology. "People that hadn't seen each other in years, because one had been at Oak Ridge, and one had been at Harvard, and one had been out on the Coast, got together," Hopper recalled. For many invitees it was also the first time that they were able to interact with people from abroad, particularly England.[34]

The need for personal communication was more pressing because of limited publications. Apart from Hopper's *Manual of Operation*, her three articles on Mark I, and von Neumann's unpublished "First Draft of a Report on EDVAC," there was little else the computing community could turn to in January 1947 other than a number of marginally informative newspaper articles. The scarcity of publication was exacerbated by enforced secrecy surrounding certain projects, such as MIT's Whirlwind, or fear that disclosure would threaten patent positions, as was the case with Eckert and Mauchly.[35]

Besides the cross-fertilization of ideas, the Symposium encouraged the development of institutional connections. Business leaders were exposed to university mathematicians and scientists who had a better understanding of how the new technology could be applied. Military and government leaders controlled funding that university scientists and mathematicians needed for the next generation of machines. Business leaders identified potential government and university customers. All groups realized that the field's future depended on continued cooperation and support.[36]

For Aiken and the original crew (Hopper, Campbell, and Bloch), the Symposium was a celebration of their hard-earned accomplishments and long hours of labor. Harvard officialdom, fellow computing pioneers, and leaders in government and the military were all in attendance to dedicate the new Harvard Computation Laboratory, to see Mark I and Mark II, and to pay homage, as the Harvard Alumni Bulletin proclaimed, to "what Professor Howard Hathaway Aiken and his staff had accomplished."[37]

For Aiken, the event marked the end of his continuous battle for legitimacy at the University. He had brazenly bypassed an unsupportive Harvard administration and turned to industry and the military in order to construct a calculating machine, and that machine had now shown its worth as a scientific and mathematical tool. Rear Admiral Joy's opening remarks praised Aiken's drive and perseverance and educated the audience on the Harvard crew's work in support of the war effort. Richard Babbage spoke of his great-grandfather's vision of automated calculation, proclaiming that Aiken had fulfilled his ancestor's dream.

But not all those in attendance were in awe of Aiken and his accomplishments. Aiken and his crew had demonstrated that computers could produce useful solutions on a consistent basis. Reliability was achieved, however, by way of conservative technical choices during hardware design. The unveiled Mark II was a disappointment, for it did not incorporate technologies that other members of the community took for granted as the state of the art. "I think Mark II was neglected because it was built out of relays and its slow speed," Hopper recalled. "Nobody paid any attention to her because by the time anybody knew anything about her, she was a dead duck, and everybody was going electronic."[38]

For a number of the younger attendees, their experience during the war made them look at computing issues from a different technical perspective than Aiken. As Maurice Wilkes recalled, wartime work in radar, ionospheric research, and television made him very comfortable with electronics. "This was the world in which I and others of my generation had grown up, and we saw the possibilities of achieving, with these means, very high speeds with elegant economy of equipment," he recalled. "Very few people of Aiken's generation developed green fingers for electronics, but not all were afraid of high speed electronics to the extent that he was."[39]

Paul Morton, representing the University of California and its budding computer project, praised the Harvard crew for developing a reliable machine, but rejected Aiken's technical choices on similar grounds. "I did give him [Aiken] a great deal of respect for the fact that he didn't make any compromises with reliability," Morton stated. "He knew everything really worked, and it did work, even though it was brute force and everybody made fun of it."[40]

Just as Aiken was criticized for choosing electromechanical relays over electronic elements, with memory, too, he found himself on the wrong side of the technical divide. His choice of latched relays for Mark II and his penchant for drum memory for the proposed Mark III ran counter to the developing consensus around the Williams tube and mercury delay lines. Frederic Williams of the University of Manchester was developing a series of cathode ray tubes that could hold electric charges that represented data. The data could be accessed rapidly and randomly, a significant advantage when working with a machine that operated at electronic speeds. Of the machines that were developed in the 3 years after the Harvard Symposium, the Manchester Mark I, Whirlwind, MANIAC, SEAC, and SWAC utilized the Williams Tube, which was in fact the first example of random access memory (RAM).

The other preferred storage technology, mercury delay lines, came by way of radar technology during the war. Delay lines stored data by converting it from an electric signal into an acoustic signal moving through a mercury-filled tube. Upon reaching the far end of the tube, the signal could be converted back to electric form, or else it could be amplified and bounced back to the beginning of the tube indefinitely until ready for use. Again, the mercury delay line's chief advantage comes in storing and accessing information at high speeds, though the information must be accessed sequentially. Mercury delay lines would be used successfully in EDVAC, EDSAC, ACE, BINAC, UNIVAC, and RAYDAC.

For the most part, Hopper defended Aiken's choice of technology, particularly for Mark II. Designing the second machine commenced in the fall of 1944, and the wartime environment hindered the team from exploring more exotic technological options. Hopper was even impressed by the creativeness of the crew despite less then optimal work conditions. "There weren't any relays that were fast enough to attain the speeds that Mark II needed," she recalled, "and those fast latch relays and the other fast relays were actually built for Mark II and Mark II only. And much of that had to be invented under pressure."[41] Bloch also backed Aiken's decisions in the face of later criticism. "Howard Aiken accomplished a great deal at a time when the tools were few and far between," he strongly asserted.[42]

For other members of the Harvard crew, however, the lack of innovative technical design at Harvard was more systemic. Fred Miller, the electrical engineer who supervised the construction of Mark II, believed that Aiken's lone wolf attitude interfered with the process of innovation. "I'm afraid that we have to blame him [Aiken] somewhere. He was so independent and the industry grew so rapidly that one man couldn't do it all himself."[43] According to Miller, the only people who had influence during the design process other than Aiken were Campbell and Hopper. Aiken's imposed hierarchical structure within the Computation Laboratory, even after he and his staff had become civilians, hindered the exchange of ideas.[44]

Despite their privileged position within the Harvard hierarchy, Campbell and Bloch concurred that Aiken was not one to seek out advice from others, especially people beyond his inner circle. "Aiken was the type of individual who could devise many of these ideas on his own," Bloch recalled, "and who also did not frequently bother to take the time to become completely acquainted with everything going on at the time."[45] If he got a concept stuck in his brain, no amount of discussion would change his mind. For instance, Aiken was convinced that the computational speeds generated by electronic machines such as the ENIAC were superfluous. Bloch, Miller, and Campbell recalled his typical argument that speed was ultimately limited by input and output, and therefore what was the use of all of that computational speed if one was limited by exogenous factors. Aiken's personal defense of relay technology on the grounds that excess speed was superfluous comes in stark contrast to Hopper's insistence that reliability and expediency were Aiken's guiding design principles.[46]

Even Aiken's uncompromising insistence on reliability and punctuality interfered at times with the design process. "Howard got to the point where he says, 'You know, on April 1st we're going to stop designing and build it anything from that time on will go into the book for our next machine,'" Miller described. "And sure enough, if somebody tried to add a feature he would stop them. I recall somebody trying to put something in on the next day and he said, 'No. That's the date. We're going to build it.'"[47] The same virtue of discipline that permitted Aiken to succeed where less focused inventors like Charles Babbage failed, had become a vice that interfered with the ability of the Computation Laboratory to explore more exotic technologies.

The Harvard Computation Laboratory at night. Courtesy of Harvard University Archives.

THE BEGINNING OF THE END: THE MIGRATION OF TALENT

In the days that followed the first Symposium on Large-Scale Digital Calculating Machinery, the *Christian Science Monitor*, the *New York Times*, and other newspapers praised the accomplishments of Howard Hathaway Aiken and his staff. Aiken once again took full advantage of the wide reach of the Harvard News Bureau to inform the world of their accomplishments. And once again, Grace Hopper found herself adorning the cover of a major newspaper. This time a well-dressed Hopper is pictured hobnobbing with Navy brass, while another photograph had her reviewing printouts from the Harvard Mark I.[48] Aiken also took full advantage of Richard Babbage's visit, and the two appeared in a photograph together inspecting the gears of Babbage's Difference Engine.

In the eyes of the educated public, Aiken, Hopper, and the rest of the Harvard Laboratory crew were situated at the forefront of a technical revolution the likes of which were only beginning to be understood. They had designed, constructed, and operated two machines before other groups had assembled one. It was only prudent that others should travel to Harvard and learn from the intellectual heir of Charles Babbage and his disciples.

For the members of the Harvard crew, the Symposium exposed them to a new world of ideas, many of which contradicted much that they had learned while working with Aiken. The Commander had created a closed system cut off from the ideas of others. "The Harvard project was sort of self-contained," Campbell recalled. "It didn't—at least through 1950—it pretty much went its own way and there was not an awful lot of interchange."[49] Aiken justified the self-containment on the grounds that Harvard had a monopoly on good ideas. "You worked with Howard," Miller recalled, "you knew everything, you had the world in your fist, and everybody else must be way out of line and out of base. In fact, I have a funny feeling that if I'd asked to spend some time at MIT to see what they were doing, he'd have seen to it that I got fired some way."[50]

But the Symposium had opened up the floodgates, and for some of the crew, there was no turning back. Weeks after the Symposium, Robert Campbell left Harvard to join Raytheon Manufacturing Company. The company had decided to set up a computer group, headed by Andy Adelson, formerly of the MIT Radiation Lab. Besides the financial incentive, Campbell would be in charge of systems design with wide-ranging authority.[51]

What shocked Campbell most upon arriving at Raytheon was the collegial environment among his co-workers. "At Harvard," he recalled, "the whole situation was dominated by Aiken. At Raytheon it was more the group of us working together."[52]

After completing a study for the Bureau of Standards, Raytheon won a contract to build a computer for the Naval Missile Test Center at Point Mugu, California. The computer, designated RAYDAC, would be a binary, electronic computer with a stored program, magnetic tape input and output, and mercury delay line memory. Before the ink on the RAYDAC contract was dry, Campbell convinced Richard Bloch to join him at Raytheon. "Aiken felt that I really should get into the professional ranks there [at Harvard] and remain in the academic environment," Bloch recalled. "I tended to feel that I was destined to move into industry and that there may be greater challenges there."[53]

Bloch left the Harvard Computation Laboratory in March 1947 to head up the software side of the RAYDAC project. Bloch basked in his newfound intellectual freedom, and soon made significant contributions to the Raytheon project. "The thing I was proudest of was the fact that I came up with the automatic error detection system," he recalled.[54] Bloch's error detection system was the first instance of an extended parity check. When Robert Campbell took a more senior position at Burroughs in 1949, Bloch was placed in charge of both hardware and software design.

THE FORMATION OF THE ASSOCIATION FOR COMPUTING MACHINERY

According to Hopper, the cross-fertilization and heightened communication generated at the Harvard Symposium made many attendees aware that the emerging computing community lacked the necessary institutions to permit a broad dialogue to continue beyond Harvard.[55] In particular, Edmund Berkeley, a former Computation Laboratory crew member, believed that a forum for sharing knowledge was needed for all those interested in computers, not just a select few. "We felt that we were not so worthwhile in the eyes of people who were making arbitrary decisions about what's worthwhile," recalled Harry Goheen, another former Harvard crew member and early supporter of Berkeley's vision.[56] Edmund Berkeley was certain that he was worthwhile and was willing to do something about it.

Berkeley received his bachelor's degree in mathematics from Harvard University in 1930. Upon graduation he worked for New York Mutual Life Insurance and then moved to Prudential Insurance. After the attack on Pearl Harbor, Berkeley joined the Navy and was assigned to the Dahlgren Ordnance Laboratory as a mathematician and a human computer. When the Bureau of Ordnance contracted with Howard Aiken to build Mark II, Lieutenant Commander Berkeley was sent to the Harvard Computation Laboratory to monitor the development of the project.

From the start, Berkeley had a difficult time adjusting to the Computation Laboratory's environment. Despite his rank, Hopper and the crew saw him as a civilian computer. "He didn't know much about the Navy," Hopper recalled. "He got scared to death of Aiken so he started sending me little notes."[57] When Hopper got tired of serving as an intermediary and Berkeley finally gained the courage to face Aiken, he exhibited a nervous habit of jotting down everything the commander was saying instead of looking at him. "This drove Aiken crazy," Hopper recalled, "so Aiken wouldn't let him take notes, and so he would go out to his desk and make notes as soon as he finished talking to the commander."[58]

Berkeley's shy disposition and penchant for order did not go unnoticed by the rest of the crew. "We used to plague the hell out of Berkeley," Hopper recalled. The crew's favorite activity was stealing Berkeley's trusty date stamp. Berkeley date-stamped every document that came across his desk, much to the amusement of some of the crew. "One day they very carefully stole his date stamp, and went up and date-stamped the whole roll of toilet paper in the men's room," Hopper recalled. "Berkeley threw a fit when he found his precious date stamp."[59]

Practical jokes aside, both Berkeley and his co-worker Harry Goheen eventually became fed up with the Computation Laboratory's "repressive" atmosphere and went their separate ways.[60] Berkeley was discharged from the Navy and returned to Prudential Insurance as the chief research consultant. During the Harvard Symposium in 1947 Berkeley and Goheen were reunited with Robert Campbell and the three began making plans for a forum for interchange between individuals and organizations at work in the computing field. "He [Berkeley] and several of us had felt that since Aiken handled most of the external contacts himself, other people in the Computation Laboratory were isolated from the rest of the world," Campbell recalled. "That was one of the motivating influences in the founding of ACM. Ed Berkeley, Harry Goheen and I from Harvard with several other people helped get the thing organized." According to Campbell, Berkeley served as the "principal instigator."[61]

It took Berkeley about 4 months after the Harvard Symposium to fashion a proposal for the new organization, at which time he attempted to enlist the support of the established members of the new field. "One day in April, 1947," Berkeley recalled,

"I went to see Archibald and Lehmer on the evening before a meeting of the National Research Council Committee on Large Scale Calculation. I persuaded Lehmer and Archibald to take the matter up at the meeting the next day, in which Stibitz and von Neumann and Aiken were . . . to meet with them."[62] Berkeley's proposal was brought up, met significant resistance, and voted down.

Howard Aiken remembered the Berkeley proposal and his strong feelings against it: "I said, 'No, we shouldn't do that because computation was a universal thing.' That our best interest and the best interests of the scientific community as a whole would be better served to assist everybody to use machinery and to publish their work, . . . von Neumann agreed with that completely, and so this proposal of Curtiss was voted down."[63] Aiken mentioned John Curtiss because he was the most ardent supporter of the Berkeley proposal on the committee. Curtiss, who at the time was the division chief of the National Bureau of Standards' Applied Mathematics Division, broke ranks with Aiken and von Neumann and joined Berkeley's quest for a computing association. That summer, Berkeley and Curtiss organized a temporary planning committee, which included Robert Campbell, Dick Bloch, and Harry Goheen. The group approached John Mauchly who, along with Presper Eckert, had recently formed the first private computer company, Electronic Control Company. Initially, Mauchly did not see the need for the organization. "John Mauchly said that there was complete freedom of interchange of information," remembered Goheen. "Well hell, he was a director of the project that built the ENIAC. Of course, for him there was complete freedom, and for people like von Neumann and Aiken—I'm sure there was never any difficulty finding out what was going on."[64] Eventually the group convinced Mauchly of the organization's potential utility, and the date was set for the initial gathering.

The first meeting of the Eastern Association for Computing Machinery took place on 15 September 1947 in a small physics laboratory at Columbia University. The majority of the meeting was spent on administrative issues, although T. Kite Sharpless reported on the design of the University of Pennsylvania's EDVAC computer. Foremost on the agenda was the selection of the Executive Council, which proved more difficult than anticipated. "There were," Goheen recalled, "people from IBM that felt that this was a ploy . . . of some of Aiken's friends to form another self-adulation society for the benefit of non–IBM people, and they were opposed to that. I mean, they didn't realize that we were a bunch of outs, I'm sure. But their attitude was: these are some of Aiken's boys." [65] According to Goheen, it took considerable reassurances on the part of Berkeley to placate the IBM crowd, and eventually all sides called for a vote. The 78 people in attendance elected Edmund Berkeley as (Prudential Insurance) acting secretary and Robert Campbell (Raytheon) as treasurer. The two most prominent figures at the meeting, John Mauchly (Electronic Control Company) and John Curtiss (Bureau of Standards), were elected vice president and president respectively. Other appointments to the executive council by the elected officials included Mina Rees (Office of Naval Research), C. B. Tompkins (Engineering Research Associates), Richard Taylor (MIT), T. Kite Sharpless (Technitrol, Inc.), E. G. Andrews (Bell Laboratories), and Franz Alt (Ballistic Research Laboratory).[66]

The assembled group agreed that the purpose of the organization was to "advance the science, development, construction, and application of the new machinery for computing, reasoning, and other handling of information." Initially, the organization would represent four geographic areas—Boston, New York, Philadelphia, and Washington—with each elected official representing one of the four chief geographical sections. The founding members agreed that the "Eastern" would be removed if and when the association had ample representation from the Mid-West and West Coast.[67]

National aspirations aside, the fact remained that other than John Mauchly and John Curtiss, the majority of the computing elite were conspicuously absent from the meeting, above all Howard Hathaway Aiken and John von Neumann. "It would have been so much better," Berkeley recalled, "if we could have gotten Howard Aiken, and John von Neumann, and Herman Goldstine, and a few other people to work with us in the society in the early days. It wasn't through a lack of trying."[68] Berkeley, in fact, sent von Neumann a letter one month before the meeting encouraging the Princeton professor to participate. Von Neumann responded in the negative, reminding Berkeley that although he felt that in theory a computing association was desirable, he believed that the overall situation had not matured sufficiently to support such an endeavor. Despite his personal views, von Neumann did end the letter on a positive note, indicating that "this does not mean, however, that I will not be very glad if you succeed in furnishing the proof of the opposite, and I want to use this occasion to wish you the best of luck in your efforts."[69]

Berkeley, through his persistence, was able to convince von Neumann to present a paper at the Association's first general meeting held 11 and 12 December 1947, at the Ballistics Research Laboratories, Aberdeen Proving Ground, Aberdeen, Maryland. Von Neumann accepted the invitation, but Goheen noted, "he was willing to appear, but as von Neumann, not as a lecturer for the ACM."[70] The famed mathematician's paper, titled "General Principles of Coding, with Application to the ENIAC," was the first example of a conference paper dedicated to programming rather than machine design.[71]

Von Neumann's presence at the Aberdeen meeting helped to legitimate the nascent organization, and by January 1948 membership swelled to 350. On 16 January 1948 the Executive Committee dropped the "Eastern" and changed the name to Association for Computing Machinery. Moreover, Curtiss arranged for the National Research Council journal, *Mathematical Tables and Other Aids to Computation*, to reserve a section for articles and papers generated by ACM members. But despite the success of the former members of the Harvard Computation Laboratory just one year after the Harvard Symposium, nothing could change the mind of their former boss. "Aiken," Campbell recalled, "was always his own man. He went his own way and he had his own idea of how to do things."[72] Eventually Campbell had to trick his former boss into joining the organization, "I asked him when he was going to pay me back the five dollars he owed me. He didn't remember, but he paid me back the five dollars. I used the five dollars to enroll him in the ACM. I don't think he ever paid another dues."[73]

HOPPER'S PLACE IN THE COMPUTING COMMUNITY

While former Harvard crew members Edward Berkeley, Robert Campbell, Harry Goheen, and Richard Bloch were off creating the Association for Computing Machinery, Grace Hopper was back at Harvard managing the operation of Mark I, training personnel from Dahlgren Ordnance Laboratory, and entertaining and educating visitors to the Computation Laboratory. Once again, Aiken took advantage of Hopper's writing ability and had his diligent assistant write the manual for the Harvard Mark II; it was published by the Harvard University Press in 1949, again with "Staff of the Harvard Computation Laboratory" rather than "Grace Hopper" as the author.

Despite the apparent injustice, Hopper was quite content, even thrilled, with her place in life. She was skilled at programming and had full access to not one but two of the only functioning large-scale calculating machines in existence. She had a passion for teaching anyone who cared to learn about her machines, and the Computation Laboratory provided an endless stream of visitors and students. Finally, Hopper, more than most, had a special bond with Aiken, especially after the departure of Campbell and Bloch. Hopper enjoyed Aiken as a person, and respected him as a boss. In turn, Aiken bestowed on Hopper unparalleled liberties in decision making, and a healthy dose of responsibility for the day-to-day operation of the Computation Laboratory. Within Aiken's microcosm, Hopper was a somebody.

Hopper's hard work and dedication had convinced a once-skeptical Aiken that a woman could do what he considered to be a man's job, but eventually Hopper could not overcome the immovable rules of Harvard University. With the expiration of the Navy contract in 1949, Aiken continued on as a tenure track professor at Harvard. He remained director of the Computation Laboratory until his retirement in 1961.[74] Hopper, on the other hand, was a faculty research fellow with a three-year contract. "They didn't promote women at Harvard at that point, so at the end of three years my time was up," she recalled.[75]

Fortunately for Hopper, by the start of 1949 the Association for Computing Machinery had taken root as the primary organization for the emerging computing community. Hopper's former co-workers Robert Campbell and Edmund Berkeley were reelected in January to serve as treasurer and secretary respectively, and the next significant meeting was planned for 18–20 April at the Oak Ridge National Laboratory in Tennessee. Hopper traveled to Oak Ridge to reunite with old friends, but also to test the job market. The talented programmer spoke with the heads of a variety of computing projects and computer-related organizations and was overwhelmed by the number of job offers she received.[76]

On the back of her conference program, Hopper jotted down her career options. She received offers from the Ballistics Research Laboratories, Aberdeen Proving Ground, Engineering Research Associates, the Eckert-Mauchly Computer Corporation, and two separate offers from the Office of Naval Research. Both Engineering Research Associates and the Eckert and Mauchly offered the most money, a substantial salary of $7,200 per year. Next to one of the ONR offers, Hopper jotted "and maybe this in uniform," followed by "they think maybe they can get me a waiver on a promotion." It seems to reason that the ONR option called for Hopper to return to active duty, a proposition that appeared to be of significant interest for the reserve officer.[77]

After some deliberation, Hopper narrowed down her choices to two. Option one reunited Hopper with her former Yale mathematics professor Dr. Howard Engstrom. Engstrom and William Norris had founded Engineering Research Associates (ERA) with financial backing from the Navy after the war. During the war both Engstrom and Norris had been commanders specializing in cryptography at the Navy's secretive Communications Annex. Engstrom and Norris transferred their development teams to St. Paul, Minnesota after the war and founded ERA with the intent of designing computing machines

for cryptological purposes. The company had substantial expertise in magnetic drum memory and in 1947 began to construct
a digital computer called ATLAS for the Navy.[78] The second
option was also a private venture. The Eckert–Mauchly Computer Corporation was a computer start-up based in Philadelphia.
Hopper first met its founders during her visit to see the ENIAC
at the Moore School of Electrical Engineering at the University
of Pennsylvania in 1945. After a dispute concerning patent rights
with the University, the two ambitious inventors struck out on
their own in the spring of 1946. By the time of the Oak Ridge
Conference, the Eckert–Mauchly Computer Corporation had
signed contracts with the Northrop Aviation to construct an
electronic digital computer, BINAC, as well as contracts with
the Census Bureau, National Bureau of Standards, and the Army
Map Service to construct a general-purpose electronic digital
computer, UNIVAC.

What made both companies attractive was the fact that
they were to have working machines available within the year.
Hopper thrived in the Harvard Computation Laboratory's
operational environment, and she hoped to find this again at
the two start-up companies. In fact, Hopper had applied for
a position at IBM, but walked out of the interview after experiencing what she perceived as the suffocating environment of
Thomas Watson Sr.'s oversized corporation. "I couldn't take it,"
Hopper recalled, "because that was back in the days when they
still had flags, an IBM flag, and sang songs about it."[79] In the end,
Hopper chose the Eckert–Mauchly Computer Corporation.
"The thing that finally tipped my decision," Hopper recalled,
"was the fact that they had BINAC running and UNIVAC I
was well underway and would be running within a year
whereas it looked as though the work out at St. Paul was going

to be quite a bit longer. Plus the fact that John Mauchly looked like a wonderful person to work for, and I would be working for him."[80]

Hopper's time at Harvard was instrumental for her development as a programmer, a manager, and a leader within the emergent computing community. The pace of the war years catalyzed her transition from a college professor to that of a computer programmer, a term that would not be applied until 1949. During that time she helped to define what programmers were, what they did, and how they did it. Along with Richard Bloch she developed a methodical system of coding and batch processing that turned the experimental Mark I from a mechanical curiosity into a useful mechanical tool. This achievement was far from trivial, for it proved that computation could be automated on a large scale.

After the war, Hopper was responsible for recording the Computation Laboratory's tacit organizational knowledge so that it could be widely disseminated. She authored the Mark I *Manual of Operation* and later the Mark II manual that documented the laboratory's technical accomplishments and placed the Harvard achievement within historical context. Her three articles concerning hardware and programming development at Harvard were widely distributed to those interested in the new field. As interest in computers grew through the 1940s, Hopper gave seminars and escorted hundreds of visitors through the Computation Laboratory. Furthermore, her close association with Howard Aiken, coupled with her growing expertise, afforded Hopper continued access to the elite of the field at a time when many women were retiring from public life. But despite her successes, Grace Hopper's career in computers had only just begun.

On a cold night in November 1949, only 6 months after leaving Harvard and joining the Eckert-Mauchly Computer Corporation, Grace Murray Hopper found herself behind bars at the central Philadelphia police station. The programming pioneer was arrested at 3 a.m. for drunk and disorderly conduct. She was eventually placed in the custody of Pennsylvania General Hospital for treatment. Hopper's life was unraveling. At the age of 43 she had accomplished much, yet her growing dependency on alcohol was jeopardizing her career and her relationships. As winter approached, Hopper even contemplated suicide by drowning herself in the Schuylkill River, something she had supposedly tried unsuccessfully in Boston's Charles River weeks before.[1]

Eight years had passed since Grace Hopper chose to reinvent herself. During those years she left her husband, quit her secure teaching position at Vassar College, joined the Navy, and aligned her future with the embryonic computer industry. The long hours and late nights she endured at the Harvard Computation Laboratory transformed the former mathematics professor into the world's premier computer programmer. She helped to prove both the viability and the utility of the new computing technology during the war, and she wrote and lectured about the

Harvard Computation Laboratory's achievements after the war. Hopper's accomplishments during her eight-year transformation, however, came at a considerable personal cost. Pioneers such as Hopper are faced with far more than technical conundrums. They must deal with a variety of social and psychological pressures associated with the very act of exploring uncharted intellectual waters. In the process of creating that which does not exist, the technical pioneer must manage not only his or her own doubts but also the doubts of colleagues, investors, managers, end users, and a skeptical public. Being an inventor is in many respects an act of faith: faith in one's own technical abilities, faith in those who work alongside, faith in the ultimate vision and purpose of the project.

The pressures associated with inventing the computer age at the Harvard Computational Laboratory were exacerbated by the special circumstances associated with the wartime environment. The war weighed heavily on Hopper and the Harvard crew, for they truly believed that their work was instrumental to the successful conclusion of the conflict. Despite the experimental nature of the Harvard machines, deadlines had to be met at an accelerated pace. On a more personal level, the war interrupted the peacetime rhythms of life: travel restrictions, food rationing, and material shortages became the norm.

But even after August 1945 and the country's gradual return to normalcy, the Computation Laboratory's overbearing director, Howard Aiken, attempted to maintain the sense of urgency associated with the war. It was during this period that Hopper's drinking problem worsened. No longer was drinking a social diversion; now Hopper found herself drinking during the week and even on the job. Flasks were hidden in closets and desks. Hopper's drinking binges and periods of recovery eventually amounted to two days per week wherein she could not function, thus undermining her productivity and placing an ever growing strain on friends and family.[2]

According to her friend and former Harvard colleague Edmund Berkeley, Hopper turned to alcohol during this period as a way to deal with the compounding pressures at the Harvard Computation Laboratory. She had dedicated herself fully to the overwhelming task of bringing Howard Aiken's machines to life. She used the machines to solve critical military problems, including one that resulted in an explosion over Nagasaki. As the psychological strains became increasingly pronounced, alcohol seemed to serve as an effective outlet, freeing Hopper to express emotions and to temporarily forget obstacles real and imagined. According to Berkeley, the expiration of Hopper's Harvard research contract was the best thing that could have happened to her, although in the short term unemployment added to the stress. During the last week of May 1949, the 43-year-old programmer packed up her belongings, headed to Philadelphia, and bet her future on two younger men who believed they could create the first commercial computer company.[3]

THE ECKERT-MAUCHLY COMPUTER CORPORATION

Leaving the caustic environment of the Harvard Computation Laboratory may have made sense to Edmund Berkeley in light of Grace Hopper's growing dependency on alcohol, but the environment of the Eckert-Mauchly Computer Corporation presented challenges too. The world of the start-up company is not for the weak of heart. Lacking the organizational constancy and financial stability of established firms, start-ups can only guarantee employees grueling hours, scant benefits, marginal pay, and a volatile future. As a rule they are the domain of the young and restless, for the vast majority fail within the first year of inception.

Even so, as of 1 June 1949 the future looked bright for Eckert and Mauchly's venture. Hopper's first days on the job were actually quite pleasant, and Berkeley noted the positive change in his friend's mental condition during her first 5 months in Philadelphia. Hopper had been ardently recruited by the company's leadership, and her reputation as a programmer, mathematician, and manager preceded her. Besides being one of the most experienced programmers in the new field, Hopper came from an operational environment. She had been instrumental in turning the Harvard Computation Laboratory into a highly efficient data-processing factory—a feat that Presper Eckert and John Mauchly had never matched with the ENIAC, given their creation's temperamental vacuum-tube technology and programming limitations.[4]

In contrast to her initial experience at Harvard, Hopper found EMCC to be very accepting of women. In fact, the majority of the programming staff as of June 1949 consisted of women. During the ENIAC project, Eckert and Mauchly arranged to have six women transferred from the Ballistic Research Laboratory (BRL) at Aberdeen to the Moore School of Electrical Engineering at the University of Pennsylvania to serve as ENIAC operators. The six had been members of a staff of about 200 mathematically inclined women who computed firing tables for artillery and rockets with desktop calculators. Three of the original six, Francis Elizabeth "Betty" Snyder (later Holberton), Betty "Jean" Jennings (later Bartik), and John Mauchly's future wife, Kathleen "Kay" McNulty, remained with Eckert and Mauchly after the two left the Moore School to form their company.[5]

The same charm and charisma that persuaded Snyder, Jennings, and McNulty to continue working with John Mauchly caught Hopper's attention when she chose EMCC. "Mauchly was one of the grandest people I have ever met," she recalled.

John Mauchly. Courtesy of John W. Mauchly Papers, Rare Book and Manuscript Laboratory, University of Pennsylvania.

"He was very broadminded, very gentle, very alive, very interested, very forward looking."[6] The man who was about to become
her new immediate boss was quite different from Commander
Howard Aiken. Where Aiken was overbearing, Mauchly was
accommodating. Where Aiken demanded, Mauchly convinced.

The sharpest distinction between the two computing pioneers,
however, was between their visions of the future. While Aiken
saw the computer primarily as a scientific instrument, Mauchly's
field of view was far more expansive. "He was looking way
ahead," said Hopper. "Even though he was a college professor he
was visualizing the use of these computers in the business and
industrial area." In fact, an inquiring customer could bring up
almost any field in business and Mauchly could ad-lib detailed
application descriptions, ranging from marketing research to
industrial process control. "He saw much more of the future of
the computer than just as a scientific tool or for the solution of
mathematical problems," Hopper recalled. "I think that's what
was exciting."[7]

Hopper marveled at the extraordinary relationship between
Mauchly and his youthful partner, Eckert. The two had met in
1941 at the University of Pennsylvania. At the time, Eckert was
a talented graduate student in the Moore School of Electrical
Engineering and Mauchly was teaching a war-related electronics
course. Two years before they met, Mauchly had experimented
with the notion of an electronic calculating machine, partly
because of the intense calculating work he was involved with for
the Army Signal Corps concerning radiation patterns for anten-
nas. The inventive physicist shared his ideas with the young
engineer and even demonstrated a simple mechanical counter
that he had constructed with gas tubes.

Eckert was drawn to the man and his computing ideas, and
the two began a dialogue concerning the feasibility of reckoning

at the speed of electricity. "Those conversations and things in 1941 gave me some confidence and assurance that I wasn't just on a wild goose chase," Mauchly recalled.[8] Eckert felt that Mauchly's theoretical concepts were plausible, but that Mauchly's engineering acumen was marginal. Mauchly saw in Eckert a no-nonsense practitioner who could turn his ideas into reality. Thus was formed a partnership that would construct the first all-electronic digital computer and establish the first commercial computer company.

According to Mauchly, the two did not expect to be business partners, for they were first and foremost academics. But with the appointment of Irvin Travis as the University of Pennsylvania's Dean of Research in January 1946, the inventors of ENIAC were forced to make a fateful decision. Travis offered Mauchly and Eckert permanent positions at the university on the condition that they sign a patent release. Travis believed that faculty and staff should not be permitted to benefit financially from research generated while working for the university. Given the potential of electronic computers, both inventors refused to sign and submitted their resignations effective 31 March 1946.[9]

Undeterred, the ambitious partners decided to build ENIAC's replacement privately, and in the spring of 1946 they formed the Electronic Control Company. "I think," Eckert recalled, "John and I wanted to get the computer out there and being used by people of every type and description for every way and every purpose, come hell or high water. We didn't care whether you called it scientific or engineering or mathematical or non-mathematical—we wanted to get this job done."[10] Their Electronic Discrete Variable Automatic Computer (EDVAC),[11] later renamed the Statistical EDVAC or Universal Automatic Computer (UNIVAC), followed the theoretical design set out in John von Neumann's June 1945 report, "First Draft of a Report on the EDVAC."

But according to both Eckert and Mauchly, the majority of the ideas in von Neumann's paper were reiterations of concepts that Eckert and Mauchly had fostered for years before the publication of the well-known mathematician's report. Von Neumann, they said, had been a beneficial sounding board because he quickly grasped concepts, and his prominence within academic and government circles permitted him to effectively broadcast ideas, but he had made few if any original contributions to the theoretical design of the EDVAC. Mauchly maintained that Eckert had written his own EDVAC report (dated January 1944), but because of government security concerns he had not been permitted to publish or even distribute it. "I was not allowed to make speeches about it, and he [von Neumann] went out and made them anyway without clearance and got out of it because nobody wanted to come down with the Espionage Act on a prestigious guy," said Eckert. "If I had done it, they would have come down on me with a ton of bricks."[12]

To add insult to injury, during the early spring of 1946 John von Neumann and Herman Goldstine (Eckert and Mauchly's trusted Army Ordnance representative to the ENIAC project, who had joined von Neumann at Princeton after the war) attempted to wholly claim the patent rights to the EDVAC. The two cited the "First Draft" as evidence of priority. Eckert and Mauchly fought their claim intensely, but in the end, on the technical grounds that one must apply for a patent within a year of publishing the results, neither party was granted a patent. Since von Neumann's "First Draft" had been distributed widely, it was considered to have been published in the legal sense; thus, both parties had exceeded the time limit.[13]

Despite the controversy surrounding the theoretical concepts for the stored-program computer, the fact remained that Eckert and Mauchly were the first Americans to bring those ideas to fruition. The UNIVAC design called for vacuum-tube technology that counted thousands of times as fast as Harvard's electro-mechanical relay machines, Mark I and Mark II. The proposed computing circuits added directly, and they replaced the subtraction operation with the addition of complements (the same numerical technique used in today's computers). Multiplication and division were achieved by successive additions— because of the tremendous speed of the processor, there was apparently no perceived advantage to applying short-cut multiplication and division methods.[14]

Similar to the architecture described in von Neumann's "First Draft," the UNIVAC's electronic circuitry processed information in a serial fashion, unlike the parallel design of the ENIAC. Since data and instructions passed one after another through the system's logic gates, circuit design was simplified and programming became less complicated. The serial flow of data also made it easy to debug hardware, for all information and instructions in a given operation had to pass through the same circuits.[15]

The UNIVAC had an experimental internal memory that could store 1,000 twelve-bit words. The technology, known as mercury delay line memory, had first been used in wartime radar systems. Electrical data from the UNIVAC was sent into a tube of mercury, where it generated small waves that bounced indefinitely until the data was reacquired by comparing the waves with a master clock. Despite the system's dependability, delay line memory had significant drawbacks. In addition to the overall size and cost, information could only be accessed sequentially, a loss of power wiped the memories clean, and the mercury had to be maintained at an uncomfortable 40 degrees Celsius for optimal performance.[16]

Electronic circuits combined with a relatively large internal memory that held both operating instructions and data would make the UNIVAC the most powerful calculating machine ever proposed. Its closest rival, the Harvard Mark II, performed 30–40 operations per second and had an internal memory of 200 words. The UNIVAC would perform more than 5,000 instructions per second with an internal memory of 1,000 words. Yet all that computational speed meant little without efficient input-output (I/O) mechanisms for entering data into internal memory. The ENIAC, for instance, was limited by the mechanical speeds of its IBM punch-card input system. Mark I and Mark II, despite their slow processors, achieved a higher I/O rate by means of paper tape.

Taking the Harvard I/O system one step further, Eckert began experimenting with a new technology initially developed by the audio recording industry: magnetic tape. The experimental magnetic-tape I/O device consisted of plate-size reels of magnetic tape, drive motors, and magnetic recording and reading heads. The magnetic heads were designed to record and read from the tape at a rate of about 400 words per second. Moreover, each 10-inch reel could hold 2,000 feet of 8-millimeter-wide tape and could store up to 2 million alphanumeric digits. High-speed drive motors and a sophisticated electronic clutch would maximize the efficiency of the tape and only 20 percent of the recording space would be wasted. The speed of the magnetic-tape system complemented the electronic circuits, permitting the user to take advantage of the hardware's calculating potential.[17]

HOW TO SELL A COMPUTER?

Although the proposed UNIVAC sounded remarkable to Grace Hopper, Eckert and Mauchly faced a considerable challenge in raising investment capital. Seed money was hard to come by, given the absence of a structured venture capital system in 1946. The only available avenue was to generate cash flow by receiving partial payment on UNIVAC purchase contracts—a difficult task with an unproven technology and an uninformed customer base. It would take all of John Mauchly's proselytizing talents to sell the vision of a computing future.[18]

Mauchly first turned to an organization with a history of supporting radical calculating technology: the United States Census Bureau. The Census Bureau was established in 1790 to track population demographics to determine the allocation of congressional seats. By the 1880 census, the population growth of the United States had outstripped the Census Bureau's manual data-processing capability, taking 1,500 full-time clerks over 7 years to produce the 21,000-page report. The Census Bureau turned to Herman Hollerith, a young engineer.

Hollerith's insight was that a person's identifying information (age, geography, etc) could be represented by holes punched in cards, which could then be processed mechanically. Hollerith's machines processed more than 60 million cards during the 1890 census, thus allowing the Census Bureau to complete the 27,000-page report 2 years early and $5 million under budget. In 1896 Hollerith formed his own company, which in 1911 merged with two other small office equipment firms to form the Computing-Tabulating-Recording (CTR) Company. In 1924 CTR's president, Thomas Watson Sr., renamed the company the International Business Machine Corporation (IBM) so that the firm's name would match his ambition.[19]

Fifty-six years after the Census Bureau purchased Hollerith's experimental punch-card machine, it signed a $300,000 contract for delivery of a UNIVAC. The Census Bureau contract marked an early victory for the fledgling Eckert-Mauchly Computer Corporation, but EMCC could not receive advance payments—government regulations only permitted the Census Bureau to award contracts for finished products. Fortunately, the National Bureau of Standards was also interested in a machine. It provided $75,000 up front to cover research costs for the mercury memory and the magnetic-tape system. The total National Bureau of Standards contract amounted to $300,000, which was to be paid in installments as the machine approached completion. Mauchly lined up a third contract with the Army Map Service, but once again money would not be released until a significant portion of the project was completed.

Eckert-Mauchly's financial situation became more precarious as the costs of developing UNIVAC crept ever higher. In October 1947, Eckert and Mauchly were forced to sign a contract with the Northrop Aircraft Company for a small Binary Automatic Computer (BINAC). The $100,000 price tag injected needed capital, but the 15 May 1948 delivery date for the BINAC would hamper progress on UNIVAC.[20]

Eckert-Mauchly's financial standing was vastly improved by an unlikely source: American Totalisator, a Baltimore-based company that supplied racetracks with machines that calculated betting odds and recorded race results. American Totalisator's senior management had heard about a new type of commercial calculating machine through George Eltgroth, EMCC's patent attorney. Eltgroth arranged for Eckert and Mauchly to meet with Henry Straus, the vice president of Totalisator. Straus, who had invented and patented the original totalisator machine, grasped the potential of the UNIVAC immediately.[21]

On 6 August 1948, Straus decided to formalize his interest in Eckert and Mauchly's start-up computing venture. Totalisator paid $500,000 for 40 percent control of EMCC, advancing the cash-strapped company $50,000 upon the closing of the contract. Straus was named chairman of EMCC's board of directors (which also included three Totalisator executives, Presper Eckert, and John Mauchly). Though outnumbered, the founding partners retained 54 percent of the common stock, with the final 6 percent dispersed among EMCC employees.[22]

Though Totalisator was formally represented on the EMCC board, strategic decisions and operational business and engineering decisions were left to Eckert and Mauchly. By 1 June 1949, when Grace Hopper arrived, the once struggling company was a flourishing organization with more than 100 employees. It had signed contracts with the National Bureau of Standards, the Census Bureau, the Army Map Service, and Northrop Aviation, and it was in negotiations with two insurance companies (Prudential and Metropolitan), with the marketing information company A. C. Nielsen Inc., and with the General Electric Company. The BINAC was close to completion, and the proposed UNIVAC (scheduled for delivery in 1951) had a technological "edge" unmatched by any potential competitor, including the established office-equipment firms IBM and Remington Rand.[23]

BETTY SNYDER (HOLBERTON)

Other than John Mauchly, Hopper spent most of her time working with Betty Snyder[24] during her transition from Harvard to EMCC. Hopper had met Snyder previously at Harvard and through the Association of Computing Machinery, but the first occasion that the two programmers had to sit down and talk was at Edmund Berkeley's home a few months before Hopper joined EMCC. Hopper was impressed with Snyder's intellect, knowledge of programming, and overall personality, all of which factored into her decision to go to EMCC.[25]

Betty Snyder (right) reconfiguring the ENIAC wiring in order to run a problem. Courtesy of U.S. Army.

Betty Snyder and Grace Hopper were similar in many respects, though Snyder was 12 years Hopper's junior. Both came from established middle-class families that emphasized learning. "I was one of eight children," Snyder noted, "and had a very delightful home life—four boys and four girls—and my father always felt that education was terribly important.[26] Also like Hopper, Snyder was influenced by her grandfather, who was a prominent astronomer. With the support of her family, Snyder attended a prestigious Philadelphia prep school, the George School, and earned a scholarship to the University of Pennsylvania, where she planned to study mathematics.

Snyder's experience at the University of Pennsylvania, however, diverged from the supportive environment Hopper found at

Vassar. During her freshman year, Snyder took analytical geometry with a well-known Russian mathematician who told the women in class that their education was a waste of time and resources. "Every day when he came into class," Snyder recalled, "he'd say 'You women should be home raising children.' Well, after you have 4 months of that every day, and you find out the next semester in mathematics is taught by the same fellow, with no alternatives, I just gave up."[27] Snyder transferred to the English Department and graduated with a degree in journalism.

Upon graduation, Snyder took a job with the *Farm Journal*. After the Japanese attacked Pearl Harbor, she wanted to join the war effort. "All of my family had joined the Service," she said. "I had two sisters in the Waves, and I wanted to join the Waves, but I wasn't accepted because of my eyes."[28] Determined to help her country, Snyder answered an advertisement in a Philadelphia newspaper for a position as a human computer for the Army's Ballistic Research Laboratory. The human computers at the laboratory spent much of their time calculating firing tables to be used by artillery units on the front lines. The advertisement specifically asked for woman with a penchant for mathematics, but added that training would be provided for those lacking a mathematical background. Snyder was interviewed by her future husband, John Holberton, who selected the young journalist and arranged for her to get extra training in mathematics.

Though Betty Snyder found calculating firing tables eight hours a day monotonous, she was motivated by the fact that she was contributing to the war effort. "I always felt it was a terrific thing we were doing," she recalled. "I really was just gung-ho on the whole thing." Gung-ho, that is, until her brother returned from the European theater and informed her that he and his men never used her tables. Instead, the gunners would shoot two or three cursory shots, make the proper adjustments on the basis of tacit knowledge and experience, and go from there. "It really burst my balloon," she recalled.[29]

Not seeing a future in human computing, Snyder volunteered for a special assignment to work on an experimental machine that supposedly would make the work of the Ballistic Research Laboratory's computer group obsolete. Snyder remembered that few people were interested in applying for the assignment, suspecting that being an operator on a machine was a demotion of sorts. "The first thing that Goldstine [said was] 'Your grades won't be decreased because you are going to be working on a machine,'" Snyder recalled. "The idea of a machine, you know, was a low-grade something or other."[30]

When Snyder reported for work at the Moore School, her experience was identical in many respects to Hopper's first days at Harvard. She remembered that no one in Philadelphia really knew what to do with her. There were no training materials or classes to teach a person to be an ENIAC operator, and from all appearances Eckert and Mauchly themselves had put little thought in how to actually operate such a machine once built. To make matters worse, Snyder's lack of numerical theory made it more difficult to understand mathematical problems broken down into component parts.[31]

The other women who arrived with Snyder recalled a similar feeling of bewilderment. Betty Jean Jennings (later Jean Bartik) remembered those first days alongside Snyder: "We knew we were supposed to run the machine and set up problems for the machine, but no one had any techniques or anything."[32] Eventually, by studying block diagrams of circuits and by taking part in long discussions with John Mauchly and with an engineer named Bob Shaw, Bartik and Snyder became proficient at running the machine. They also became quite familiar with the machine's hardware, for two reasons. First, unlike Mark I, the ENIAC was "programmed" via hardware manipulation. Much like the Moore School's analog differential analyzer, the ENIAC was physically reconfigured to correspond to the problem to be solved. Second, because of the unreliability of the vacuum-tube technology, much of their time was spent debugging the hardware.

By the winter of 1946, Betty Snyder was a valuable member of the ENIAC staff. She thoroughly enjoyed her new career, though there was no name for it. In February, after Eckert and Mauchly decided to set up a private company, she asked Mauchly if she could be a part of it. According to Snyder, for ethical reasons Mauchly was not soliciting staff members of the Moore School, even though he desperately needed trained people. "He wasn't willing to offer me a job until I made the overture," Betty Snyder Holberton later recalled.[33]

Through the spring of 1946, before the company received funding, Betty Snyder met with the other founding members at John Mauchly's house. "We used to go up there on weekends, I guess about five or six of us," she recalled. "We would hold the meeting starting Friday evening . . . maybe seven o'clock after dinner, and we worked until four in the morning." The original members of the team defined their roles and responsibilities during the design phase of the UNIVAC. Snyder and Mauchly assumed joint responsibility for constructing the operating code. Snyder would also work closely with Eckert to develop the magnetic-tape I/O system.[34]

LEARNING THE ROPES AT EMCC

After arriving in the early summer of 1949, Grace Hopper worked closely with Betty Snyder, who exposed her to new techniques and procedures. First and foremost was the practice of meticulously planning out the logic of a program with flow charts. "We didn't use flow charts [at Harvard], because everything was a perfectly simple sequence of operation because it just rode right along that tape," said Hopper.[35] BINAC and UNIVAC I were stored-program computers with the ability to modify instructions during a program run, and so the programmer could write much more complicated, non-sequential algorithms. Without a flow chart, the programmer was apt to lose her way when coding.

A flow chart, also called a flow diagram, is a graphical representation of the steps involved in a program. It systematically breaks down the algorithm and represents the flow of operations by means of geometric symbols. Snyder standardized the symbols used in flow charts, such as a rectangle for a process of action (e.g., Add *a* and *b*) and a diamond to represent a decision (e.g., Is *a* greater than *b*?). Because there were no index registers to allocate memory, memory locations had to be defined and tracked within the chart. Arrowed lines indicated the path of computational flow. The overall flow of the chart was from top to bottom and from left to right.[36]

A flow chart represents the logical analysis of a problem separate from a specific computer code or language. Hopper could draw up a single flow chart for coding an inventory control program, and that same flow chart then could be used as a guide to code two distinct computers with different object programs. Moreover, flow charts were a useful form of documentation. They permitted other programmers to quickly grasp or check a colleague's work by tracking the states of variables at crucial points during the flow of a program, thus helping to uncover errors in logic. Ultimately, flow charts were a powerful tool that helped standardize the process of program design.[37]

Although Grace Hopper emphasized that Betty Snyder developed the system of flow-chart analysis for EMCC, the historical record is not as clear. Herman Goldstine has credited himself and John von Neumann with the invention and development of the programming tool:

In the spring of that year [1946] von Neumann and I evolved an exceedingly crude sort of geometrical drawing to indicate in rough fashion the iterative nature of an induction. . . . I became convinced that this type of flow diagram, as we named it, could be used as a logically complete and precise notation for expressing a mathematical problem and that indeed this was essential to the task of programming.[38]

In 1947, Goldstine and von Neumann published a paper on the subject titled "Planning and Coding of Problems for an Electronic Computing Instrument." Years later, when questioned why she did not publish her original ideas at the time in order to receive the proper credit for them, Betty Snyder Holberton replied: "I did not write for publication because I wasn't out to push my name ever." Regardless, the practice of flow-charting programs began in Philadelphia and was passed to Hopper by Snyder during the summer of 1949. "She taught me that . . . and got me thinking in another dimension because you see the Mark programs had all been linear," said Hopper.[39]

Snyder also taught Hopper C-10, the instruction code for the UNIVAC, which she had developed with Mauchly over a two-year period. An instruction code, or operational code, constitutes the most basic set of commands that can be executed by the computer. In December 1947, Mauchly wrote to Snyder suggesting that "the instruction code should use symbols which are easily learned and identified with the operations by already existing mental associations: 'a' for add, etc." By replacing a sequence of binary numbers with a single letter to represent an operation,

Mauchly and Snyder were simplifying the coding process and making it much more intuitive for users. The philosophy would have a tremendous effect on Hopper's own breakthrough work during the 1950s. "I felt that people couldn't understand what we were doing because we were using such bizarre terminology," said Snyder. "I felt that we would never get anywhere unless we could really make people understand . . . you would see the word *s* and it meant subtract, and *t* meant test, and this kind of thing." Snyder chose to have the code coincide with the 26 letters of the alphabet so that the computer code paralleled concepts that all English-speaking users were familiar with, regardless of their mathematical background.[40]

Snyder thoughtfully created the code, constructing sample problems to see what instructions appeared most often. She hoped to create a type of language that a programmer could write fluently without constantly referring to a code manual. Three digits that designated memory location accompanied each code. The memory location, like the numbers entered as data, were written in decimal rather than binary or octal, another attempt to make the code adjust to the human instead of the other way around.[41] Hopper was impressed by Snyder's C-10 code, combined with the versatility of a stored-program computer, and she found the system far easier to use than what she had experienced at Harvard. "After coming from Mark I, I slipped into UNIVAC I like duck soup," she said. "I felt as if I'd acquired all of the freedom and all of the pleasures of the world; the instruction code was beautiful."[42] (See table 7.1.)

Hopper was impressed by C-10's advantages over the other machine codes. On both Mark I and Mark II she had to translate alphanumeric codes into octal digits that the computer could understand. Likewise, storage locations were written in octal.

TABLE 7.1
Examples of UNIVAC I's C-10 code instructions.

rA	Register used to store result of addition, subtraction, etc.
Am	Add (m) to (rA), result in rA
Mn	Multiply (rL) by (m), rounding off the product to 11 digits; result in rA
Nm	Multiply (rL) by negative (m); result in rA
Tm	Test to determine if (rA) > (rL); if so, transfer control to m

The difficulty of coding in a computer-centric numeric code made programming time-consuming, tedious, and prone to error. Furthermore, it had detrimental effects on Hopper's personal accounting. Each month her checkbook would be unbalanced because she would slip into octal addition and subtraction when balancing her accounts. The C-10 code, on the other hand, was much more intuitive. "We had decimal storage locations and it was heaven," she recalled. "It was all the difference in the world."[43]

After Hopper quickly familiarized herself with flow charts and C-10 code for UNIVAC, her main task during the summer and fall of 1949 was to begin to prepare a library of useful applications for the UNIVAC. Hopper brought to EMCC 5 years' operational experience that she applied to the task of developing a series of useful subroutines and generic programs. Like the relative code packages developed at Harvard, Hopper and her new team of programmers first constructed subroutines that could generate square roots, sine, cosine, tan, log and other transcendental functions. Each routine had flexible addresses so it could be placed into any specific portion of memory, and accuracy was made available up to eleven decimal places. During this time Hopper also developed a unique package of programs to solve Laplace boundary value problems that was ideal for solving heat and wave equations in engineering.[44]

In order to validate the efficacy of programs written for a computer that did not yet exist, Hopper employed the recently completed BINAC. The small binary stored-program electronic digital computer was supposed to be delivered to Northrop Aviation on 15 May 1948, but the machine was not operational until a month after Hopper's arrival. The machine was smaller but similar in design to the proposed UNIVAC, with a fast vacuum-tube processor and 512 words of memory provided by mercury tanks. "I would write in the C-10 code a subroutine to compute the sine and I'd transliterate it into BINAC code and check it out on BINAC so that we would have something ready to run when we got UNIVAC running," said Hopper.[45] Although the machine calculated in binary and could not represent alphabetic characters, UNIVAC I programs written in C-10 could be translated into octal and thus processed.

As Hopper settled into her new position, she took it upon herself to enhance the EMCC staff with talented programmers. "Some of the Harvard people I managed to attract to come down there, like Dick Waltman and Charles Katz," she said. "I brought a lot of people in down there." Other key additions included Hugh Livingston who was one of the enlisted operators assigned to Mark I, and most notably, Herb Mitchell, the first person to receive a doctorate from Aiken's Computation Laboratory.[46]

Hopper soon realized, however, that as of 1949 the pool of competent programmers was hardly larger then her immediate circle of friends, and that in the immediate future EMCC would have to "create" programmers. To make such a training program less hit or miss, Hopper and Mauchly attempted to identify the traits and abilities that they should look for when interviewing candidates. In the end they agreed on fifteen different characteristics, with three of the fifteen highlighted as essential. These included a systematic nature and methodical approach to new problems, careful reasoning without jumping to conclusions which are unwarranted, and imagination and creative ability. John Mauchly even devised an "aptitude test" for candidate assessment, though the subjective nature of some of the traits made personal interviews necessary. In the end, Hopper and Mauchly's efforts helped to identify the aptitude boundaries for a new profession, and EMCC began to make programmers, one at a time.[47]

Unbeknownst to Hopper, her efforts to build a team of programmers in order to build libraries of applications and subroutines were being mirrored by another group thousands of miles away at Cambridge University. Maurice Wilkes was assembling Britain's first stored-program electronic binary computer, the EDSAC, and in June 1949 he organized a group of programmers headed by David Wheeler to construct a library of programs. "We settled down to work on the library of subroutines and programming research in real earnest," wrote Wilkes. "The group of programmers—for they could now be called that—met regularly, and each member undertook the production of one or two subroutines."[48] Wilkes, Wheeler, and Stanley Gill eventually published the first work on programming in 1951. Titled *The Preparation of Programs for an Electronic Digital Computer*, it recorded the fruits of their efforts. It became standard reading for the next generation of computer programmers.

One year before the publication of their seminal work, Wilkes visited the United States to get a sense of developments there.

While visiting Eckert-Mauchly, he noticed the similarities in work between EMCC's programming group and his own. "I do remember some stimulating discussions with the group, led by Grace Hopper, who were concerned with programming." he recalled. "I found that they had a full appreciation of the importance of programming and of the need to develop organized and disciplined methods. I felt I was among people who looked at things in the same way that I did myself."[49]

Hopper's focus on the UNIVAC I's library of programs left Betty Snyder time to develop another important yet unheralded contribution to early programming advances. This was the sort-merge generator for a magnetic-tape computer.[50] In order for the UNIVAC I to be useful as a business machine, it had to be able to sort through and order data as effectively as existing punch-card technologies. Snyder first began working on the problem during the summer of 1947. With no formal training in logic, she applied common sense to figure out a binary method of sorting. "I remember bringing a deck of cards to the office on 1215 Walnut Street and turning them face down and making decisions and building piles," she recalled. "I built the logic of binary sorting from a deck of cards without ever having . . . anybody tell me anything about how it ought to be done."[51]

Once Snyder had developed the theory behind efficient binary sorting, she created a program that she called a generator. The generator contained the characteristics of the data to be sorted: number of items, length of items, categories or fields of information within the data set, etc. When a specific query was entered, the generator would "generate" another program, which would instruct up to ten different tape drives to take certain data off several reels and feed it back in a specific order onto another set of reels. The process was continued until a final tape contained the desired information in the proper order it was requested.

The coordination and automation of high-speed tape drives by means of a computer program was a monumental task that required a variety of technical problems to be solved. Working with the UNIVAC I engineers, Snyder developed a series of "interlocks" that scheduled the operation of input and output devices. Thus, only one magnetic-tape reel could function at a time, and a reel could not function simultaneously as an input and an output device. Like Hopper, Snyder took advantage of a functioning BINAC to aid in the design of UNIVAC I's tape system, which represented a new development itself in computer design. "The first time a computer was used to design a computer," remarked Hopper.[52]

AN UNTIMELY DEATH

By the fall of 1949, the future of the Eckert–Mauchly Computer Corporation looked bright. So did Grace Hopper's own future. Hopper had found a new home among the diverse members of a start-up company with the only functioning stored-program computer in America. She had a far-sighted boss in John Mauchly, one of the finest engineers in Presper Eckert, and around her a team of talented engineers and programmers. Betty Snyder had helped her learn to program the first commercial stored-program computer. In return, Hopper shared her 5 years of programming and management experience, and helped build a strong programming team by bringing in some of her former Harvard colleagues.

But just as the company was poised to become the first significant mover in a new and potentially lucrative business sector, the unthinkable happened. On 25 October 1949, a plane carrying Henry Straus, the chairman of the EMCC's board of directors, crashed just outside of Baltimore. As John Mauchly stated in his annual president's report to the shareholders of

EMCC, "Not only did the Corporation lose a wise and far-sighted leader, but the entire personnel of the company felt keenly the loss of an understanding and sympathetic friend."[53]

And sympathy was something EMCC's senior management needed as the company moved into a new decade. Despite the technical successes achieved in hardware development and programming, cost overruns, poorly negotiated contracts, and production delays threatened the financial solvency of the company. To make matters worse, the provisions of the contract between Straus's company and EMCC were no longer adequate to see through the construction of the first UNIVAC. "It is now apparent that, even if the American Totalisator Company were to continue to supply operating capital in return for preferred stock up to the limit contemplated in their contract with us, we would not have adequate funds to carry through the test period of the first UNIVAC," stated Mauchly in his report to shareholders.[54]

Mauchly's appeal for more funding after Straus's death could not have been more poorly timed. The accident killed the person at Totalisator who believed most in the potential of the electronic computer. The Munn brothers, the majority owners of Totalisator, had little interest in or understanding of digital computers, and instead of answering Mauchly's plea, immediately placed EMCC up for sale. To make matters worse, Totalisator demanded repayment of a $62,000 advance by January 1950.[55]

Both Hopper and Snyder remembered the shock of losing such a "marvelous man," as well as the malaise that came over the company. Instead of concentrating on the UNIVAC, Eckert and Mauchly were now forced to focus on the immediate need for an infusion of funding. They initially turned to loan companies and research foundations, but with little success. With their backs against the wall, the neophyte businessmen hoped to sell EMCC to a major corporation that specialized in calculating equipment (National Cash Register, IBM, Burroughs), or to a firm that had a need for advanced calculating technology (Hughes Aircraft).

If there was any glimmer of hope, the successful demonstrations of BINAC during the late summer were attended by executives and engineers from many of these companies. Among the attendees were representatives from International Business Machines Corporation, and soon after Straus's death Eckert and Mauchly were invited to meet with the aging Thomas Watson Sr. and his heir apparent, Thomas Watson Jr. In his memoirs Watson Jr. vividly recalled his meeting with the two young inventors, and his impression of them would stay with him from that point on:

> I was curious about Mauchly, whom I'd never met. He turned out to be a lanky character who dressed sloppily and like to flout convention. Eckert, by contrast, was very neat. When they came in, Mauchly slumped down on the couch and put his feet up on the coffee table — damned if he was going to show any respect for my father.[56]

Eckert explained the technology behind their work, while Mauchly shared his vision of the computing future, a future that jeopardized the technological monopoly held by mechanical punch-card machines. Because of the slow speeds and limited storage of punch cards, they were not an optimal input-output system for electronic computers. For instance, a handful of UNIVAC's magnetic-tape discs could store the policy records of an entire insurance company, while an individual punch card was needed for each policyholder. Moreover, those individual punch cards could only be sorted and processed at mechanical speeds. Electronic circuits, combined with Betty Snyder's sort-merge system, could process, store, erase, move, and save magnetic records quickly and securely.[57]

At the end of the meeting, Thomas Watson Sr. thanked Eckert and Mauchly for their presentation, but frankly told them that, for anti-trust reasons, IBM lawyers advised that IBM's purchasing the Eckert-Mauchly Computer Corporation could have negative legal ramifications. According to Thomas Watson Jr., the real reason that Watson Sr. rejected Eckert and Mauchly's offer ran far deeper:

Having built his career on punch cards, Dad distrusted magnetic tape instinctively. On a punch card, you had a piece of information that was permanent. You could see it and hold it in your hand. Even the enormous files the insurance companies kept could always be sampled and hand-checked by clerks. But with magnetic tape, your data were stored invisibly on a medium that was designed to be erased and reused.[58]

An aging CEO had built his career and corporation on mechanical punch-card systems, and he wholeheartedly believed that Eckert and Mauchly's electronic computer was an interesting but unproven business machine destined for the technological ash heap. IBM's engineers at Endicott, Watson Sr. believed, should focus on building a better punch-card system, not on experimenting with marginal technologies.

Up until the 1949 meeting with Eckert and Mauchly, Watson Jr. had shared his father's sentiments. In fact, he had attended the formal demonstration of the ENIAC in February 1946 with the number-two man at IBM, Charles Kirk, and had walked away unimpressed by and unconcerned with the temperamental monstrosity. "The truth," Watson Jr. recalled, "was that I reacted to ENIAC the way some people probably reacted to the Wright brothers' airplane: it didn't move me at all. I couldn't see this

gigantic, costly, unreliable device as a piece of business equipment. Kirk felt the same way."[59] But by 1949 the younger Watson
had begun to reconsider. Besides the increasing attention the
popular press was giving to computers and electronics, Watson
Jr. acknowledged the unexpectedly robust sales of a marginal
IBM product. "It was the success of the 604 Electronic Calculator
that convinced me that electronics was going to grow much
faster than anyone had anticipated," he recalled.[60] The IBM
604 was an electronic version of a popular IBM desk calculator.
It had been developed by a small group of electronics experts
working in Poughkeepsie rather than in IBM's main laboratory
in Endicott. The group, headed up by Ralph Palmer, had applied
experience gained with radar during the war. Standard IBM
plug-in boards were mounted with vacuum tubes and supporting
circuitry in such a way that the new electronic innards could
be mass-produced at a reasonable cost. "Palmer and his men,"
Watson Jr. recalled, "had produced an amazingly elegant design
that made it easy to cope with vacuum tubes, which were constantly burning out or otherwise going haywire."[61]

Although the unexpected sales of the 604 were seen as an
anomaly by many of IBM 's top executives, Watson Jr. viewed it
as a sign that, at the least, IBM had to learn more about the new
technology. He offered Presper Eckert a prominent position at
the Poughkeepsie laboratory, where he would be able continue
work on his envisioned computer. With so few options, and with
bankruptcy looming, Eckert seriously considered the offer, but
in the end he decided to remain with Mauchly. "I certainly was
influenced by him [Mauchly] and by my wife," Eckert recalled.
"My own feelings about doing it [alone] were much less stronger
than his. . . . I don't think Mauchly recognized the difficulties in
doing it ourselves. I think I had a better sense of that."[62]

Since EMCC was not joining the International Business Machines Corporation, they were competitors. "The IBM Company," Mauchly recalled, "was telling its customers that it's absolutely ridiculous for the tape machines they're talking about down there, because you know you can't sort data on tape. You can only sort it with cards because you move the cards around." Watson Jr. confirmed Mauchly's suspicions in his memoirs: "Dad told the marketing men to call on Prudential and persuade them that the UNIVAC idea was not sound."[63]

A PERSONAL SHORT CIRCUIT

With the decision to keep EMCC intact for the time being, Eckert and Mauchly spent the remaining months of 1949 seeking financing. Hopper remembered the period as one of uncertainty, scarcity, and low morale. Not only was the future in question; there was no money to pay the bills in the present. Hopper and others accepted salary reductions, and purchases of equipment for the UNIVAC were put on hold. Instead of dreaming about the coming computer revolution, discussions now turned to what to do if EMCC were to fold.[64]

Hopper had thrown herself wholeheartedly into Eckert and Mauchly's business venture, and its deterioration sparked a crisis in her life. The 43-year-old programmer's furtive addiction to alcohol resurfaced, and on a cold Saturday night in November she was arrested for public drunk and disorderly conduct. Released to Philadelphia General Hospital for treatment, she was eventually placed into the custody of her friend Edmund Berkeley. It was far from the first time Berkeley found himself covering up his friend's growing addiction. The incident prompted Berkeley to write a passionate "intervention letter" to Hopper, copies of which he sent to John Mauchly and to other close friends and relatives. Berkeley emphasizes from the onset that the letter was not written to hurt his friend's feelings, but rather out of deep love and sincerity. He justifies distributing copies of the letter under the pretext that there is nothing to hide, because so many people know Hopper's "secret"—even marginal acquaintances who, according to Berkeley, routinely ask "Has Grace stopped hitting the bottle?" Though Berkeley emphasizes that "a person changes not for rational reasons but for emotional reasons," the rest of the letter provides a detailed and rational analysis of Hopper's worsening addiction.[65]

Grace Hopper's drinking, according to Berkeley, was the result of a variety of factors, many of them shadow sides of her most admirable traits. For instance, Hopper's ability to persevere in the face of obstacles, be they intellectual, organizational, or cultural, was a characteristic that Berkeley and others deeply admired. Her career thus far had been punctuated by personal choices that demonstrated this trait: the first woman to graduate with a doctorate in mathematics from Yale, one of the first women to become an officer in the Navy, the third programmer of the first modern computer, and now a senior manager at the first commercial computer start-up company. Even her divorce could be seen as a break from the norm, given the cultural climate of the 1940s. According to Berkeley, it was the intensity of Hopper's strengths, such as her perseverance, that paradoxically fueled her addiction:

What are the sources of these dammed-up emotions, worry prohibitions, and proud self-imposed laws? These ways of behaving are chunks of immaturity, of infantile habits, baby ways of dealing with grown-up situations. The biggest chunk of all the immaturities I think is your determination to be your own boss, decide for yourself, and to hell with doing anything you don't choose to do. Oh, I don't mean that you are consistently head-strong; of course you often do things you do not choose to do, but you do them in cases where you have not involved all your personality, all of yourself. This biggest chunk of immaturity I believe probably derives from revolt against family constraints while you were young, coupled with your innate tendency to be stubborn.[66]

Berkeley truly believed that Hopper did not intend to become an alcoholic, but that her potent intellect worked against her and kept her from seeing her problem for what it was: a disease that was slowly destroying her ability to work and to interact with family and friends. "Your alcoholic habit however is of such long standing that it has warped most of the intellectual processes that you would ordinarily use to attack your alcoholism," he wrote. "Your fierce passion to reject authority has enlisted very many of your intellectual capacities to defeat all intellectual approaches."[67]

Berkeley strongly condemned Hopper's growing tendency to use her drinking as a means of manipulating friends and family for attention. After one of her "episodes," Hopper was in such a desperate physical and psychological state that she typically had to persuade friends to stay with her until she recovered. Since most of her friends were also hard-working people, her drinking problem began to interfere with their productivity. What had started as a personal problem, according to Berkeley, had become a community issue, and one that threatened the very thing that Hopper craved most: love and attention from those around her.[68]

More disturbing, according to Berkeley, were Hopper's recent threats of suicide, which he believed were cries for help and attention:

Committing suicide cannot solve the problem you have taken into your feelings, of more financing for EMCC; but several hours of sober, resolute intellectual effort might result in your giving some very useful suggestions to John [Mauchly]. To fill up one's head with vague pleasant ideas about committing suicide and other people being sorry is also a lot easier, more childish, and more "ego-stroking," than concentrated thinking right on the point of an objective problem.[69]

Berkeley truly believed that Hopper could cure herself. She needed to enlist her powerful mind to overcome the addiction that gripped her more with each passing day. She needed to find a different way to deal with her emotions and her worries, openly communicate with her friends and family, and maybe even find a less stressful job with more stability. "The EMCC strain is building up greatly. I think it is wiser for you to avoid that strain," wrote Berkeley. "One definite and good possibility for you is another job soon in some other company, where there will be less strain."[70]

Berkeley's motivations for helping Hopper to defeat her addiction went beyond friendship. A pioneer in the computer industry himself, Berkeley recognized Hopper's talent:

I and many other people know full well what a wonderful intellectual and emotional endowment you have. Even when you function properly only 70 percent of the time, you are worth to Eckert-Mauchly Computer Corporation all of the $6500 salary they pay you. . . . I can see in my mind's eye the marvelous things you could accomplish with the 30 percent of the rest of your time (now wasted), such as writing, teaching, living, and any other of the other things at which you are so competent.[71]

Grace Murray Hopper had played a pivotal role in the early years of the computer industry. Edmund Berkeley sensed rightly, however, that her most important contributions to the field were yet to come.

A POTENTIAL SAVIOR: THE REMINGTON RAND CORPORATION

As winter set in, the future looked bleak. While Hopper and other EMCC employees fought their own personal demons, the company as a whole headed steadily toward bankruptcy. With few options, Presper Eckert and John Mauchly accepted a less than generous offer from James Rand, the aging president of the Remington Rand Corporation. At the time of the purchase, in February 1950, Remington Rand was an established leader in the office equipment business, selling everything from file cabinets to punch-card calculating machines. Rand reimbursed American Totalisator $70,000 less than it had paid for its 40 percent share in 1948, even though EMCC had already produced the BINAC, was in the process of constructing the UNIVAC, and had six pending orders. Eckert and Mauchly received another $100,000, which was promptly disbursed to employees and suppliers for salary and back payments. Rand also agreed to pay EMCC 59 percent of monies received from its patents, with a minimum annual guarantee of $5,000.[72]

Unlike Henry Straus, the aging James Rand had little interest in computers. Though an inventor himself,[73] he had only a limited knowledge of electronics. Rand's special assistant, Arthur Draper, had persuaded him to purchase the struggling Eckert-Mauchly Computer Corporation, but Rand viewed the acquisition as a niche product line to add to his company's diverse product catalogue. Lou Wilson, an EMCC engineer, recalled Rand's first visit to the laboratory. After being briefed on the technical aspects of UNIVAC and the potential of computers, Rand responded "That's very interesting, but why is that an IBM typewriter?" Rand was pointing at the proposed UNITYPER, the output source for the UNIVAC. The UNITYPER was a reconfigured IBM typewriter, and Wilson's new boss wanted to know why he was not using a Remington Rand. "Take that label off that machine! I don't want it seen here!" said Rand on his way out.[74]

In the reorganization that followed, the Eckert-Mauchly Computer Corporation became a subsidiary of Remington Rand and was listed as a separate division. The new EMCC division was far from autonomous, however, and Remington Rand's management was grafted onto the organization. "We were just peons," Betty Snyder Holberton recalled. "When [Remington Rand] came in, they set up this hierarchy, and I finally had a boss that I worked for. That was a disaster too, because I'd go to him with decisions and he'd make the wrong decisions and I had to live with them."[75]

Part of the problem, according to Hopper, was that the majority of the Remington Rand management had little understanding of computing in general and programming in particular. Hopper and Snyder found themselves defending the technological choices made by EMCC in the face of management schooled in mechanical punch-card machines. Typical arguments that they had to deflect were "We don't think those tapes are ever going to work" and "We didn't put tapes on our machines; the card is the thing." Sadly, according to Hopper, Remington Rand management was looking at information processing from a different mental paradigm. Theirs was a world of specialized mechanical machines dedicated to a specific processing task: one machine for accounting, another machine for inventory, a third machine for billing. All the input and output used by these machines could be found on paper punch cards. Punch-card information was "real" because it could be seen and verified with one's own two eyes. According to the experts, there was no place for bits, Boolean algebra, logic gates, internal memory, subroutines, and machine code in the office machine marketplace.[76]

A difference of opinion concerning UNIVAC's potential also existed between Eckert and Mauchly and their new boss, General Leslie Groves. Mauchly in particular had a vivid vision of a commercially viable general-purpose machine that would help transform science and business. Groves, the former head of the Manhattan Project, saw an unreliable, unproven, and costly piece of equipment, which was now his headache as Remington Rand's director of advanced research. As the man in charge of overall operations of the Eckert-Mauchly division, Groves had the final say on strategic business decisions and on funding for research and development.

For Groves, the first thing to do was clean up the financial mess that Eckert and Mauchly created. The novice businessmen had gravely underestimated the development costs of UNIVAC, which now approached $1 million per unit, and Groves sent Remington Rand lawyers to renegotiate the UNIVAC contracts. Even though the three government agreements for $300,000 each could not be changed, Remington Rand successfully broke contracts with Prudential Insurance and A. C. Nielsen Inc., who expected to purchase UNIVACs at the implausible price of $150,000 each.[77]

Next, Mauchly was transferred to the sales department when a Remington Rand security check revealed that the co-founder of EMCC did not have proper security clearance. According to Eckert, not only had Mauchly attended Communist meetings during the 1930s; there was evidence that his secretary had Communist affiliations as well. "[The secretary] was sleeping with a guy who was a Communist," Eckert recalled. "As a matter of fact, he would take her to Communist meetings. Therefore they decided maybe she's a Communist, and maybe John's a Communist."[78]

Not only did EMCC's new bosses look unkindly on potential Communists; it also appeared that Remington Rand was no place for women. "Women, as far as I could see, had absolutely no future under Remington Rand, absolutely none," Betty Snyder Holberton recalled. EMCC's programming expert remembered how poorly Remington Rand salesmen and management had treated her because her salary rivaled their own: "You felt it. There was some resentment against a woman because you had essentially moved up all the way from the bottom."[79] Grace Hopper too sensed the tide turning against women after the takeover: "There were not the same opportunities for women in larger corporations like Remington Rand. They were older companies, and the jobs had been stereotyped." When Hopper had joined Eckert and Mauchly, the sky was the limit because the field was new, the company was small and flexible, and there were no gender-based roles. "Eckert and Mauchly were singularly unprejudiced, but also they were trying to gather together a team to build that first computer, which no one believed in," she said.[80] Betty Snyder Holberton also recalled a tolerant, flexible company with few traditions or defined job classifications. "Some days," she said, "you would be programming, sometimes you would be doing logic, sometimes you would go out with Mauchly selling. In fact, I can't remember anybody really telling me what to do. I just did what I felt had to be done and then went to somebody with what I had done."[81]

But by the summer of 1950, Snyder was so disillusioned with her new circumstances that she contemplated leaving Remington Rand and computers for good. She felt that her new masters were milking her for information, and that eventually she would be kicked to the curbside, especially since she did not have a doctorate. That summer, she decided to marry John Holberton, the man who in 1944 had interviewed her for the ENIAC programming position. After an intimate ceremony with friends and family, the couple went on an extended honeymoon to England, where they visited Maurice Wilkes at Cambridge and inspected the EDSAC. Upon their return, Betty Snyder Holberton decided to leave Remington Rand rather than be transferred to New York. She eventually accepted a job at the Navy's David Taylor Model Basin in Annapolis. (Her husband worked in Washington.)[82]

Although Betty Snyder Holberton continued to work with computers at the David Taylor Model Basin, her brilliant career at the first computer start-up company had come to an unexpected end. During her time at EMCC, she had worked with John Mauchly to develop C-10, the object code for the world's first commercial computer, and her pioneering work with sort generators would have important ramifications throughout the 1950s. Despite her accomplishments, the weight of Remington Rand's misogynistic culture, combined with her newly perceived obligations as a wife, tempered her enthusiasm for computing.

Betty Snyder Holberton's departure and John Mauchly's political struggles put the new company's programming burdens on Grace Hopper's shoulders. Hopper, however, had only recently recovered from her struggle with alcohol addiction. The unexpected death of Henry Straus and the resultant near bankruptcy of the Eckert-Mauchly Computer Corporation had thrown Hopper into a deep depression that nearly ended her career. But sometimes a person's darkest moments in life serve as the catalyst for change and establish a foundation for future success. Paradoxically, the takeover of EMCC by Remington Rand would mark the beginning of the most productive and creative chapter of Hopper's career.

One of the more difficult concepts for historians of technology to explain is that of invention. From patents and other written evidence, it may be simple to determine *when* and *where* a certain technology came into being. What remains difficult for the historian is to determine *how* and *why* a certain technology was created. Answering *how* requires insight into the process of invention. If we believe Thomas Edison's maxim that invention is 99 percent perspiration and 1 percent inspiration, then it follows that invention is not a completely serendipitous event. The inventor patiently prepares for inspiration to strike in a variety of ways. These include being well versed in the field of inquiry, having access to the essential equipment, and acquiring skill in empirical learning through long hours of trial and error.

Even more difficult for the historian is determining the moment and source of inspiration. Often the historian is left with just faint reflections of the moment as it is recorded in memoirs and interviews after the event. The accuracy of such reflections may be questionable, in view of the passage of time between the event and its recording. Moreover, errors can be magnified by the mind's ability to organize the past into a coherent progression of events.

Tied to the question *how* is another question: *Why* was a certain technology created by a particular person at a given time and place? Understanding the motivations for why the inventor added her perspiration to the process of invention goes beyond altruistic notions of improving one's society. Personal impulses are conjoined with a variety of external forces generated by a multitude of actors, be they individuals, organizations, or social groups. Since these groups often provide the knowledge, the funding, and the demand that propel the process of invention forward, it is necessary to understand the underlying milieu in which the inventor works.[1]

THE INVENTION OF THE COMPILER

It is generally accepted by historians of technology that Grace Hopper wrote the first compiler during the winter of 1951–52. According to interviews and speeches she gave years later, she began working in her spare time on the programming invention in October 1951. Hopper's recollections point to motivations ranging from an altruistic desire to allow "plain, ordinary people" to program to dealing with her own laziness. Naturally one must be skeptical of such claims, for they were made years after the fact. In 1951 it was difficult for even a visionary like Hopper to imagine the eventual ubiquity of computer technology, and one can be pretty confident that Hopper was not a lazy person.[2]

Likewise, the inspiration leading to Hopper's compiler design seems to be blurred by the passage of time. On occasion Hopper has credited Howard Aiken's Mark III coding machine as the source of her inspiration; at other times, Betty Snyder's sort generator has been mentioned as providing the inventive spark. In one speech, Hopper went so far as to credit her experience

"Captain Marvel and the Incredible Calculator." Courtesy of Archives Center, National Museum of American History, Smithsonian Institution.

playing basketball in college as the inspiration for a program that "passed" subroutines back and forth.[3] To get a better sense of the compiler's roots, let us first take a look at conditions at the Eckert-Mauchly Computer Corporation just after the merger with Remington Rand in 1950. We will then turn to the articles and papers Hopper wrote on compilers during this same period.

REMINGTON RAND AND THE CHALLENGE OF SALES AND CUSTOMER SUPPORT

As was discussed in the previous chapter, the purchase of EMCC by Remington Rand brought with it a multitude of organizational challenges. EMCC, a small computer start-up focused on innovation, did not mesh well with the culture of a large, corporate organization concerned primarily with quarterly revenue targets. To get a sense of the conditions at EMCC, let us turn to Hopper's own assessment and to the views of more than 30 computing pioneers associated with UNIVAC computers during the 1950s.[4] From their collective memories emerges a narrative that highlights Remington Rand's difficulties with constructing a sales and customer support structure for UNIVAC during the first half of the 1950s. These difficulties weighed heavily on Hopper and her staff, and generated the conditions that propelled Hopper to search for a radical technological solution to ease EMCC's mounting programming crisis.

From the first days of the merger, Remington Rand senior management was reluctant to invest heavily in what they viewed as an unproven technology. Instead of embracing a strategy to increase UNIVAC sales in order to bring down unit costs, the director of advanced research, General Leslie Groves, decided to cut EMCC's costs and to reduce the production quota from twelve units per year to six.

With such low sales expectations, there was little incentive to educate Remington Rand's sizable sales force about the new technology. According to Cecil Shuler, at the time a Remington Rand tabulating machine salesman in Nashville, the company did not establish a training program for tabulating machine salesmen who were interested in learning about the UNIVAC.[5] Moreover, Remington Rand failed to define a commission policy for sales of UNIVACs, thus depriving salesmen of a financial incentive to sell the computers. Hopper's former Harvard colleague Fred Miller remembered the difficulty he had inquiring about purchasing a UNIVAC for the Naval Proving Ground: "You had to find a salesman and buy him a drink before he'd talk to you."[6]

Eventually, in the summer of 1950, Remington Rand's senior staff established a UNIVAC sales training program. David Savage, referred to as "the most brilliant person in the Remington Rand Sales organization" and "comparable to Professor Eckert" in the company's internal newspaper, the *Remington Rand News*, was placed in charge of training the sales staff and preparing UNIVAC marketing materials. To the amazement of EMCC personnel, Savage developed the programming and applications course material and marketing handouts during the fall of 1950 without ever contacting anyone familiar with the UNIVAC, and when Hopper and others offered assistance, they were viewed as "meddlesome." In an angry memo to senior Rand executives, John Mauchly wrote: "It is not to [Savage's] discredit that he has had no previous experience in programming automatic computers, but we are at a loss to understand how anyone, having accepted a position demanding experience which he does not have, would fail to seek all possible help in preparing himself to discharge his duties."[7]

Tensions between Remington Rand's sales force and the EMCC staff continued to mount as Hopper and other EMCC programmers found themselves filling the sales, marketing and customer service void left by a sales department with neither the knowledge nor the motivation to sell the expensive, unproven machines. When Rand salesmen did attempt to represent UNIVAC, their incompetence did more harm than good, prompting Herbert Mitchell, Hopper's former student at the Harvard Computation Laboratory and a senior programmer at EMCC, to send a venomous open letter to senior management:

November 16, 1950

Dear Sales Division,

Please allow me to congratulate you upon your vast knowledge of psychology. You were faced with the task of convincing the EMCC technical people that they should be the ones to popularize the UNIVAC System. However, knowing that they were loath to do a "selling" job, you conceived the brilliant approach of preparing a presentation for customers that was so fantastic, bizarre, and childish that the EMCC would be shocked into the position of demanding to undertake this responsibility. . . . You have succeeded admirable.

We at EMCC are frantic. Faced with the alternative of being made the laughing stock of the entire professional computer field, of losing all possibility of selling any of the computing systems, and hence of being put out of business, we are eager-no, demanding to be given this job. We are convinced and ready.

Very truly yours,
Herbert F. Mitchell Jr.[8]

In response to the new initiative, members of Hopper's staff were distributed among regional sales offices in order to answer customers' questions concerning UNIVAC. Jean Bartik, an original ENIAC programmer, was sent to the Washington sales office in 1950 as the UNIVAC representative. "They didn't know what to do with me," she recalled. "Generally, the attitude in the Washington sales force was that Eckert and Mauchly were a bunch of dreamers and didn't know what they were talking about."[9] Eventually the Rand salesmen got the idea to employ Bartik and her fantastic machine as a ploy to gain entrée into government agencies in hopes of selling other office equipment. "I used to got out and describe UNIVAC and then they would hustle me out of the room, and then the salesmen would sell them typewriters."[10]

Another Hopper programmer, Adele Mildred Koss, was assigned to Commonwealth Edison when the utility approached the Chicago sales office concerning a potential purchase of a UNIVAC for billing and payroll. At the time, Koss was 7 months pregnant and working part time. Since her pregnancy precluded travel, Commonwealth Edison management was forced to come to Philadelphia in order to discuss their billing needs. In the end, the utility did not buy a UNIVAC, but instead purchased an IBM 701 when it became available. Koss recalled: "I remember Grace Hopper's memo to management saying 'This is a multi-million-dollar client and you are not treating them like one. You have only assigned a part time programmer to work with.'"[11]

The Commonwealth Edison fiasco was not the only matter that made Hopper's blood boil over the lack of support from Remington Rand management. Beginning with the delivery of the first operational UNIVAC to the Census Bureau on 30 March 1951, the Eckert-Mauchly division was now faced with the task of customer support. According to Hopper, "nobody had realized what it was going to take to support the new user."[12]

Eckert-Mauchly's programmers scrambled to help the new customers in any way they could. Besides developing subroutine packages, Hopper and others visited installations in order to assess computational needs and plan application programs. Much of their effort was spent educating the personnel assigned to operate UNIVAC. Hopper once again relied on her teaching experience, developing curriculum and writing lectures in order to get UNIVAC customers up to speed. Her operational experience at Harvard also served her well as she attempted to set standards and operating procedures both for Eckert-Mauchly and for customers' installations. "We had to introduce some kind of system and discipline to it," Hopper recalled, "and that's how I eventually got put in charge of them. I realized the things that had to be done and I pounded on management until they too accepted the concepts."[13] As the demand for programming and application software increased with each installed UNIVAC, so too did the pressures on Hopper and her programming staff.

THE EDUCATION OF A COMPUTER

For Hopper, the two years that followed the merger with Remington Rand were some of the most trying of her career. The senior programmer's abilities were stretched to the limit, not to mention the added pressures associated with her managerial duties in the maturing company. But out of crisis flowed resourcefulness, and starting in the fall of 1951 Hopper spent what little spare time she had searching for a technical solution for her predicament.

The mathematician-turned-inventor documented her seven-month creative journey in a paper aptly titled "The Education of a Computer," which she presented on 3 May 1952 at the Pittsburgh meeting of the Association of Computing Machinery.[14] Though Hopper had been sharing her thoughts and ideas with John Mauchly, Betty Holberton, and other close colleagues, it was at the ACM meeting that "automatic programming" was introduced to the greater computing community. Hopper claimed that many in the audience that day were skeptical of her automated coding aspirations. She also noted that about 100 copies of the paper that she had brought from Philadelphia were distributed, which suggests that even those who were skeptical about automatic programming had an interest in finding easier ways to program computers.[15] The paper itself represents Hopper's views circa May 1952, which differ in some respects from her recollections in later interviews and speeches. First and foremost, the central motivations for automatic programming were far more personal in the 1952 paper. With the construction of a functioning compiler, Hopper hoped, "the programmer may return to being a mathematician." Though Hopper had sincerely enjoyed the challenge of coding since first being introduced to computers 8 years earlier, she wrote, "the novelty of inventing programs wears off and degenerates into the dull labor of writing and checking programs. The duty now looms as an imposition on the human brain."[16] By teaching computers to program themselves, Hopper would be free to explore other intellectual pursuits.

In accord with the first chapter in the Mark I Manual for Operation, the paper begins with a historical narrative identifying the significant figures in computing history. Pascal, Leibniz, Babbage, Aiken, Mauchly, and Wilkes get special mention, while von Neumann, Eckert, Holberton, and Goldstine are notably absent. Hopper writes that her time with Aiken was instrumental in developing the earliest form of subroutines, and that the unique coding machine developed for Mark III represented a hardware solution to the concept of a library of subroutines that could be called upon by means of a mechanical button. Once again she mentions Mauchly's influence concerning symbolic programming solutions represented by short-order code, and she praises Wilkes for his book, which gave the programming community a shared vocabulary for the concepts of subroutines and subroutine libraries.[17] These computing pioneers, according to Hopper, created machines and methods that removed the arithmetical chore from the mathematician. This chore, however, was replaced by the new burden of writing code, thus turning mathematicians into programmers. Hopper's paper boldly offers the next step in the history of computing: shifting the human-machine interface once again so as to free the mathematician from this new burden, and making "the compiling routine be the programmer and perform all those services necessary to the production of a finished program."[18]

Hopper utilizes the metaphor of a factory to make abstract programming concepts more concrete for her audience. On a production line, inputs were raw materials that were acted upon by an assortment of instruments and tools. Human beings dictated the controls that organized the process, and the operation produced output ranging from automobiles to cans of tomatoes. Solving mathematical problems, according to Hopper, was no different. Inputs were alphanumerical data and tools consisted of formulas, tables, pencil, paper, and the arithmetic processing power of the brain. The controls of the process were provided by the mathematician, and the output was the final result.[19]

The achievement of Aiken, Mauchly, and Wilkes replaced pencil, paper, and the brain with mechanical hardware. But the human was still left to analyze and break down a mathematical problem into its constituent parts, provide step-by-step controls for the process via a program, write that program in notation best understood by the machine, and coordinate the introduction of input. The user was also faced with the significant problem of identifying and correcting for errors. The more complicated the problem, the greater the chance of error.

With the use of a compiler supported by a library of subroutines, Hopper offered to fully automate the computing process:

> He [the mathematician] is supplied with a catalogue of subroutines. No longer does he need to have available formulas or tables of elementary functions. He does not even need to know the particular instruction code used by the computer. He needs only to be able to use the catalogue to supply information to the computer about his problem.[20]

The "catalogue of subroutines" was a menu that listed all the input information needed by the compiler to look up subroutines in the library, assemble them in the proper order, manage address assignments, allocate memory, transcribe code, and create a final program in the computer's specific machine code.[21] A subroutine entry in the catalogue consisted of a subroutine "call-number" and the order in which arguments, controls, and results were to be stated. The call-number identified the type of subroutine (t for trigonometric, x for exponential, etc.), specified transfer of control (entrance and exit points in each subroutine), and set operating and memory requirements. In fact, language such as "call-number" and "library" compelled Hopper to name her program generator a "compiler," for it compiled subroutines into a program in much the same way that historians compile books into an organized bibliography.[22]

For Hopper, the benefits of such an automated programming system were enormous. She describes a future in which programs could be written and debugged in hours instead of weeks. The generated results would be accurate, since all subroutines in the library would have been fully debugged and tested. The greatest benefit, however, excited the imagination of the most ardent skeptic. A program generated by a compiler could not only be run as a stand alone program whenever desired; it also "may itself be placed in the library as a more advanced subroutine." This suggested that subroutine libraries could increase in size and complexity at an exponential rate, thus enabling mathematicians to solve problems once deemed impossible or impractical.[23]

Hopper ends the paper by establishing a short-term roadmap for the future development of compilers. She describes a "type-B" compiler, which, by means of multiple passes, could supplement computer information provided by the programmer with self-generated information. Such a compiler, she imagines, would be able to automate the process of solving complex differential equations. To obtain a program to compute $f(x)$ and its first n derivatives, only $f(x)$ and the value of n would have to be given. The formulas for the derivatives of $f(x)$ would be derived by repeated application of the type-B compiler.[24]

Hopper also admits that the current version of her compiler did not have the ability to produce efficient code. For example, if both sine and cosine were called for in a routine, a smart programmer would figure out how to have the program compute them simultaneously. Hopper's compiler would embed both a sine subroutine and a cosine subroutine in sequence, thus wasting valuable memory and processing time. Hopper states boldly that the skills of an experienced programmer could eventually be distilled and made available to the compiler. She concludes as follows:

With some specialized knowledge of more advanced topics, UNIVAC at present has a well-grounded mathematical education fully equivalent to that of a college sophomore, and it does not forget and does not make mistakes. It is hoped that its undergraduate course will be completed shortly and it will be accepted as a candidate for a graduate degree.[25]

DISTRIBUTED INVENTION: COMPILER RESEARCH EXPANDS

After publicly announcing the compiler concept, Hopper asked members of her programming staff to help turn her invention into something more substantial. Since there was no formal support from Remington Rand management at this time, those from Rand's Computation Analysis Laboratory who joined Hopper did so on their spare time.

In the summer of 1952, Hopper's assembled team began to test the programming aptitude of the compiler (aptly named A-0) against teams of seasoned programmers. Richard Ridgway, a Hopper programmer who joined Eckert-Mauchly in 1950, reported the results of one of these studies on 8 September 1952 at a meeting of the Association of Computing Machinery in Toronto. The equation tested was $y = e^{-x} \sin(x/2)$. Given a set of input parameters for x, the Computation Analysis Laboratory first solved for y using what Ridgway referred to as the "conventional" method, which was similar to the batch process method developed by Hopper and Bloch at Harvard. First, a mathematician analyzed the equation and broke it down into a series of arithmetic steps (20 minutes). A programmer then reduced the steps to computer instruction code, utilizing a code manual, tables, and formulas in the process (480 minutes). The completed program was checked for errors (240 minutes), transcribed onto magnetic tape (45 minutes), and rechecked for errors (40 minutes) after printing out the tape's content (20 minutes). Finally, an operator, following operation instructions, fed the program into computer memory along with pertinent inputs (31 minutes). UNIVAC then ran the program and produced results (4 minutes). In the end, Ridgway reported, the problem was solved from start to finish by a team of three people in 860 minutes.[26]

The same problem was then solved with Hopper's A-0 compiler. Once again a mathematician analyzed the problem and broke it down into arithmetic steps. This time, however, the mathematician selected corresponding subroutines from the subroutine library and wrote down the appropriate information to describe these subroutines with the aid of the subroutine library catalogue (20 minutes). The resultant information sheet was transcribed on tape (10 minutes) and proofread (5 minutes) after generating a printout of the tape's content (5 minutes). The tape was then fed into the computer (2 minutes), which prompted the compiler to look up the appropriate subroutines from the library tape, assemble them in the proper order, manage addresses and memory, and generate a program in C-10 UNIVAC machine code (90 seconds). UNIVAC ran the compiler-generated program and produced the final results (5 minutes). In the case of the A-0 compiler, one person, a mathematician, solved the problem in 48½ minutes.[27] (See table 8.1.)

Although the test results appear to be a smashing endorsement of the A-0 compiler, Ridgway dedicates a substantial amount of his paper to the inefficiency of run-programs. (A "run-program" was the final product of the compiler process. Today, such a program is called object or machine code.) During the 5 months since Hopper had introduced compilers, critics had pointed out that run-programs generated by compilers were less efficient than those created by seasoned programmers. Hopper's experience with Richard Bloch at Harvard was evidence that a creative

TABLE 8.1

Time preparation comparison: A-0 compiler vs. conventional programming.

	Conventional programming	Compiler programming	Efficiency ratio
Mathematician/ programmer's time	740 minutes	20 minutes	37:1
Mathematician/operator's time	105 minutes	20 minutes	5.3:1
UNIVAC processing time	35 minutes	8.5 minutes	4.1:1
Total preparation time	880 minutes	48.5 minutes	18.2:1

programmer could use a variety of tricks and tactics to generate code that was 30–40 percent more efficient than that produced by the A-0.

At first glance, program inefficiency did not appear to be significant in Ridgway's example, for the more inefficient compiled program ran for 5 minutes whereas the programmer-generated code took only 4 minutes. But, programmers argued, that extra minute was relevant if the same program had to be run multiple times. In fact, the vast majority of problems solved by data-processing facilities in the early 1950s were repeated computations. If Ridgway's compiled program were to be run 1,000 times, 1,000 extra minutes of computer time would be required.[28] The extra computer time generated by the 1,000 runs made the conventional method more time-efficient overall. Furthermore, an hour of computer time was far more costly in 1952 than an hour of programmer time. In most cases it was both more efficient and more cost-effective to hire a team of programmers and operators in order to limit computer use. (See table 8.2.)

TABLE 8.2

A-0 compiler vs. conventional programming method: 1,000 program runs.

	Conventional programming	Compiler programming	Efficiency ratio
Mathematician/ programmer's time	740 minutes	20 minutes	37 : 1
Mathematician/operator time	105 minutes	20 minutes	5.3 : 1
UNIVAC processing time	4,000 minutes	5,000 minutes	4 : 5
Total preparation time	4,845 minutes	5,040 minutes	1 : 1.1

Ridgway acknowledged that using compilers took up more computer time, both as a result of compiling a program and as a consequence of inefficient code. But "in this case," he argued, "the compiler used was the 'antique,' or A-0, the first to be constructed and the most inefficient." Ridgway was confident that Hopper and her team at the Computation Analysis Laboratory would construct new compilers that "squeezed" coding into "neat, efficient, and compact little packages of potential computation."[29]

In the months that followed the presentation of Ridgway's paper, the Computation Analysis Laboratory addressed the problem of compiler efficiency. Hopper admitted that the A-0 compiler, despite its inherent logic, was cumbersome to use.[30] For instance, if the A-0 was processing a subroutine and that subroutine required transfer of control to another subroutine, the A-0 did not know where the second subroutine began. This forced the compiler to transfer control from the first subroutine to a temporary storage location while keeping track of the fact that a control transfer to the unprocessed subroutine was still necessary. Since a programmer could create a flow chart of the entire program before coding, such intermediate steps could be avoided.

The group's research efforts were rewarded in the early winter of 1953. The A-1 compiler was completed and tested by January, and much of the cumbersomeness of A-0 had been refined and eliminated. By the spring of 1953, an even cleaner compiler, the A-2, was developed by Margaret Harper, Frank Delaney, Mildred Koss, James McGarvey, and Richard Ridgway under the direction of Herbert Mitchell and Richard Woltman. Hopper had recruited Mitchell and Woltman from the Harvard Computation Laboratory and felt comfortable turning over the day-to-day project management of compiler development to them.[31]

A closer look at the manual for the A-2 compiler (produced by the Computation Analysis Laboratory during the summer of 1953) suggests that, despite the significant improvements over the A-0 compiler, automatic programming had its limitations. Hopper's vision of intuitive, user-friendly, hardware-independent pseudo-codes generating efficient running programs was far from realization. The A-2 provided a three-address "pseudo-code" specifically designed for the UNIVAC I 12-character standards. The manual defined "pseudo-code" as "computer words other than the machine (C-10) code, designed with regard to facilitating communications between programmer and computer."[32] Today we refer to it as source code. Since pseudo-code could not be directly executed by the UNIVAC I, the A-2 compiler included a translator routine which converted the pseudo-code into machine code. (See table 8.3.)

The manual states that the pseudo-code is "a new language which is easier to learn and much shorter and quicker to write."[33]

TABLE 8.3
Examples of pseudo-codes from the A-2 compiler subroutine library.

Add	AA0004 F00001	Logarithm	LAU118 F00001
Subtract	AS0004 F00001	Root	RNA154 F00001
Multiply	AM0004 F00001	Exponential	X+A096 F00001
Divide	AD0004 F00001	Change sign	AN1002 F00001
Cosine	TC0100 F00001	Input generator	GMI000 F00001
Sine	TS0106 F00001	Test	QZ0004 F00001
Arctan	TAT118 F00001	Type in	BTI002 F00001
Raise to a power	APN048 F00001	Print out	YT0004 F00001

Indeed, it was easier compared to manually writing machine code. If the user wanted to solve for the cosine of a, for instance, she would look up the appropriate pseudo-code in the subroutine library catalogue.

The familiar notation

$$y = \cos a$$

was written

TCO(A) 000(Y).

Note that the pseudo-code call-words conformed to UNIVAC I's twelve-character structure, with parentheses in the first example signifying the relative working storage address of the quantity called for. In most cases the second character correlated with the subroutine operation it depicted, such as S for sine and M for multiply. But Hopper admitted years later that her team, at the time, could not see very far past the constraints of the UNIVAC hardware:

I think we often forget how much our surroundings influence our research decisions. All those things that we're aware of and yet are not aware of when we make decisions. And the fact was that we were living in an environment which consisted of a 12 alpha-decimal word, and it became perfectly obvious to us that the entire world operated in 12 alpha-decimal characters of which the first three defined an operation, the next three one input, the next three another input, and the last three the result.[34]

Despite the limitations of A-2 pseudo-code, Hopper and her team incorporated innovations that made the compiler more user-friendly. Unlike the A-0, the A-2 now made two sweeps of the pseudo-code. The first pass generated a record to help the compiler make more efficient code on the second pass. The record, which was a list of operations, could also be printed out and serve as a general check of the compilation before the final running program was completed. Normal printouts during compiling, such as "end translation," "end sweep 1," and "end compile," informed the user about the stage of the process. The most groundbreaking change was the A-2's ability to debug pseudo-code and flag errors automatically. The compiler generated twelve-character error codes that captured the nature of the error, a miraculous innovation for any programmer who had experienced the pain and monotony of debugging computer code. (See table 8.4.)

Although the A-2 compiler had been designed for novice programmers, Hopper understood that in order for it to be more widely adopted her team would have to add features that would be appreciated by skilled programmers. The A-2 made it easier

TABLE 8.4
Examples of error messages generated by A-2 compiler.

RINFOΔ WORD?R	A word of information fails tests: transcription error.
RTΔMCH ΔINFOR	The compiler can store no more than 60 descriptive words: memory exceeded.
RNOTΔI NΔLIBR	The word of information is a call word for a subroutine not in the library.
RFULLΔ TAPEΔR	The 1955 data blocks on the running tape have been used.
ROPΔSE QΔOUTR	The information lists an operation number that is not in the proper sequence.
RNOTΔS TOREDΔ	The programmer called for a generative routine that is not in the library.

to modify compiled programs. Entrances, exits, and references to working storage could be manipulated manually, thus allowing parts of a program to be reused with other operands in another section of the run program. For instance, if the A-2 generated the same subroutine in two different segments of the run program, a skilled programmer could now remove one, producing a more efficient final run program. Furthermore, modifying programs was easier, and changes could be made without the need to restructure the entire routine.[35]

COMPILING ROUTINES

In the May 1953 issue of *Computers and Automation*, Grace Hopper heralded the laboratory's successes in an article titled "Compiling Routines." She predicted that the next generation of compilers, coupled with efficient subroutines that had been tested and proved, would produce machine code as efficiently as the average programmer. Subsequent tests had shown that "the reduction in programming time for those classes of problems upon which compilers have been tested is incredible, actually little short of fantastic." Nonetheless, Hopper reminded the programming community that these compilers were still in the prototype stage, with limited availability of tested subroutine libraries."[36]

Hopper focused attention on another major benefit of compilers: pseudo-code. Pseudo-code freed the user from the constraints of the machine's hardware, for the compiler, not the user, was responsible for changing the pseudo-code into machine-specific code that the computer could process. In her first paper she had focused on the time benefits for the mathematician/programmer, but by the time of the May 1953 paper Hopper had realized that pseudo-code exhibited two revolutionary attributes.

First, the designer of the compiler now was a linguist. That is, the compiler programmer had the ability to design the syntax of the pseudo-code. Hopper noted that for mathematical problems this was comparatively easy to do, since mathematical symbolism had become standardized over the years. Therefore, a compiler designer could have the pseudo-code match accepted mathematical terms: cos, add, sin, exp, and so on. Hopper emphasized that what was relatively straightforward for mathematical pseudo-code was problematic for the pseudo-code of other imagined commercial compilers. For example, a logical, intuitive pseudo-code would have to be planned out and standardized for accounting and payroll compilers. "If 'cos' indicates cosine," Hopper writes, "why not use 'foa' for 'federal old age' or 'ssd' for social security deduction?"[37] A well-constructed pseudo-code had the potential to make computers available to users other than programmers and mathematicians. Not only would it be far easier to learn than machine code; its intuitive logic would help users debug their work. "I felt," Hopper recalled, "that sooner or later . . . our attitude should be not that people should have to learn how to code for the computer but rather the computer should learn how to respond to people because I figured we weren't going to teach the whole population of the United States how to write computer code, and that therefore there had to be an interface built that would accept things which were people-oriented and then use the computer to translate to machine code."[38]

The second benefit of pseudo-code, program portability, would have far more meaningful ramifications for the future, though it appears that at the time the article was written Hopper thought of the benefit more as a nicety. She mentioned that compilers could be designed to program the machine code of any computer. "A problem stated in a basic pseudo-code can thus be prepared for running on one or more computers if the corresponding compiler and subroutine library is available," she wrote. Just as the compiler freed the user from knowing how to program in machine language, pseudo-code was now liberated from a specific type of hardware. A payroll pseudo-code could run on a UNIVAC or an IBM computer, so long as the appropriate compiler was running on both. Hopper stated that as of May 1952 such a benefit was theoretical, insofar as her laboratory had tried it only once, with inconclusive results.[39]

In the same article, Hopper compared compilers to another example of "automatic programming" that had gained momentum since her "Education of a Computer" presentation: the interpreter. An interpreter is a program that executes a pseudo-code much like a compiler. The difference lies in the output of the execution. Whereas a compiler generates a program, an interpreter "interprets" a pseudo-code that refers to a subroutine and immediately performs the subroutine, thus generating intermediate results. Therefore, no permanent set of machine instructions is produced. Hopper listed the following steps as occurring during the interpreter process:

1. Transfer arguments to the subroutine or to some standard location
2. Mark position in the main routine
3. Transfer control to the subroutine
4. Carry out the subroutine
5. Transfer control back to the main routine
6. Retrieve results from the subroutine or standard location

Though interpreters were simpler to use than programming in machine code, Hopper believed the approach was a step in the wrong direction. Compiling the A-2 pseudo-code was time consuming in the short term, but the resultant run-program eliminated these six interpretive steps and thus could run more efficiently. In her final comparison of interpreters and compilers, Hopper wrote: "In both cases, the advantage over manual programming is very great, once the basic subroutines have been tested and proved. The saving of time for a compiler is usually greater."[40]

DISTRIBUTED INVENTION: EXPANDING THE NETWORK OF INNOVATION

The A-2 compiler, though still cumbersome in many respects, was, in Hopper's opinion, robust enough to be distributed to UNIVAC I installations for evaluation. But convincing people to use the experimental programming system turned out to be far more difficult than Hopper anticipated, for the advantages of compiled programs were not readily apparent to most: "We found that we had to change from being research and development people and turn ourselves into salesmen and get out and sell the idea of writing programs this way."[41]

On 16 July 1953, the Computation Analysis Laboratory turned its attention from inventing to selling and sponsored the first automatic programming workshop in Washington, D.C. With the Census Bureau as a co-sponsor, Hopper invited about 90 programmers and technicians from the various UNIVAC I installations to the one-day event. Hopper's staff presented lectures on the A-2 compiler and provided demonstrations on the Census Bureau's UNIVAC machine. Hopper believed the overall reaction to be favorable, and many of the installations agreed to test the compilers during actual day-to-day operations.

Through the fall and winter, installations with experienced UNIVAC programmers fared better than those without, which suggested that the A-2 was not as simple to use as had first been believed. Betty Holberton, now a senior programmer at the Navy's David Taylor Ship Basin in Annapolis, had little difficulty applying the A-2 to problem solving. But Emil Schell, the head of mathematical computation at the Air Force's Office of the Air Comptroller, was less successful in applying the new technology. "The writing of the pseudo-code words, the specifications for generating subroutines, and the use of the modifying indicator in 'own codes' involve decisions of a sort we are ill-equipped to make," wrote Schell. In order to help his installation get up to speed, he requested that Hopper send more and better expository materials and operating instructions.[42]

By December 1953, the Census Bureau, the Office of the Air Comptroller, the Army Map Service, the David Taylor Model Basin, Lawrence Livermore Laboratory, New York University, and the Bureau of Ships were experimenting with the A-2 compiler. The Computation Analysis Laboratory gained valuable feedback from these installations, including the identification of subroutine and pseudo-code errors and suggestions concerning future iterations of the compiler system. Some installations went as far as to rewrite code, which was then evaluated by Hopper and incorporated into later versions of A-2. For example, during the winter of 1954 Nora Moser of the Army Map Service sent Hopper a list of innovations that the Army Map Service had incorporated into the A-2, including more efficient input and output generators, rerun provisions, and an editing subroutine library. Moser had also copied the changes onto magnetic tape and sent them to Betty Holberton at the David Taylor Model Basin for further evaluation.[43]

Hopper's constructed network of compiler developers was unique for a variety of reasons. Whereas Howard Aiken had isolated the Harvard Computation Laboratory from other computer projects, Hopper realized that the process of invention could not be confined to the artificial boundaries of her staff or even her company. Information flowed smoothly between Remington Rand and other organizations, with Hopper serving as the conductor of invention rather than its dictator. Though she insisted that copies of all correspondence be passed through her, Hopper did this in order to better orchestrate the efforts of others rather than to control the direction of compiler development.[44]

Moreover, Hopper's network of invention attracted the enthusiastic participation of many women in the programming field. Nora Moser (of the Army Map Service), Betty Holberton (at the David Taylor Basin), Margaret Harper (of the Remington Rand/ Naval Aviation Supply Office), and Mildred Koss (of Remington Rand) viewed the compiler as more than just a new programming concept. Indeed, they saw it as the centerpiece of an innovative automated system of programming that they had a hand in creating. Though posterity identifies Hopper as the leader of this programming revolution, one must not forget the many men and women who helped to transform Hopper's original proto-type into a viable commercial automated programming system.

Hopper nurtured her growing distributed network of inven-tion by arranging a second workshop on automatic program-ming, held on 1 December 1953 at the Pentagon and co-sponsored by the Air Force. Hopper kicked off the workshop with a paper titled "Progress in Automatic Programming." Once again her staff provided descriptive lectures and demonstrations, but this time multiple UNIVAC installations reported on the benefits and dif-ficulties associated with applying compilers to real-world com-putational situations.[45]

The audience of more than 100 also included many people not associated with UNIVAC installations. Hopper recalled that representatives from government agencies and businesses equipped with IBM machinery came to learn more about the new concept in programming. In fact, the December conference was not the first attempt by Hopper and her team to educate the wider computing community about the A-2. At a September 1953 meeting of the Association of Computing Machinery at MIT, Hopper organized a panel that served as a "coming out" party for her automatic programming faithful.

The fact that Hopper wholeheartedly welcomed non-UNIVAC personnel to learn about the A-2 compiler sheds some light on her beliefs concerning intellectual property. Hopper did not view software as a commodity to be patented and sold. Rather, she took her cue from the mathematics community. Like most other academics, mathematicians shared information uni-versally, in order to advance knowledge. Though individual efforts were acknowledged by colleagues, advancement in the field was contingent on a communal view of information, community validation, and evolutionary advancement based on previous work. In the same way, software, according to Hopper, was a public good to be shared freely among all users. Complicating software development with secrecy would only inhibit innovation. Learning from the Harvard Computation Laboratory's tendency to isolate itself from other computer developments, Hopper came to realize that a distributed network of inventors, each with his or her particular technical perspective,[46] could sustain a faster rate of innovation in the long term compared to an individual inventor or even an isolated team of inventors. The freeware and open source movements of the present day preserve this doctrine. The roots, however, go back to Hopper and her team of distributed inventors.

After Hopper's remarks concerning general compiler developments, two of her protégés, Adele Mildred Koss and Harry Kahrimanian, presented compiler-related papers. Koss discussed an "editing generator" that could manipulate raw results into a form suitable for printing. That is, the editor supplied titles, headings, and page numbers, suppressed unnecessary zeros, and inserted decimal points and plus and minus signs. Koss's editor did this by means of a special type of compiler called a generator. The generator contained what Hopper referred to as "coded coding," which, on the basis of specifications inserted by the user, expanded into a limited subroutine containing the controls necessary to process the data.[47]

Kahrimanian's paper, titled "Analytical Differentiation by a Digital Computer," described a differential compiler that represented the fulfillment of the type-B compiler that Hopper had written about in "The Education of a Computer."[48] In view of the difficulty Hopper experienced solving for differential equations on the Harvard Mark I, including von Neumann's famous implosion problem, Kahrimanian's differentiator seemed too good to be true. The user had only to provide a specific function in the pseudo-code and indicate the number of n derivatives, either complete or partial, to be generated. The operator routine of the differentiator would then guide the computer to produce the subsequent formulas for the nth derivative. The formulas derived by the operator routine could be immediately compiled to construct a program for numerical evaluation. Comparing the work of Koss and Kahrimanian with other papers presented at the ACM conference, and considering the nature of the discussions that followed, Hopper came to this conclusion: "It was evident that Remington Rand's Programming Research Group had progressed considerably further in the development and application of automatic programming techniques than had any other single or combined effort in this field."[49]

MAKING CONVERTS

One of the non-Remington Rand participants impressed by the A-2 and the differentiator was Carl Hammer. Hammer had first been exposed to data-processing equipment as a research associate in the T. J. Watson Scientific Computing Laboratory at Columbia University. During the fall of 1953 he was employed by the Franklin Institute to study the industrial applications of computers. Hammer successfully used the differentiator and the A-2 compiler to solve a difficult differential equation concerning roller bearings and oil viscosity. Much to his amazement, he solved the problem in a day. "I wrote twenty lines of coding for an A-2 compiler to solve the whole problem," he recalled, "and here they'd been working for months and years sometimes on these things."[50]

Hammer was so impressed, in fact, that he wrote an article for an engineering magazine describing the A-2 compiler and its revolutionary consequences for engineering and science. "I tried to point out to the people that this was a remarkable thing," he recalled. "We could speed up industry, science, all the applications we could learn more, and all that from the power of this machine."[51] In 1955, Hammer quit his job and joined Remington Rand. From 1955 to 1957, he headed the European UNIVAC Computing Center.

Not all programmers were as enthusiastic as Hammer about the potential of automatic programming. Herb Grosch,[52] a notable computer pioneer who headed up computer operations at General Electric (a UNIVAC customer in 1953), became a vocal opponent of automatic programming. Grosch and his fellow "Neanderthals" (as they came to be called as the debate intensified during the 1950s) continued to argue that programming took far too much creativity and dexterity for the human being to be replaced by the very machine he was manipulating. Furthermore, most commercial programs were task-specific or company-specific, so it made more sense for a team of experienced programmers to design and implement handcrafted codes that met the particular needs of the client.

Reflecting on the negative reactions of some of her fellow programmers, Hopper expressed the belief that arguments focusing on "efficiency" and "creativity" covered far baser motivations: "Well, you see, someone learns a skill and works hard to learn that skill, and then if you come along and say, 'you don't need that, here's something else that's better,' they are going to be quite indignant." In fact, Hopper felt that by the mid 1950s many programmers viewed themselves as "high priests," for only they could communicate with such sophisticated machines. They served as the intermediaries between user and computer, and automatic programming jeopardized their exclusive position.[53]

Hopper was not the only one who came to this conclusion. John Backus, developer of Speedcode and later of FORTRAN, was conscious of the programming community's reaction to his contributions: "Just as freewheeling westerners developed a chauvinistic pride in their frontiersmanship and a corresponding conservatism, so many programmers of the freewheeling 1950s began to regard themselves as members of a priesthood guarding skills and mysteries far too complex for ordinary mortals."[54] But the more the likes of Backus and Hopper preached the benefits of automatic programming, the more concerned the programming priesthood became about the spreading technology.

WINNING THE HEARTS AND SOULS OF MANAGEMENT

If convincing fellow programmers of the benefits of automatic programming was challenging, persuading senior management at Remington Rand to invest money in the new technology was nearly impossible. For many executives in the 1950s, the very notion of the computer as a business technology itself was hard to grasp, aside from the question of how these machines worked. "It was totally hopeless," Hopper recalled, "to explain to anybody that you thought computers could put together programs because it was obvious to everyone that computers could only do arithmetic; they couldn't write programs. And no matter how much you explained they weren't really writing a program, they were only piecing one together, people just didn't understand that."[55]

By December 1953, Hopper felt it was critical to make management understand the importance of automatic programming

Grace Hopper. Courtesy of Library of Congress.

Until then, Hopper and her network of programmers had worked on compiler technology during their spare time. But the success of the prototypes and the growing demand required full-time resources and personnel. On 31 December 1953, Hopper drew up a report aimed at convincing Remington Rand to invest in her concept of automatic programming. Her "plea for a budget," as she referred to it, not only chronicled the development of compiler technology but also addressed the commercial potential and implications of automatic programming in far more depth than any of her writing up to that point.[56]

Hopper's report highlights a growing reality that few in or out of the computer industry comprehended as of 1953: the cost of programming, operating, and maintaining computers was increasing and would continue to do so at an alarming rate. These rising costs resulted from a variety of factors. First and foremost, the accepted method for constructing programs was labor-intensive. Creating a basic commercial application such as a payroll routine required a team of mathematically trained programmers. By 1953 they were in short supply. Those with experience commanded high salaries, and those without experience required expensive and time-consuming training. As computer hardware proliferated, the shortage of skilled labor would only intensify.

Worse, Hopper reminded her audience of executives, there was no such thing as a static commercial program, for changing business conditions required continuous modifications. "A change in government regulations, city ordinances, union contracts, or requirements of company management, even a simple change, such as income tax exemptions, may invalidate not only parts of runs, but whole runs in such a base problem," she wrote.[57] The problem was exacerbated by the fact that most commercial program rewrites had to be made on extremely short notice, thus requiring companies that operated computers to maintain permanent teams of programmers. The way out of this costly conundrum, according to Hopper, was through the implementation of compiler techniques. A pseudo-code for payroll could be updated quickly, and the run-program could be recompiled at a moment's notice. The changes were checked automatically and human error was eliminated, thus ensuring the accuracy of the computed results. Hopper concluded that the reduction in staff would result in a significant reduction in costs.

The most striking and innovative aspect of Hopper's report, however, concerned a radically new way to think about executive decision making:

In any business or industry a large quantity of information exists on paper. This information in random, unprocessed form is of little or no value to management as a basis for decision making. When information is organized and processed, it becomes "intelligence." Effective management, then, relies on the ability to process information to be used in decision making.[58]

Not only did the information have to be processed accurately; it had to be processed quickly. Hopper noted that there existed a whole set of statistical studies and tabulations—known to be useful to management—that were not typically made. Even with the aid of a computer and a programming staff, this set of problems could not be calculated rapidly enough to supply the needed intelligence before a decision had to be made. Compiling routines, combined with the speed of electronic circuits, opened unexplored intellectual territory not only for scientists and engineers but also for business leaders. Automatic programming could precipitate a revolution in decision making.[59]

"A monumental effort," Hopper told Remington Rand management, "is being expended by IBM, RCA, Raytheon, CPC (National Cash), Consolidated Engineering, Burroughs and all their users and prospective users, and by their affiliated university installations, to develop similar [automated programming] techniques for use with their digital computers." Though she did not reveal her sources, Hopper said: "Through personal contacts, it has been determined that our closest competitors are making an all-out effort to approach the level that Remington Rand has attained and to surpass us."

In her final call to arms, Hopper demanded that "personnel be devoted 100% of their time to the development of the compiler techniques and particularly to the development of the A-3 compiler."[60] Risking her position at Remington Rand, Hopper was ultimately successful in creating a separate department to further explore automatic programming. In a letter to the Army Map Service dated 10 February 1954, the new Director of Automatic Programming thanked her distributed development team and shared with them her success in institutionalizing automatic programming at Remington Rand:

The fact that there is today some hope of building an automatic programming group is due to your efforts on A-2. I cannot tell you how grateful I am. If I had not been able to report the success of your efforts, automatic programming would have been a very dead duck in Remington Rand.[61]

On the eve of 1954, Hopper believed Remington Rand had the ability to seize and maintain the lion's share of the computer industry, a market that appeared to be on the verge of rapid expansion. Remington Rand held a substantial lead in both hardware and software technology. But its closest competitor, the International Business Machines Corporation, was demonstrating a growing interest in computer technology.

In the summer of 1949, when Grace Hopper joined the Eckert-Mauchly Computer Corporation, the International Business Machines Corporation controlled 90 percent of the market for mechanical calculators and punch-card machines, with annual revenues of $300 million. Apart from experimental work on the Harvard Mark I and the Selective Sequence Electronic Calculator, IBM leadership firmly believed that the company's future growth would be driven by mechanical punch-card technology. But within 10 years IBM was the undisputed leader in electronic computers, with more than 70 percent of the global market. IBM's dominant position in the marketplace helped to drive annual revenues to $1.8 billion by 1960.[1]

How IBM came to control the early computer industry has been thoroughly explored by economists and historians. What is more important here is how IBM's success, as well as Remington Rand's loss of market share, affected the direction of programming's development during the 1950s. In particular, how did Remington Rand react to the IBM challenge, and in what ways did this reaction influence Grace Hopper and her work?[2]

IBM: HARD-WORKING UNDERDOG, OR RUTHLESS
MONOPOLIST?

On 17 January 1969, the U.S. Department of Justice filed an
antitrust lawsuit against International Business Machines. The
IBM lawsuit became the longest and most arduous court case in
U.S. history, coming to a sudden end in 1982 when the Reagan
administration withdrew the antitrust charges. In hindsight the
case appeared to have wasted both IBM's and the government's
money and manpower, but for business historians the trial offered
a documented history of the computer industry. Secondary
literature published in the 1980s relied heavily on the thousands
of papers made public and the hundreds of testimonies generated
during the 13-year trial. These first attempts to capture the
industry's early history tended to follow closely the opposing
positions outlined during the antitrust trial. Authors aligned with
the Justice Department's perspective depicted IBM as a ruthless
monopolist bent on controlling the computer industry. Cash flow
generated by the company's punch-card monopoly permitted
it to underprice the 700 series and other early computers.
According to the economist-turned-historian Richard Thomas
DeLamarter, IBM's pricing policies hurt Remington Rand's
bottom line while expanding IBM's market share: "Remington
saw its share of the expanding market plunge irretrievably during
the next few years as customers flocked to the IBM 701 and 702."[3]
The economists Franklin Fisher, James McKie, and Richard
Mancke, on the other hand, asserted that IBM was just one of
many companies that had the potential to enter the new industry
during the 1950s. The knowledge needed to build computers was
widely dispersed, thus creating a level playing field on which IBM
competed. According to Fisher, McKie, and Mancke, IBM became

dominant because the company's leadership consciously committed more resources and personnel to the new industry. This risky investment translated into better products and better service, and ultimately IBM was rewarded with market leadership.[4]

REMINGTON RAND'S MARKETING COUP

Neither DeLamarter's account nor that of Fisher et al. pays much attention to developments outside IBM. Interviews with Grace Hopper and with 30 other people associated with UNIVAC during the 1950s suggest that IBM did not win the computer market so much as Remington Rand lost it. The difficulties of merging Remington Rand with EMCC and ERA during the first part of the 1950s kept Remington Rand from capitalizing on its technological lead. As Remington Rand stumbled, IBM's far more sophisticated sales and customer support system quickly came to dominate the fertile market. This is a tidy summary, but further inspection reveals a far more complicated story.

In November 1952, on the night of the Eisenhower-Stevenson presidential election, Remington Rand seized the imagination of the country and positioned itself to become, in the eyes of the American public, the undisputed leader in computer technology. A mock-up of a UNIVAC machine had been installed in the headquarters of the CBS television network, next to the desk of CBS's anchorman, Walter Cronkite. In the days leading up to the election, Hopper's programming team had entered demographic and voting data from previous elections into a working UNIVAC. On election night, these data were associated with real-time voting results. With only 5 percent of the votes tallied, the UNIVAC predicted an Eisenhower landslide and a final electoral-vote count of 438 to 93. Because UNIVAC's prediction differed so markedly from the findings of the Gallup and Roper opinion polls, executives at CBS decided to inform Americans that UNIVAC predicted a close race, with Eisenhower slightly in the lead. In the end, Eisenhower defeated Stevenson soundly.[5]

The uncanny accuracy of UNIVAC's prediction during a major televised event sent shock waves through the nation. At the conclusion of the election coverage, a Remington Rand spokesman appeared on CBS and informed viewers that UNIVAC's original prediction had been suppressed. As Thomas Watson Jr. recalled, "millions of people were introduced to the UNIVAC by Edward R. Murrow, Eric Sevareid, and

J. Presper Eckert Jr. (center) discussing UNIVAC output with Walter Cronkite. U.S. Census Bureau.

Walter Cronkite, who called it 'that marvelous electronic brain.' "[6] In the months that followed, "UNIVAC" gradually became the generic term for a computer.

UNIVAC's election-night heroics had significant ripple effects. Morale was boosted within the Eckert-Mauchly division, and Remington Rand management began to take the machine more seriously. Furthermore, the demand for UNIVACs swelled considerably in the months after the election, despite Remington Rand's lack of investment in sales and marketing. More and more, members of Hopper's team found themselves fielding sales inquiries from potential customers rather than programming. In fact, one of the programmers (George Danehower) later recalled that the vast majority of UNIVAC contracts were generated this way: "The machines were not really sold. Certain companies had certain kinds of problems . . . they heard about the computers, so they made inquiries."[7] The ultimate sale was actually made through the process of responding to inquiries. In 1953 and 1954, Remington Rand received more than 40 UNIVAC orders.[8]

Two of the more significant commercial orders of this period came from the General Electric Company and from the Pacific Mutual Life Insurance Company. Both companies conducted feasibility studies and concluded that the UNIVAC was superior to IBM's comparable machine, the 701/702. Pacific Mutual's reasons were highlighted in a paper given by Wesley Bagby, the company's controller, to the Controller's Institute of America in November 1955:

There were three items of difference . . . which influenced our final decision. Remington Rand's UNIVAC could be leased or purchased outright. IBM's 702, which they were competing against, could only be rented. Second, UNIVAC, one of the specific models we were considering, had been thoroughly field-tested. The other, IBM 702, had not yet been used by any customer. Third, it appeared to us that UNIVAC had some technological advantages.[9]

According to Ken Garrison, a member of Pacific Mutual's evaluation team, those technological advantages centered on the reliability of UNIVAC's mercury delay memory and the machine's ability to buffer input and output, which permitted offline tape processing and printing.[10]

The surging demand for UNIVACs in 1953 and 1954 added to Remington Rand's growing customer support problems. Many talented members of Grace Hopper's staff were assigned to clients or were hired away by clients. Hopper asked John Mauchly to inform her superiors at Remington Rand of her growing attrition problem. Mauchly put it this way:

Some of the members of Dr. Grace Hopper's staff have already left for positions with users of IBM equipment, and those of her staff who still remain are now expecting attractive offers from outside sources. . . . The Eckert-Mauchly Division has not, however, been able to make offers sufficiently soon enough, or good enough, to prevent the depletion of her staff, because there is no budget allowance in the Eckert-Mauchly Division for such personnel.[11]

Pressure from Mauchly, Hopper, and others prompted Remington Rand to organize more structured UNIVAC customer support. During the summer of 1953, a UNIVAC National Sales Headquarters was established in New York, with a training office, a customer service bureau, and a maintenance office. Paul Chinitz left Hopper's programming group to head up the initiative. The training office offered an intensive two-week course on computers that included an overview of UNIVAC I's capabilities and seminars on programming and systems analysis. According to Chinitz, the fee-based course attracted mostly middle and upper-middle managers who were familiar with the data-processing requirements of their companies.[12]

The customer service bureau, under the direction of Arthur Katz, helped potential clients determine their computing needs. The service bureau conducted surveys, prepared proposals, and organized customer-specific demonstrations. A demonstration usually involved a critical aspect of the client's proposed need. Once defined, the problem was sent to Hopper's team in Phila-delphia, and two or three programmers worked on it for a month or two. The finished program was then run for the potential customer, either at the New York service bureau, at the Phila-delphia factory and laboratory, or at the Census Bureau in Wash-ington. If the demonstration was a success, the service bureau followed up to sign a contract.[13]

Eventually the maintenance department came under the direc-tion of engineers from the newly acquired Engineering Research Associates (ERA). Remington Rand purchased the Minnesota-based company in early 1953 for a variety of reasons. First, ERA had 400 experienced technicians and engineers who could be used to augment Remington Rand's customer service staff. Second, ERA's president, John Parker, would be appointed head of the National Sales Office, so Presper Eckert could remain in the laboratory. Third, ERA's magnetic drum memory technology was the most advanced in the industry. Finally, ERA's computers were scientific in their orientation, thus augmenting Rand's product offering and complementing UNIVAC I's more com-mercial slant.[14]

Though Remington Rand's efforts to reorient itself were commendable, the 1950 decision to cut production capability came back to haunt the firm. The UNIVAC engineer Lou Wilson later acknowledged the almost impossible situation in which he and his fellow engineers had found themselves during 1953 and 1954: "In spite of having the production capability of only six machines a year, within 2 years they sold 42 machines. The result was they couldn't deliver the damn things."[15] And if Remington Rand did deliver on time, what showed up was not always a fully functioning machine. Gene Delves recalled, for example, that a UNIVAC was to be delivered to a General Electric facility in Louisville in December 1953. With the delivery date quickly approaching, the machine was still in production. "So December 15 they just crated it all up and brought it to Louisville and delivered it along with all the engineers who were still building it."[16]

Despite manufacturing challenges, in the winter of 1953–54 Grace Hopper believed that the dearth of trained programmers was the chief limit on the growth of the computer market. As has happened often in the history of technology, labor scarcity became a central external driving force behind technical innovation, prompting Hopper to ask Remington Rand management to allow herself and her team to dedicate themselves full-time to finding a way to automate the programming process.[17] In light of Remington Rand management's unwillingness to make the necessary budget allowances to maintain an adequate programming workforce, Hopper's 31 December 1953 proposal was approved and the Computation Analysis Laboratory was renamed the Automatic Programming Department. The new department shed its more mundane task of UNIVAC customer support and focused entirely on automatic programming research and development related to automatic programming. Hopper was named the department's director.[18]

IBM BENEFITS FROM THE COLD WAR

The historical evidence shows that during the first half of the 1950s Remington Rand competed successfully with IBM. Not only did UNIVAC lead in sales; even such traditional IBM customers as General Electric and Pacific Mutual picked the UNIVAC over the IBM 701/702 on technical grounds. Furthermore, all competitors in the computer market were faced with the same shortage of talented programmers. Unwillingness to pay a premium to keep programming talent may have cost Remington Rand a chance to build a commanding lead within the industry, but the firm's efforts to build a customer training and support system were commendable, and senior management's willingness to support Hopper's automatic programming research was farsighted.

If Remington Rand held its own during the first half of the 1950s in an area of relatively open competition in the nascent industry, what explains IBM's sudden ascendancy? Paradoxically, government funding of private research and development became a pivotal factor in IBM's rise to dominance, for it subsidized IBM's computer investment and transferred protected knowledge from the Massachusetts Institute of Technology to IBM's Poughkeepsie Laboratory. That funding came courtesy of the SAGE (Semi-Automatic Ground Environment) early warning defense system.[19]

SAGE was a consequence of the growing tensions between the Soviet Union and the United States. In 1949 the Soviet Union exploded its first atomic bomb. The communist nation's newfound nuclear capability, combined with its long-range bomber technology, threatened the North American continent, and the Truman administration called upon America's scientists and engineers to devise a counter to the perceived threat. The associate director of MIT's Servomechanisms Laboratory, Jay Forrester, proposed a network of radar installations across Northern Canada and Alaska to track enemy bombers and provide real-time intercept information to friendly fighter aircraft. The Forrester proposal mapped out a 15-year research and development effort with a price tag exceeding that of the Manhattan Project.[20]

The only way to deal with a mass attack of bombers was to fully automate the tracking and intercept system—something that could be accomplished, Forrester believed, with high-speed digital computers. During World War II, Forrester had worked on a flight simulator for the Navy. After the war, that project retained funding under a new name: Project Whirlwind. With the continued backing of Mina Rees at the Office of Naval Research, Whirlwind became the most elaborate, expensive general-purpose computer project of its day. Forrester now saw a purpose for the theoretical machine. The Whirlwind computer—a real-time information-processing system capable of automating command and control—would serve as the brain of the SAGE radar network.[21]

Late in 1952, Forrester received authorization to pick a subcontractor for an unprecedented 50 Whirlwind computers. Forrester and his team spent the early part of 1953 interviewing engineers, programmers, and management from three prospective subcontractors: Remington Rand, the Raytheon Manufacturing Company, and the International Business Machines Corporation. Thomas Watson Jr. believed that the SAGE contract was the answer to the UNIVAC challenge. "I thought it was absolutely essential to IBM's future that we win it," Watson recalled. "The company that built those computers was going to be way ahead of the game, because it would learn the secrets of mass production."[22]

Unknown to Watson Jr. at the time, efficient computer mass production was not the only secret to which the contract winner would be privy. Between 1948 and 1951, at the cost of more than $1 million, Forrester and his team had invented high capacity, real-time, random-access memory. Not satisfied with mercury delay lines or electrostatic storage, Forrester's team experimented with magnetic memory in 1949. Starting from the knowledge that certain materials could be magnetized and demagnetized by pulses of electricity, the MIT team constructed a matrix of small doughnut-shaped magnetic ferrite cores that performed much like binary switches.[23] Not only could these switches hold more information than other memory technologies; the information could be accessed far more rapidly in a non-serial fashion.[24]

IBM executives were well aware that Remington Rand was the top candidate for the SAGE contract. Not only had Remington Rand's machine proven itself in the marketplace; Leslie Groves, the much-respected former director of the Manhattan Project, was the head of advanced research at Remington Rand. "I tried not to worry about Groves or the other competitors," Thomas Watson Jr. remembered. "I took Forrester to see our plants and introduce him to our most gifted people. He was under extreme pressure to get the system into production as soon as possible, and I think what impressed him was the fact that we were already building computers in a factory."[25]

Though IBM's internal computer technology left something to be desired, Forrester was impressed by the Poughkeepsie lab's integration of research and production. Forrester also took note of IBM's "degree of purposefulness, integration, and esprit de corps."[26] Remington Rand's superior technology and talented engineering and programming staff were overshadowed by concerns about the company's production capabilities. Forrester concluded that IBM was better equipped to manufacture, in a limited period of time, 50 of the most complex machines ever produced. In April 1953 he offered the contract to Thomas Watson Sr.[27]

The contract to build 50 Whirlwind computers was a technological watershed for IBM, and Thomas Watson Jr. was the first to admit that "SAGE saved the 702 design team."[28] IBM immediately assigned more than 300 engineers and scientists to Poughkeepsie in order to design and manufacture what would be called the AN/FSQ-7. During the first year alone, MIT transferred more than 1,000 confidential technical documents to Poughkeepsie, while IBM personnel spent upwards of 950 person-days at MIT's Lincoln Laboratory learning about Whirlwind.[29]

Not only did IBM engineers take away knowledge about random-access magnetic core memory; they also learned how the Whirlwind team had pushed the technological envelope in a number of other areas. Forrester's staff had figured out a variety of ways to lower the frequency of vacuum-tube failure, thus increasing system reliability. Cathode-ray-tube displays were ingeniously employed to display processed information, index registers made programming easier, and real-time information from radar sensors could be processed without the need for a slow input medium such as punch cards.

Not surprisingly, Whirlwind technology quickly found its way into the next generation of IBM's commercial computers.[30] The IBM 704 was announced on 7 May 1954. Its redesigned circuitry was twice as fast as its 701 predecessor and far more reliable. Although it was shipped with two electrostatic and two magnetic drums for storage, the 704 was designed so that core memory could be installed at a later date. Then, on 1 October 1954, the

IBM 705 was announced. The 705 was manufactured with fully integrated random-access magnetic core storage and a buffered magnetic tape input/output (I/O) system that could read and write simultaneously.[31]

To appease disgruntled customers, IBM filled standing orders for 701s and 702s with the superior 704s and 705s. The market quickly embraced the new IBM machines, and there were far more new orders than had been anticipated. "In a little over a year we started delivering those redesigned computers," wrote Thomas Watson Jr. "They made the UNIVAC obsolete and we soon left Remington Rand in the dust."[32] By the start of 1957, IBM had 87 computers in operation and 190 on order. Remington Rand, in contrast, supported 41 operational UNIVACs and had back orders for 40 more.

In only 3 years IBM had met the Remington Rand challenge, mainly because of the benefits accrued from winning the SAGE contract. Not only did SAGE inject Whirlwind technology deep into IBM's DNA; the magnitude of the contract permitted IBM to hire more than 8,000 more engineers, programmers, and administrators. An astonishing 80 percent of the company's revenues from stored-program computers were generated by the SAGE contract, which amounted to more than $500 million by the completion of the project.[33] In view of the Justice Department's antitrust case against IBM during the 1970s, it is paradoxical that a large government contract appears to have been the basis for IBM's ability to dominate the computer market by 1960.

Besides providing IBM with a market advantage, the SAGE contract transmuted computer programming from an esoteric craft to a well-funded profession. The massive programming task required hundreds of thousands of lines of code, written by more

The 28 March 1955 cover of *Time*.

than 800 programmers. Since resources were not an issue, IBM subcontracted much of the programming work to the RAND Corporation, a non-profit, military-sponsored research center. RAND hired and trained so many programmers that the SAGE development division soon outnumbered the rest of the RAND Corporation, prompting RAND to spin off the division as the System Development Corporation.[34]

The sharp increase in the number of programmers sparked by the SAGE contract did not directly affect Grace Hopper and her work, but it did indirectly make it more difficult to sell the idea of automatic programming. Some of the most outspoken opponents of Hopper's automatic programming vision through the 1950s were programmers. By automating the programming process, Hopper was threatening to make programmers redundant at a time when their numbers and importance within the computing community were growing exponentially.

On 13 May 1954, a little-known moment in computer history
significantly affected programming development at both Remington Rand and IBM. Charlie Adams, a long-time member of
MIT's Project Whirlwind, presented a paper at an Office of Naval
Research (ONR) symposium on automatic programming. Grace
Hopper had organized the meeting in conjunction with the
Navy in order to assess the state of the programming field. Adams
described computer developments at MIT, including the work
of J. Halcombe Laning Jr. and Neal Zierler. Laning and Zierler
had applied emerging compiler techniques and had created what
they called an algebraic compiler. The compiler accepted standard
mathematical symbols and converted them into machine language. Thus, with a limited amount of training, a first-time user
could simply write an equation and its parameters, and the computer would generate the answer.[1]

For the most part, Laning and Zierler's efforts were ignored.
To many the algebraic compiler sounded nothing short of
chimerical. IBM programmer John Backus captured this senti-
ment in a paper he presented at the same conference, "IBM 701
Speedcoding and Other Automatic Programming Systems."
Backus stated that most programmers had at one time or another

thought about how nice it would be to write $X + Y$ instead of a more complicated code, but "no doubt if he were too insistent next week about this sort of thing he would be subject to psychiatric observation."[2] As of 1954, programmers in general were skeptical of most forms of automatic programming, let alone ones that claimed to be capable of the direct translation of mathematical equations. "To them," Backus later recalled, "it was obviously a foolish and arrogant dream to imagine that any mechanical process could possibly perform the mysterious feats of invention required to write an efficient code."[3] But in fact there were dreamers in the audience that day, including the newly appointed director of automatic programming at Remington Rand, Dr. Grace Hopper. Her own A-2 compiler, though a milestone in the field, was difficult for even skilled programmers to use.

Laning's and Zierler's work demonstrated the possibility that computers could be operated by laymen. Two years later, while serving as the keynote speaker for the second ONR-sponsored Symposium on Advanced Programming Methods, Hopper stated that the MIT compiler represented the most comprehensive language ever developed, since it not only assisted the original programming of the problem but even partially automated the debugging process.[4] MIT's achievements in the field of automatic programming effectively changed the trajectory of Hopper's work in automatic programming between 1954 and 1956, leading to her most significant contributions to date.

THE AUTOMATIC PROGRAMMING DEPARTMENT AND MATH-MATIC

By 1954, "computer programmer" was a well-defined job description. Most programmers were mathematically trained and knowledgeable about computer hardware. The programming craft involved coaxing accurate output out of a temperamental machine handicapped by input/output and memory limitations. The complexities surrounding the "black art" of programming translated into escalating computer costs that both users and manufacturers of computer equipment hoped to lower with the implementation of automatic programming. This mounting economic quandary eventually moved Remington Rand management to back Hopper's research efforts by forming the Automatic Programming Department. The new department afforded Hopper the chance to implement her own unique approach to management. Combining a sense of purpose and direction from the Harvard Computation Laboratory with the flexibility and freedom of the Eckert-Mauchly Computer Corporation, Hopper instituted a decentralized management style that unleashed a certain level of self-direction, encouraged playfulness in the work environment, and provided her subordinates with an overarching vision of the computing future. Time and again people who worked with Grace Hopper during this period spoke about how they loved what they were doing. "It was," Mildred Koss recalled, "really a place where you felt a lot of loyalty to the people who were there, wanted to make it work, wanted to be a part of that exciting environment."[5] Grace Hopper had somehow captured the unity and sense of urgency that existed during the war and transferred it to Philadelphia in the 1950s.

Just before the May ONR symposium, the Automatic Programming Department's efforts focused on improving the A-2 compiler. The resultant A-3 wrote more efficient machine code, but it was far from user-friendly. According to Hopper, Laning and Zierler's efforts opened her eyes to the full potential of pseudo-code[6] and confirmed in her mind that automatic programming could bridge the gap between user and computer, thus eliminating the need for programmers outside of research and development laboratories.[7]

Hopper and her colleagues explored the possibility of an equation-based programming language, and by 1956 they had modified A-3 to the point where it could support a user-friendly source code. The resultant AT-3 compiler was later named MATH-MATIC. Hopper had finally freed programmers from UNIVAC's awkward three-address coding format. MATH-MATIC pseudo-code was quite natural to write and further separated the user from the eccentricities of hardware.

MATH-MATIC also appeased more experienced programmers, for it had the ability to handle lower-level languages. That is, the compiler could process statements written in A-3 pseudo-code or even in C-10 machine code alongside the new source code. This flexibility enabled experienced programmers to manually modify compiler code output, thus ensuring the production of the most efficient final code possible. This was feasible because MATH-MATIC first translated its source code into A-3 pseudo-code as an intermediate step. A-3 was then translated into machine code.

In many respects MATH-MATIC outstripped the capabilities of the hardware for which it was designed. The 1,000-word internal memory was so limited that Hopper was forced to create an elaborate system of "virtual" memory. That is, MATH-MATIC made full use of the UNIVAC's ten magnetic servo tapes, automatically orchestrating their use to make the machine appear as if it had more internal memory. For instance, if a generated object code was too large to fit into internal memory or on a single magnetic tape, the compiler automatically inserted the necessary control transfers and input/output statements to reload memory from other tapes as often as required.[8]

Sadly, for all their creative efforts, MATH-MATIC's designers could not overcome the programming language's one glaring shortcoming: unbearably long run times when compiling. MATH-MATIC, like Laning and Zierler's algebraic compiler, had identified the paradox associated with automatic programming during much of the 1950s: the more user-friendly the source code, the longer the run times. Until this was rectified, automatic programming had no comparative advantage over teams of skilled programmers writing machine code.

SOLVING THE EFFICIENCY PARADOX: JOHN BACKUS AND FORTRAN

Charlie Adams's short description of Laning and Zierler's algebraic compiler did not go unnoticed by another ONR symposium attendee, John Backus. The 29-year-old Backus had joined IBM as a programmer in 1950 and had spent his first years there developing Speedcode for the IBM 701. An avid student of Hopper's automatic programming work, Backus was impressed by the A-2 compiler's speed but frustrated by its awkwardness. Part of the A-2's inefficiency, Backus believed, was attributable to the limitations of the UNIVAC hardware. The 1,000-word memory and the lack of an index register caused the A-2 to spend much of its processing time on "housekeeping chores."[9] If automatic programming was to be accepted on a larger scale, Backus believed, the efficiency paradox had to be solved.

In January 1954, John Backus, Harlan Herrick, and Irving Ziller set out to develop a more "streamlined" compiler for IBM's proposed 704 computer. The MIT-inspired hardware design, complete with core memory, floating decimal processor, and index register, provided the IBM team with unprecedented design flexibility. But despite these advantages, Backus recalled, the group spent months debating the theoretical design limits of automatic programming. Though he did not mention Hopper's name directly, Backus suggested that one of the reasons the computing community as a whole was skeptical of automatic programming in the mid 1950s "came from the energetic public relations efforts of some visionaries to spread the word that their 'automatic programming' systems had almost human abilities to understand the language and needs of the user."[10] But, as the case of the A-2, on further inspection most compiling systems proved to be "complex, exception-ridden performers of clerical tasks."[11]

Laning and Zierler's algebraic compiler served as evidence that prestigious institutions such as MIT were taking automatic programming seriously, prompting Backus to write Laning a letter shortly after the May symposium. In the letter, Backus informed Laning that his team at IBM was working on a similar compiler, but that they had not yet done any programming or even any detailed planning.[12] To help formulate the specifications for their proposed language, Backus requested a demonstration of the algebraic compiler, which he and Ziller received in the summer of 1954. Much to their dismay, the two experienced firsthand the efficiency dilemma of compiler-based language design. The MIT source code was commendable, but the compiler slowed down the Whirlwind computer by a factor of 10. Since computer time was so dear a commodity, Backus realized that only a compiler that maximized efficiency could hope to compete with human programmers. Despite this initial disappointment, Laning and Zierler's work inspired Backus to attempt to build a compiler that could translate a rich mathematical language into a sufficiently economical program at a relatively low cost.[13]

On 10 November 1954, Backus submitted a report titled "Preliminary Report: Specifications for the IBM Mathematical

Formula Translating System, FORTRAN" to his boss, Cuthbert Hurd. The report stipulated that FORTRAN would "comprise a large set of programs to enable the IBM 704 to accept a concise formulation of a problem in terms of a mathematical notation and to produce automatically a high-speed 704 program for the solution of the problem."[14] The report also suggested that a novice programmer would be able to manipulate FORTRAN's notation after a one-hour course. In effect, Backus was promising ease of coding with unprecedented speed of execution.

Backus initially thought the time from specifications to prototype would be 6 months. It turned out to be 30 months. During that time, Backus and his team of twelve programmers developed a variety of compiling techniques that increased both the efficiency of the generated machine code and decreased the computer time needed to compile. These advances included separate compilation of commonly used subroutines, detection of identical sub expressions (thus eliminating duplicate calculations), methods to avoid recompilation during the debugging phase, and self-checking mechanisms that flagged user-based errors when preparing source code.[15]

Though the FORTRAN operator's manual was completed by the fall of 1956, the compiler itself was not distributed to IBM 704 installations until April 1957. Within a year after distribution, half of the IBM 704 installations were using FORTRAN to solve more than half of all mathematical problems.[16] Subsequently, compilers were produced for the IBM 705 and the IBM 650, quickly making FORTRAN the most widely used automatic program of its day. By 1961, UNIVAC users demanded a compatible FORTRAN compiler and abandoned Hopper's MATH-MATIC. Backus's focus on compiler efficiency, coupled with IBM's growing market share in hardware,

Grace Hopper at a UNIVAC keyboard, 1960. Courtesy of Smithsonian Institution.

resulted in the first programming-language standard. For the first time, programmers on different machines could speak the same language.

CREATING A BUSINESS LANGUAGE: B-O AND FLOW-MATIC

FORTRAN, like MATH-MATIC, was designed to permit engineers and mathematicians to write source code using standard mathematical symbols. But in the winter of 1955–56, while these two languages were still being developed, Grace Hopper was planning a far more radical programming language. She believed that computers were more than just elaborate calculators—that they were also data-processing and decision-making tools. There-fore, she wanted her Automatic Programming Department to create a unique compiler that would enable managers and admin-istrators to write business programs using standard business vocabulary.

On 31 January 1955, Hopper submitted to Remington Rand management a report (titled "The Preliminary Definition of a Data Processing Compiler") that outlined the original specifica-tions for the first B-0 business language. The most significant concept outlined in this report concerned the nature of the compiler's pseudo-code. The report stated that both symbols and abbreviations should be replaced with understandable English words. "Oh, I loved the symbols, but I saw there were a lot of people that didn't, and I wanted them to be able to use the computer as well," Hopper recalled.[17] The typical business admin-istrator or manager, she argued, would rather use standard busi-ness vocabulary to delineate both operations and data names. Therefore, $A \times B = C$ should be written as

MULTIPLY BASE-PRICE AND DISCOUNT-PERCENT
GIVING DISCOUNT-PRICE

At first glance the latter description seems verbose, but Hopper defended English source code on several counts. Mathematics utilized a widely accepted set of symbols; business language did not. According to B-0 co-developer Mary Hawes, Hopper first directed the design team to study business expressions used by different UNIVAC users in order to generate a suitable business vocabulary. "When we tried mnemonic abbreviations," Hawes recalled, "we found different abbreviations for the same term in different departments of the same company, not to mention the differences among companies."[18] Instead of attempting to invent symbols and abbreviations to represent basic business terms (e.g., tax, gross pay, and price), Hopper came up with an elegant solution that would allow programmers to define their own pseudo-code language by assigning program variables to any desired English name. For example, X_1, X_2, and X_3 could be assigned "number of employees," "numbers of hours worked," and "hours at 1½ times pay."

Such unprecedented source-code flexibility created significant challenges for the B-0 design team. First, the habit of using fixed word lengths had to be broken, which was easier said then done after years of programming with this constraint. Additionally, a single variable could now be defined by more than one word. How would the computer know that "employee number" was one rather than two variables? "The contingency was taken care of by defining a word . . . as a group of letters preceded by a space symbol and followed by another space symbol," Mary Hawes explained.[19] Sometimes, shifts in perspective yielded simple, elegant solutions.

Hopper also noted some of the unintended positive by-products of pseudo-code. English-based programs were self-documenting, permitting a second programmer or technician to pick up where a colleague left off. This changed programming from an individualistic endeavor to a group activity, thus setting the foundation for teams of programmers to work on more complex projects. In addition, managers with limited computer skills could understand the logic and purpose of a given program, making administrative assessment possible (much to the chagrin of some programmers).[20]

To help Remington Rand management accept the seemingly strange concept that computers could translate and compile source code written in English, the Automatic Programming Department prepared a series of small demonstration programs. The first program, a simple inventory control application, contained only 20 lines of English-based code. Upon compilation, the English sentences were successfully expanded into machine code. To make the demonstration more impressive, and thus to increase the probability of funding, Hopper had her team rewrite the test compiler so it could also translate pseudo-code written in either French or German[21]:

IF GREATER GO TO OPERATION 1
OTHERWISE GO TO OPERATION 2

SI PLUS GRAND ALLEZ À OPÉRATION 1
AUTREMENT ALLEZ À OPÉRATION 2

WENN GRÖSSER GEHEN ZU BEDIENUNG 1
ANSONSTEN GEHEN ZU BEDIENUNG 2

Each of these three lines of pseudo-code generated the same machine code, despite the language differences. Hopper had proved that compiler pseudo-code could be designed to meet the needs of any business, even one in another country. Surprisingly, Hopper's theoretical linguistic demonstration was not well received. Management was concerned that Hopper's plans were too ambitious, and that the Automatic Programming Department was wasting time and energy exploring such marginal areas as multilingual programming. "It was completely self-evident [to management] that an American computer built in blue-belt Pennsylvania couldn't possibly be programmed in French or German," she recalled.[22] Hopper had to assure her superiors that the proposed business language would only be in English.

B-0, as the business language compiler was designated, became available to UNIVAC customers at the start of 1958. Before its completion, Remington Rand merged with Sperry Gyroscope Corporation to form Sperry Rand. The marketing department of the new company renamed the business language FLOW-MATIC. (In addition, AT-3 was renamed MATH-MATIC.) The completed version of FLOW-MATIC had a rich library of operational verbs that appeared to meet the application needs of most businesses.[23] These verbs included editing commands so information could be formatted before output. Furthermore, FLOW-MATIC provided unparalleled flexibility in data designation, thus allowing file names to be given complicated descriptions.

As they had had to do with previous UNIVAC compilers, Hopper and the staff of the Automatic Programming Department had to "sell" FLOW-MATIC to a skeptical programming and business community. "We finally got it running," Hopper recalled, "and there we were, research and development group, with a product, and nobody to use it. We had to go out and sell the idea of writing programs in English."[24] The group turned immediately to dependable UNIVAC customers, and by the spring of 1958 US Steel, Westinghouse, the Air Force Comptroller, and the Navy Bureau of Ships were writing payroll and inventory applications in FLOW-MATIC.

Once again, the harshest critics of the new programming language were programmers. Many programmers believed FLOW-MATIC English phraseology to be superfluous, especially when basic operations such as MULTIPLY and SUBTRACT had to be written out. Moreover, the length of commands increased the time needed to compile the pseudo-code into machine code. Most important, the pseudo-code was so far removed from the inner workings of the machine that even the most gifted programmer could not express all needed operations. By making FLOW-MATIC accessible to a wider group of users, its designers had sacrificed a certain amount of flexibility and control.

Faced with a skeptical programming community, Hopper dedicated much of her time to communicating the benefits of automatic programming. Between 1955 and 1959 she published ten articles on the subject, with titles such as "Programming Business-Data Processors," "Computer Programs in English," and "From Programmer to Computer." Hopper emphasized that automatic programming was economical, easy to learn, easy to debug, and easy to maintain, and that it reduced the time needed to build applications and solve problems. During this same period, Hopper gave dozens of papers at various conferences and symposiums and encouraged members of her staff to do the same. She continued to help organize programming symposia.

Hopper remained active in the Association of Computing Machinery. From 1956 to 1958 she served as on the association's council, and in 1957 and 1958 she was a member of the editorial board for the association's main publication, *Communications of the ACM*. By 1960, Hopper had indeed navigated her way to the center of the computer revolution. She would use her prominent position to help guide the development of COBOL, which remains to this day the most successful computer programming language.

11 DISTRIBUTED INVENTION MATURES: GRACE HOPPER AND THE DEVELOPMENT OF COBOL

By the late 1950s, Grace Hopper's style of invention had taken full form. Though she had created the original A-0 compiler on her own, subsequent iterations of her prototype evolved out of a distributed process of invention and development. A-1, A-2, A-3, MATH-MATIC, and FLOW-MATIC were "invented" by Hopper in the sense that she coordinated the creative efforts of a heterogeneous group of programmers and users. Many of the co-inventors worked for her in Sperry Rand's Automatic Programming Division, but Hopper did not limit her innovative alliances to her company's borders.

Input from users was a essential component of the development process. Hopper freely distributed code and provided user manuals. In return she received feedback and suggestions for compiler improvement. Some users went so far as to rewrite or expand the original code. Hopper would review these changes and incorporate the best practices. The end result was a computer language that continually improved in an organic fashion, nourished by the collective insights of Hopper's group of innovators.

During the 1950s, maintaining and expanding that network became a central activity for Hopper. The diversity of the expanding computing industry called for a person who could bridge a variety of subgroups within that community. Hopper moved freely in many of these disparate worlds, and could speak about computers and programming in both technical and non-technical terms, depending on her audience. Her position as the director of automatic programming development at the largest computer manufacturer afforded her access to senior management throughout the entire industry, while making her aware of the requirements of influential customers. As a reserve officer in the Navy, she personified the growing bond between industry and the military during the Cold War era, and she spent 2 weeks per year on active duty assessing the Navy's computing needs. And in 1958 she returned to her academic roots, taking a position as an adjunct professor at the University of Pennsylvania, where she lectured about programming to a new generation of computer enthusiasts.

Hopper also became a leading figure in the ever-growing Association of Computing Machinery. She headed the association's Programming Committee, which was tasked with keeping track of the latest developments within the field and disseminating this information in the programming community. Much to her credit, ACM conferences allocated a growing number of panels and papers to issues related to programming. Hopper chaired many of these panels, and she encouraged members of her programming team at Remington Rand to speak about their latest work. During 1953 and 1954, Hopper also headed up the ACM's Nomenclature Committee and was responsible for publishing the first complete computer glossary of terms. Though at first glance "Nomenclature Committee Chair" is not the most striking title, the position gave Hopper an opportunity to define a common language for the industry as a whole.

Every mature profession, such as medicine or law, has a shared language that members have internalized. A common language serves a variety of purposes. On the most basic level, it identifies and defines important terms and concepts within the community of practitioners. These terms and concepts locate the broad intellectual boundaries of the profession and magnify the subtle details within the landscape. For instance, during her time as the head of the ACM's Nomenclature Committee, Hopper attempted to move the community away from "words of the *magic brain* class." While she was working at Harvard in the 1940s, influential academics such as Norbert Wiener and John von Neumann tended to describe computers as "giant brains" and applied descriptive language that perpetuated this metaphor. Hopper purged these words from computing in the 1950s, replacing "memory" with "storage" and "thinking" with "processing."[1]

On a deeper level, a common language helps forge a sense of identity among members of the profession. It facilitates coordination of effort, defines roles, and sustains a feeling of cultural kinship. Hopper found herself at that rare moment during the early years of a budding community when language had not yet precipitated into a more solid, stable state. Fittingly, the person most skilled at communicating with computers was also the central figure in the effort to facilitate communication between people within the maturing profession.

Any discussion of identity brings up questions of power, and Hopper seemed to have been completely aware of that connection. Feminists have long recognized that male-oriented, male-defined language has contributed on some level to the subjugation of women. Hopper was less concerned with gender dominance than with other types of bias built into the language. She readily admitted that the 1954 glossary was UNIVAC oriented and feared that others would reject it out of hand. With that in mind, Hopper opened the language to scrutiny. "It is our earnest plea," she wrote to fellow members of the Association for Computing Machinery, "that we receive comments, both mild and violent, suggestions, and criticisms as soon as possible." By broadening participation during the development phase, Hopper increased the odds that the computing community would freely adopt the resultant language.

INVENTION BY COMMITTEE

By 1959, Hopper had proved herself as a businesswoman, a programmer, a naval officer, and an academic. Her multifaceted career, combined with an inventive style that encouraged broad participation, made her the ideal person to orchestrate the creation of a universal, standardized general business language. Hopper's vigorous efforts to further the cause of automatic programming led to the development of COBOL (Common Business Oriented Language). Although some widely distributed publications (including the *New York Times* and the *Washington Post*[2]) have listed Hopper as COBOL's inventor, the development of the popular business language is a far more complex story, involving a number of individuals and organizations.

Besides Hopper, the person most cited as the creator of COBOL is Charles Phillips, Director of Data Systems Research at the Department of Defense between 1958 and 1962.[3] Yet in a paper presented at the annual conference of the ACM on 1 September 1959, Phillips himself admitted that the idea for COBOL did not originate with him. "We were embarrassed," Phillips said, "that the idea for such a common language has not had its origin by that time in Defense since we would benefit so greatly from the success of such a project."[4] Phillips credited Grace Hopper and her "idea team" for coordinating the COBOL effort. Hopper, an adjunct professor at the University of Pennsylvania in the spring of 1959, organized a meeting of users, manufacturers, and teachers at the university's Computer Center on 8 April 1959 to discuss the feasibility of co-developing a common business language.[5]

Phillips's account coincides with Hopper's own recollection of the event.[6] According to Hopper, she, Robert Bemer of IBM, and Howard Bromberg of the Radio Corporation of America had been discussing the possibility of creating a common business language for industry. At the time, Bemer was an assistant manager for programming research at IBM and Bromberg was the head of automatic programming at RCA. Before joining RCA, Bromberg had worked under Hopper as a programmer at UNIVAC. "We all knew each other," Hopper recalled, "but we couldn't work together and agree on anything because we were breaking antitrust laws. The only way we could all work together and not throw our companies into fits was under the jurisdiction of a university or the government."[7]

In order to create a legal forum, Hopper, Bemer, and Bromberg asked Dr. Saul Gorn, Director of Computing at the Moore School of Engineering, to call a meeting to discuss the issue. Gorn, who had been attempting to write a universal computer language himself, invited representatives from industry, government, and academia to the Penn campus. Industry attendees included representative of the main computer manufacturers, as well as the primary users of computers. "We all were in agreement that we would like to have one language for data processing," said Hopper.[8]

The chief concern that motivated both manufacturers and users was the rising cost associated with programming. The expenditure for defining business applications, writing, debugging, documenting, and maintaining code, and transferring the program to a second computer accounted for an ever-increasing percentage of total computer outlays. This growing consensus was confirmed by a 1959 survey of prominent user organizations, which concluded that the average programming cost for any large data-processing installation exceeded $800,000. If programs had to be translated in order to run on upgraded hardware, an additional investment of $600,000 was needed. The study also estimated that if the original programs had been constructed in a machine-independent common business language, a full translation could be completed in 6 months (versus 2 years) at a cost of $50,000.[9]

The daunting question Hopper and the other attendees faced at the 8 April meeting was how to go about crafting a common business language. The group was well aware of the recent development of separate but similar automatic programming languages (among them FLOW-MATIC, COMTRAN, and AIMACO), and that the number of languages would continue to increase if left to the whims of market forces. To avoid the seemingly inevitable "Tower of Babel," Hopper insisted that users and manufacturers should put aside their private agendas in the name of collaboration. But developing a common, problem-oriented, hardware-independent business language could take more than 10 years, and asking a wide array of organizations to coordinate their efforts for such a long period seemed naive at best.[10]

After the 8 April meeting, Hopper and the "idea group" searched for an appropriate sponsor for such a formidable undertaking. In order to ensure wide-ranging support from both users and manufacturers, an appropriate sponsor would have to be neutral and would have to possess enough stature to encourage participation. Hopper first solicited the advice of her long-time friend Eugene Smith, a civilian employee of the Navy who had been the Bureau of Ships' liaison to the Harvard Computation Laboratory during World War II. Smith advised that the Navy was unable to support such an ambitious endeavor, and eventually the group turned to the Department of Defense.

Charles Phillips, who at the time was the DOD's director of data systems research, recalled being approached by the delegation and being impressed by the "dedicated naval reserve officer who thoroughly understood the DOD problems."[11] As of 1959, the DOD operated 225 internally programmed computers and had ordered 175 more. More than $200 million, according to Phillips, had been spent on application design, flow charting, programming, and debugging. Any means of speeding up software development and reducing operation costs would be welcomed.[12]

Because the DOD operated a variety of computers from different manufacturers, Phillips was also interested in the possibility of program portability. In 1959, a program written for an IBM machine could not work on a UNIVAC. Hence, each change in hardware necessitated the rewriting of program libraries. Program portability would permit programs to run on different computers, regardless of differences in hardware.

Program portability was well suited to the DOD's plan to streamline and consolidate its archaic supply system. For example, in 1959 the military was attempting to reduce costs by unifying its medical supply system across service branches. The Navy had overall management responsibility and coordinated ten major supply depots: four for the Army, five for the Navy and the

Marine Corps, and one for the Air Force. Five of the ten depots used five different computers from two different manufacturers; the other five were awaiting computer delivery to replace aging punch-card machines. Since all ten depots used the same stock-distribution system, the savings gained from using one computer program for all ten would be considerable.[13]

Program portability also could generate other savings for the Department of Defense. According to Hopper, the military's unique personnel policies added to the costs of programming. Personnel, be they Navy pilots or Air Force computer programmers, served two- to three-year tours of duty. When a tour was completed, the person was sent to a new duty station. Owing to the proliferation of various makes and models of computer hardware, the military spent a considerable amount of money and time retraining personnel. One solution would have been to standardize hardware purchases, but this was impractical because of the dynamic state of the industry. Grace Hopper and the "idea team" convinced Charles Phillips that the best solution would be a portable, common business language that a DOD programmer could learn once. Phillips agreed to put the weight of the military behind the project.[14]

Phillips tasked Hopper and her colleagues with drafting the agenda for a DOD-sponsored meeting to discuss the feasibility for such an unprecedented approach to program development. Invitations to this meeting were to be "restricted to a nucleus of well-qualified key people who would provide adequate representation for both users and manufacturers."[15] For Hopper, this nucleus was easy to identify, for it coincided with the same distributed group of users, manufacturers, and programmers that she had helped to organize over the previous 8 years.

The more difficult task was to decide on an appropriate agenda. First and foremost, general agreement had to be reached among the meeting's participants in regard to both the desirability and feasibility of a common business language. Desirability could probably be gauged at the 28 May meeting, but study groups would have to be created in order to make an educated decision concerning feasibility. These groups would have to specify the requisite elements of a common business language and identify the types of problems that such a general language would be able to handle.[16]

The idea team also faced difficult organizational problems. If a variety of subcommittees were formed to study feasibility issues, how would they be organized to foster effective communication? Would the sub-committees' responsibilities overlap? How would consensus be determined? These and other questions would be answered at a two-day meeting in the spring of 1959.

On 28 and 29 May 1959, the Department of Defense hosted the organizational meeting of the Conference on Data Systems and Languages (CODASYL). Forty representatives from seven government agencies, eleven companies (users), and ten computer manufacturers attended. The computer manufacturers were Sperry Rand, IBM, Honeywell, RCA, General Electric, Burroughs, National Cash Register, Philco, Sylvania, and International Computers and Tabulators. Charles Phillips chaired the meeting, and Grace Hopper attended as a representative of Sperry Rand and as Phillips's technical advisor.[17] Hopper was impressed by both the number and the quality of the attendees: "I don't think ever before or ever since have I seen in one room so much power to commit men and monies as I saw that day."[18]

After discussing the feasibility of such an ambitious project, Phillips hoped to gain a sense of the proposed business language's desired characteristics. Betty Snyder Holberton, Hopper's longtime friend and confidant, offered this recollection: "Phillips . . . asked each of us to make some statement what we thought about the language plan. . . . I began to hear exaggerated claims, many unrealistic hopes, and I wondered what I would say."[19] Holberton and other professional programmers in attendance winced at the enthusiastic yet naive suggestions made by attendees with less coding experience. The group imagined a straightforward language that could be effectively applied to banking, utilities, insurance, production, and inventory control, not to mention medical and government applications.[20] But Hopper viewed the same relaxed forum as an essential preliminary stage in the innovation process, a process that was consciously removed from the hands of professional programmers and included users and managers. The concerns of users differed considerably from those of professional programmers, as listed in a 1959 paper by E. J. Albertson (a member of CODASYL's executive committee and a representative of the U.S. Steel Corporation):

• The majority of the group favored maximum use of simple English language.

• The majority preferred a language that was easy to use, even if somewhat less powerful.

• The majority agreed that the language should be initially open-ended and capable of continuous change.

• The majority agreed that the language should be problem-oriented and machine independent.

• All participants agreed that it was necessary to broaden the base of those who could state problems to computers.

• All agreed that the envisioned language characteristics should not be biased or limited by the limitations of present compilers.

The most significant disagreement concerned the use of mathematical symbols and algebraic expressions. Some participants believed that some business concepts were better expressed with mathematical symbols than with English words; other participants, including Hopper, felt that maximizing English expressions broadened the set of potential users, served a second role as program documentation, and made debugging easier.[21]

With some guiding principles in place, attendees focused their attention on how to create such a language. Three committees were formed, each with a defined set of objectives. The short-term committee, chaired by Joseph Wegstein of the National Bureau of Standards, would study existing business compilers, survey users about their experiences, and generate the initial specifications for an interim language. The intermediate-term committee, led by Hopper's close friend Eugene Smith of the Bureau of Ships, would consist of two task groups; one would study the syntax of language and the other would study trends in business language. At the time of the May meeting it was believed that the more abstract knowledge gleaned by the intermediate-term committee would be incorporated into the final version of the language. The long-range committee, whose members were not determined during the May meeting, would then explore the fundamentals of all language and consider the merger of scientific and business languages into a universal computer language. The work of the three committees would be reviewed and approved by a CODASYL executive committee consisting of Charles Phillips, Joseph Cunningham (Air Force), E. J. Albertson (U.S. Steel), Gregory Dillon (Dupont), M. Grosz (Standard Oil), and the three committee chairs. Grace Hopper (Sperry Rand) and Robert Bemer (IBM) would serve as the executive committee's chief technical advisors.[22]

THE SHORT-TERM COMMITTEE AND THE COBOL
SPECIFICATIONS

The short-term committee was given a September deadline to come up with the specifications for an interim language, a deadline that experienced members of the committee knew was impractical from the onset. "To expect the short-range committee to develop a language and write the report in 3 months was gross optimism on the part of the executive committee," recalled Betty Holberton (who had been a member of the committee). At best, initial findings would be reported in September, and the executive committee would have to accept the fact that it could not put such a strict deadline on the process of invention.

Having developed programming tools and languages in the past, Holberton instinctively knew that there was no such thing as an "interim" language. Manufacturers and users alike would implement a language only if they believed that it would be around for a while. To prove her point, Holberton turned to her old friend to supply the necessary data. "I asked Grace Hopper if she could send me a cost estimate for implementing the compiler. She estimated that it would cost Sperry Rand $945,000 and 45½ man-years of effort," she recalled. "In no way was this language going to be an interim solution. This language was it!"[23] In the weeks after the initial meeting at the Pentagon, it became readily apparent to most members of the short-term committee that the burden of inventing the common business language rested squarely on their shoulders, despite the stated roles of the three committees.

The first round of meetings took place 7–9 July at a lakeside resort near Battle Creek, Michigan. Nora Taylor, another member of the short-term committee and a close colleague of Hopper's, thought it amusing that committee members were instructed to bring bathing suits to the meeting. Though the majority of the committee's time was spent wading through the surveys sent out to a multitude of computer facilities, the group did find time to enjoy the resort.

The survey of users verified that automatic programming had become both an accepted and a desired method. Half of the users surveyed were already employing Hopper's FLOW-MATIC business language. Companies and organizations that used automatic programming reduced average training time of new users from 2 months to 2 weeks, and applications were up and running in 2–3 weeks rather than the more typical 2–3 months. Users cited time savings in coding, debugging, and testing, and compiled programs were considered about 80–90 percent as efficient as human-generated programs. The complaints cited most often were lengthy compile time, awkward language structure, and subroutine limitations. The most common business application requests were for payroll, sales statistics, pension plans, premium billing, inventory control, and production control.[24]

After confirming user's preferences, noting complaints, and identifying the most common applications, the short-term committee assigned a smaller statement language subcommittee to assess the strengths and weaknesses of existing automatic business compilers. The three main candidates for review were FLOW-MATIC, AIMACO, and COMTRAN, although Autocoder III, SURGE, FORTRAN, RCA 501 Assembler, Report Generator (GE), and APG-1 (Dupont) were also to be considered. As of July 1959, FLOW-MATIC and AIMACO were operational, while IBM's Commercial Translator (COMTRAN) existed only on paper. Jean Sammet, a former UNIVAC programmer who supervised the advanced programming department at

Sylvania, prepared a comparative study of language functions for FLOWMATIC I, FLOWMATIC II, COMTRAN, and AIMACO that was presented at the 22 July meeting in Washington. The untiring efforts of Sammet and others that summer earned the short-term committee the nickname "The P.D.Q. [Pretty Damn Quick] Group."

The criteria the study used to judge the languages were naturalness of language, effectiveness in structuring data-processing problems, and ease of implementation. For example, when looking at language structure, the study considered how many individual sentences could be combined, whether a sentence could contain more than one function word, and to what extent the language could tolerate extraneous words and misspellings. Data management was also considered, especially data descriptions and the movement of data (input, output, sorting).[25]

AIMACO was an Air Force derivative of FLOW-MATIC, so it differed only marginally from the UNIVAC languages. COMTRAN's specifications, on the other hand, included flexible GOTO and IF-THEN functions and a search function, and permitted programmers to use mathematical symbols instead of English when describing formulas. Roy Goldfinger, the author of the COMTRAN manual and a member of the intermediate-term committee, attended the statement language subcommittee's meeting (held 22–24 July in Washington) to support his creation and to encourage the use of algebraic expressions.[26]

When word of the direction of the committee discussions got back to Grace Hopper, she responded with a heated memorandum to the short-term committee (dated 28 July 1959). Hopper reiterated that since 1954 Sperry Rand had led the industry in its effort to develop "problem-oriented, user-oriented languages" that aimed to use basic English as the chief input. "It is not the intention of Sperry Rand," Hopper wrote, "to progress backwards by introducing mathematical symbols and banning adjectives, etc. etc." Therefore, it was imperative that the committee focus on creating the specifications for a compiler suitable for the commercial customer, not for mathematicians and programmers. "If the language developed by the statement language committee continues in the direction in which it is headed," Hopper threatened, "Sperry Rand will not implement it." Instead, Sperry Rand would break from the CODASYL effort and would "supply its customers the first and the best use of English possible at any given stage of the art." Hopper ended the memo with a caustic challenge to the short-term committee: "Sperry Rand would like to support the development of a common data-processing language, but suggests that such a language will probably have to be developed by people familiar with business data-processing problems and not by mathematicians and programmers."[27]

According to Hopper, throughout the fall of 1959 the short-term committee took her advice to heart and used FLOW–MATIC as the blueprint for the new language's specifications. In fact, Hopper asserted that entire sections of the FLOW–MATIC manual itself had been copied because of time constraints imposed by the executive committee and the DOD.[28] The most significant concept that the short-term committee borrowed was the application of basic English to describe both data and the procedures to be executed.[29] This meant that FLOW–MATIC-type operational verbs, sentence structure, and full alphanumerical descriptions of data (no abbreviations) found their way into COBOL. Jean Sammet, a member of the short-term committee, concurred with Grace Hopper's claim that COBOL was highly influenced by FLOW–MATIC, though she also maintained that the languages were not one and the same.[30]

As for the other two languages reviewed by the short-term committee, little could be gained from AIMACO, itself a derivative of FLOW-MATIC. In 1958, Colonel Alfred Asch (a member of the short-term committee) and his programming team at the Air Force Air Materiel Command in Dayton had modified FLOW-MATIC to run on a UNIVAC 1105. At the time of the first CODASYL meeting, Asch was attempting to improve on the original by introducing limited portability. According to Sammet, the project was never completed once COBOL was accepted as the DOD standard.[31]

IBM's Commercial Translator (COMTRAN), like many of the company's other products, was "announced" to IBM customers and potential customers well before it was close to completion. The technique permitted the powerful firm to gauge the receptivity of the marketplace while the potential product was still in the design phase. To the dismay of IBM's competitors, many customers rejected rival products on the promise that IBM would produce what it pledged.[32] As of 1959, COMTRAN existed only as a series of specifications, but the short-term committee regarded it as a competitor to FLOW-MATIC. Much like FLOW-MATIC, COMTRAN was to be an English-based language, but its specifications included some notable differences, which were incorporated into COBOL's design. These included a powerful conditional IF-THEN that enhanced the naturalness of the language (by making it unnecessary to write multiple JUMP or GOTO commands) and a more robust file-management system that included suffixing, searching, and layered data description.[33]

FACT AND THE POLITICS OF LANGUAGE STANDARDIZATION

In the fall of 1959, another business programming language was much farther along in the development process than

IBM's COMTRAN, yet its characteristics were not incorporated into the initial COBOL specifications. The creative mind behind FACT (Fully Automatic Compiling Technique) was Roy Nutt, who had developed the specifications for the language 5 months before the first CODASYL meetings. Nutt, who had worked on FORTRAN's development while on loan to IBM from United Aircraft, was an extraordinary programmer with an ability to anticipate errors just by looking at the code.

Nutt and his associate Fletcher Jones (of the newly formed Computer Science Corporation) approached Richard Clippinger, the head of software development for the Honeywell 800 computer, concerning the construction of a powerful business data-processing language. Nutt's design represented the most complex and robust computer language to date, requiring several hundred thousand instructions to complete.[34]

By October 1959 (according to Jack Strong, a member of the intermediate-range CODASYL committee), Roy Nutt's FACT manual had found its way into the hands of members of the short-range committee and members of the intermediate-range committee. Serious programmers on both committees admired FACT for its flexible input/output system and its intuitive data-description and record-retrieval functionality. Built-in error-checking and information-compression capabilities impressed the intermediate-range committee to the extent that it passed the following resolution on 14 October 1959 by a vote of 15 to 1, with two abstentions:

IRTF II recognizes that the Honeywell Business Compiler represents the most advanced compiler specifications existent at this date, and recommends to the executive committee that the Honeywell Business Compiler specifications be the basis for the first stage Common Business Language.[35]

After the resolution vote, Jack Strong recalled, "we all went home, secure in our thoughts that significant improvements would be incorporated in the design of COBOL."[36] But much to Strong's surprise, supporters of a FLOW-MATIC-based COBOL would overturn the intermediate-range committee's resolution, leaving FACT, CSC, and Honeywell out in the cold.

Jean Sammet remembered that the intermediate-range committee resolution "had the effect of a major bombing" on the spirits of the short-term committee. The short-term committee was well along in defining its specifications by October 1959, and to scrap the work done thus far and make FACT the basis for COBOL was unthinkable. Sammet freely admitted that FACT was indeed the technically superior language by the fall of 1959. The language's advantages, however, were diminished by the fact that its creators did not concern themselves with machine portability, nor did they build consensus among manufacturers and users.[37]

But not all motivations for blocking FACT in favor of FLOW-MATIC were so innocent. Howard Bromberg (RCA's representative and a member of the original "idea team" that approached Charles Phillips) worked many hours with Sammet and the short-term committee to create COBOL's specifications. At the same time, Bromberg fed technical data to his RCA team. "We kept about one week behind the committee," he stated later. "RCA wanted to commercialize COBOL as a product to have a marketing edge."[38] By scrapping COBOL and starting over with FACT, RCA would lose both its technical and its economic advantage.

As tensions mounted and Honeywell threatened to develop FACT on its own, IBM's commitment to COBOL began to waver. On the one hand, IBM, as the largest computer manufacturer, had much to gain from an easy-to-use common business language. Expanding access to computers via COBOL would increase the size of the hardware market. But because of IBM's growing dominance within that market by 1959, there was a strong chance that COMTRAN, once operational, would evolve into the standard common business language. This hope was supported by the growing popularity of FORTRAN by the end of the 1950s. FORTRAN was the most widely used language on IBM equipment,[39] and UNIVAC was planning a FORTRAN compiler for its next generation of computers, signaling the demise of Hopper's MATH-MATIC.[40]

Mounting tensions among the manufacturers prompted one of the more colorful moments in the history of programming. Sometime during November 1959, a depressed Howard Bromberg was driving in New Jersey when he came across a place where cemetery monuments were sold. As he slowed the car, a child's marble tombstone with the image of a lamb engraved on it caught his eye. Bromberg stopped the car, purchased the tombstone, and had the letters COBOL carved and gold-leafed below the lamb. Bromberg took the tombstone home, built a crate for it, and shipped it express to Phillips's office in the Pentagon. Grace Hopper recalled that the tombstone was meant to remind Phillips of the precarious position in which the infant common business language found itself during the late fall of 1959: "COBOL is about to die, do something."[41] But according to Phillips, the tombstone represented a much different message. "Obviously," Phillips recalled, "someone did not wish the COBOL program well, and was very kindly providing the chairman with a marker for the grave."[42]

As the December deadline for technical specifications approached, a FLOW-MATIC-based COBOL had enough supporters to avoid an early grave. For one thing, Howard Bromberg's connection to FLOW-MATIC ran deeper than the economic advantage accrued by RCA. Bromberg—a former member of Grace Hopper's Computation Analysis Laboratory— had designed the RCA Automatic Programming Group in its image. "Having worked for Grace Hopper, I worked for RCA carrying her banner and using the techniques that she taught me," wrote Bromberg.[43] A closer inspection of the short-term committee's makeup reveals a substantial number of Hopper protégés. Jean Sammet worked for Sperry Rand before going to Sylvania. Betty Holberton, Nora Taylor, and Mary Hawes were longtime colleagues of Hopper's, and in particular Holberton and Hopper worked side by side to create the original programming department at the Eckert-Mauchly Computer Corporation. Colonel Alfred Asch was responsible for AIMACO, the Air Force language derived directly from FLOW-MATIC. Finally, committee members E. F. Somers, William Finley, and Dan Goldstein were all gainfully employed by Hopper at UNIVAC as of 1959.

The pro-FLOW-MATIC short-term committee approved the final specifications despite objections from individuals and organizations inside and outside CODASYL. The final report outlined the specifications for COBOL and insisted that it be the only common business language sponsored by CODASYL. No modifications of the language would be permitted except through consultation with a permanent COBOL maintenance committee whose initial membership, unsurprisingly, would be made up of members of the short-term committee.[44]

The final report also contained a letter from Honeywell reject-ing the short-term committee's findings. C. H. Gaudette, manager of Honeywell's Automatic Programming Department, praised the short-term committee's efforts and admired the collaboration of traditional competitors. Ultimately, however, the committee's findings could not fulfill the needs of Honeywell's business customers. Gaudette noted these deficiencies:

(1) The lack of a powerful output processor
(2) The inability to process card input files directly
(3) The absence of built-in sort routines
(4) The weakness of handling records of a highly variable nature

Naturally, these deficiencies could be corrected by making FACT, Honeywell's business language, the nucleus of a revised COBOL.[45]

On 17 December 1959, the COBOL report was sent to the CODASYL executive committee for final approval. Much like the short-term committee, the Executive Committee was made up of people who were already familiar with FLOW-MATIC. E. J. Albertson (U.S. Steel) and Gregory Dillon (Dupont) represented UNIVAC customers. Eugene Smith (Navy) and Joseph Cunningham (Air Force) were friends of Hopper, who herself was the committee's senior technical advisor. In January 1960, the executive committee approved the report of the short-term committee and assigned Betty Holberton to edit the document for publication. Changes that were made to COBOL from that point on were reviewed by the newly formed COBOL maintenance committee and approved by the executive committee. In April the official COBOL report was published and distributed by the Government Printing Office.

During the summer of 1960, RCA and the UNIVAC Division of Sperry Rand turned the April report into a functioning language. The first complete and accurate COBOL compilation (17 August 1960) was done on an RCA 501. By December 1960,

RCA and Sperry Rand had confirmed the portability potential
of the new language. The two companies each wrote a business
application program in COBOL source code, interchanged the
programs, and ran them successfully on a UNIVAC II and an
RCA 501.[46]

The executive committee's approval of COBOL (60) coupled
with RCA and RAND's efforts did not stop the controversy, and
the battle over the standard raged throughout the year, prompting
Jean Sammet to author a passionate plea for support. In a report
dated 2 December 1960, Sammet wrote:

The lack of completion of final and complete COBOL specifications
is due primarily to certain companies and individuals who have refused
to work from the present language and prefer to "start all over." These
persons and their companies have done a great disservice to the COBOL
effort by refusing to face the fact that the present specifications do exist,
are being implemented, and are being used to write and run successful
data processing problems.[47]

The main culprits were the manufacturers who had invested
heavily in developing other English-based business languages,
hoping instead that their own language would become the de
facto standard. But according to Sammet, some users were also
undermining the COBOL effort. In particular, companies and
organizations that operated only one type of machine were less
concerned with portability and hoped to see the establishment
of a much more powerful language than that proposed by
CODASYL. For instance, D. A. Nelson of the Lockheed Aircraft
Corporation wrote to Charles Phillips shortly after the executive
committee's approval of COBOL to express "dissatisfaction with
the lifeless camel of a language which is to become . . . the programming language for business data processing." Nelson echoed

Grace Hopper running COBOL on a UNIVAC II. Courtesy of
Computer History Museum.

the concerns of others, accusing the short-term committee of being "derelict in their duties" in failing to define a truly revolutionary language and instead offered one with a "scope barely wider than that of FLOW-MATIC."[48] Through the firestorm of opinions, Sammet expressed hope that "those who now oppose COBOL—either actively or passively—will stop condemning it long enough to give it a chance to succeed."[49]

COBOL: THE SUCCESS OF A PROGRAMMING LANGUAGE

In the years that followed the publication of COBOL, scores of people predicted the demise of the experimental common business language. Their forecasts were not the unapprised views of a pessimistic few but rather the sound, informed observations of computer community elite, ranging from master programmers to computer industry executives. The critique of COBOL included complaints about the language's semantic verbosity, its syntactical redundancy, and its overall lack of linguistic elegance. Mathematically inclined users cursed the upstart language's inability to accept formulas and symbols. Astute programmers felt disconnected from the hardware of the machine. What was supposed to empower the user seemed to restrict programming creativity and hampered one's ability to commune directly with the computer.

Even a few members of the short-range committee averred the claims of COBOL skeptics. The first compilers had some serious limitations, especially when conjoined with the available hardware of the day. State-of-the-art processors had difficulty dealing with the verbose, high-level language. Moreover, inefficient object code generated by the COBOL compilers used up internal computer memory, a precious resource that in 1960 was measured in dollars per byte. (At 1960s rates, today's average laptop computer contains millions of dollars of memory.)

More surprising, criticisms of COBOL were aimed at the very process of its technical invention, a process that mirrored Hopper's own style of distributed innovation. Many did not feel comfortable with the prospect of "innovation by committee," including some who were part of that process. As Howard Bromberg stated, "little control was exercised over the development effort and the degree of guidance normally expected from a group of top-level technical managers was not forthcoming." The COBOL process of invention did not correlate well with preconceived notions of invention. There was no heroic inventor like Thomas Edison or Elmer Sperry who passed down a singular guiding vision. Instead, "the COBOL committee was plagued by discontinuity of personnel and more often than not by a lack of talent."[50] Howard Bromberg's comment concerning talent is particularly troubling, in view of the fact that committee members such as Betty Holberton, Jean Sammet, Mary Hawes, and Nora Taylor were the most experienced programmers in the business. None of them had a traditional pedigree of the kind more commonly held by their male counterparts in the industry, but few women of their generation did. Indeed, some COBOL skeptics concluded that the fruits of such an unstructured, female-dominated process could not be expected to survive, let alone flourish.

But COBOL did flourish on an unprecedented scale, despite the warnings of the experts. In the 10 years after its introduction, COBOL became the most widely used programming language throughout the world. By the turn of the millennium, it was estimated, 240 billion of the 300 billion lines of computer code (about 80 percent of all code worldwide) was written in COBOL.

Because 95 percent of finance and insurance data was processed in COBOL, the fear of computer glitches on a global scale mounted as the year 2000 approached. "Y2K" anxieties were based on the fact that the CODASYL committee, for reasons probably connected to memory conservation, adopted a two-digit convention to represent that year. Hence, as year fields worldwide switched from "99" to "00," the potential threat of an array of arithmetic, comparison, and sorting errors emerged. The efforts of thousands of COBOL programmers, may of whom came out of retirement in the years leading up to 2000, fixed the vast majority of the Y2K bugs, and the millennium began with little cyber-fanfare.[51]

As with all technologies that proliferate, COBOL's long-term success was far from inevitable and rested on a combination of interrelated factors. The most obvious were specific actions by Charles Phillips, chairman of the CODASYL committee. In effect, Phillips used the economic weight of the Department of Defense to put pressure on uncooperative companies. On 12 August 1960, Phillips wrote a personal letter to computer manufacturers asking for a commitment to support, develop, and implement the common business language created by the CODASYL committee. This request was given financial gravity when Phillips required all future DOD computer procurements to be bundled with a working COBOL compiler.

In view of the purchasing power of the Department of Defense in the early 1960s, even the largest manufacturers were forced to fulfill the DOD's requirement.[52] This did not mean, however, that IBM put other initiatives on hold. Shortly after Phillips's DOD policy announcement, a senior IBM executive wrote to inform Phillips that IBM intended to complete COBOL processors for its line of computers by the third quarter of 1961.

He also mentioned that IBM's customers were still interested in using COMTRAN, and that IBM had distributed Commercial Translator manuals 3 months earlier.

Phillips's actions may have created a temporary demand for COBOL compilers, but, as IBM's actions proved, DOD policy in no way guaranteed the sustained use and subsequent spread of the contentious language. For Betty Holberton and its other creators, COBOL's successful proliferation could be attributed in part to the design of the technology itself. For all of the slights about COBOL's capabilities, Holberton was a true believer in the language. She had attended the first CODASYL meeting, had been a member of the short-term committee, and had edited the final COBOL specifications. Her fondness for the language was personal as well as professional. Having dedicated a year of her life to the creation of the common business language, she was convinced that the committee had done its best to find a technological solution to the future needs of users and manufacturers.

Holberton's 15 years of programming experience, matched only by Hopper's longevity in the field, contributed to her belief that COBOL's positive design aspects outweighed the technical limitations identified by a variety of other computer experts. She defended the English-based pseudo-code (criticized by many as verbose and inefficient) on the ground that the language had been developed for future users, not for present programming experts. The next generation of computer users needed a language that could be learned quickly. The self-documenting nature of the English pseudo-code permitted a programmer to easily understand the work of another and build upon it, which made COBOL ideal for collaborative programming efforts in which multiple people worked on the same data-processing problem. The flexible file nomenclature did not require the user to change the definitions on preexisting data files, only the style of writing the program. This was important when converting older programs to the new COBOL format. Holberton's experience in managing data-processing installations, combined with her deep knowledge of programming, helped her to appreciate these more subtle COBOL design characteristics. During the 1950s an elite of mathematics-oriented programmers dominated the field, but with the exponential spread of computers during the 1960s others gained access to computers. The new users, less interested in the "art" of programming, just wanted to solve data-processing problems. They were the first generation of programmers who knew little about the workings of computer hardware and who therefore appreciated a computer language that served as an intermediary between them and the machine.

GRACE HOPPER AND THE SPREAD OF COBOL

No matter how well designed a new technology appears to be, it cannot spread spontaneously. A new technology spreads by means of the continuous actions of hundreds and thousands of users, manufacturers, and intermediaries. But not everyone associated with a new product or idea is equal in his or her ability to influence the expanding technological system. Some individuals are connected in special ways throughout the technological system. They have the ability to influence both micro and macro outcomes, and their actions have ripple effects. Despite Betty Holberton's accolades for the technology itself, she and others continually acknowledged Grace Hopper as the person most responsible for the success of COBOL during the 1960s.

How can a single person influence widespread technical change? Modern society appears too large and complex for individual actions to carry much weight. This is especially true in the realm of technology, where new products and practices seem to appear and proliferate of their own accord. Technological progress is something that simply happens. It is the inevitability of society focused on the future.

Hopper understood that technology did not exist apart from society. A technology's logical design would not guarantee its ultimate acceptance. A multitude of cultural, social, political, and economic factors figured in the acceptance or rejection of a given technology, be it a car, a camera, or a computer language. "Because of early difficulties . . . prejudices, inertia, normal reluc-tance to change procedures, some remaining technological imperfections," Hopper wrote in a detailed report to the Navy explaining why the institution's leadership needed to make a concerted effort to push COBOL as the service's business lan-guage standard, "it will be necessary to *supply motivation* for the use of COBOL." COBOL would not sell itself; the concerted efforts of a variety of people were needed. This brings up an interesting point concerning the process of invention. Invention does not stop with the creation of a prototype. Prototypes must be actively marketed by their creators, or by proxies for their creators, in order to gain acceptance. The marketing process, ideally, feeds back into the technology's design, embedding in the physical artifact social, economic, and political attributes that further its chance of survival. In effect, Hopper's support of COBOL did not begin in 1960; it began in 1951 with the inven-tion of the A-0 compiler. Since then Grace Hopper had been automatic programming's most energetic proponent, and COBOL was the next iteration of that grander vision.[53]

What had changed by 1960 was Hopper's status within the maturing computer industry. The prominent pioneer had levers that few within the computing community possessed during the 1960s. Her position as director of automated programming at the number-two computer manufacturer conferred on her influence over senior management within Sperry Rand and over other senior computer executives. She was also one of the most senior women in the Naval Reserve, serving as a technical advisor to the largest consumer of computers, the Department of Defense.[54]

Within the world of computers, Hopper was a connector, a role that few people were capable of playing during the 1960s. Malcolm Gladwell, a science writer for the *Washington Post* and *The New Yorker*, eloquently describes the importance of "connectors" in technological revolutions in his 2002 book *The Tipping Point*. Gladwell employs the biological theory of epidemics as his chief metaphor to relate how new technologies propagate rapidly. Epidemics are a function of the particular attributes of the infectious agent, of the behavior of the carriers of the infectious agents, and of the environment in which the infectious agent is introduced. The three elements interact to determine how quickly the epidemic spreads.

For instance, the AIDS virus spreads via exchange of fluids. Activities that facilitate such exchange, such as unprotected sex and the sharing of needles, are the chief vehicles for the virus. At the beginning of the epidemic, it was not the actions of all those infected but the activities of a handful of "connectors" who engaged repeatedly in high-risk behaviors that influenced the early progression of the virus.

To shine a more positive light on the epidemic metaphor, Gladwell substitutes for the spread of disease the flow of information, and tells the story of the most honored "connector" of the American Revolution: Paul Revere. During the night of 18

April 1775, America's famous equestrian was not the only person riding into the Massachusetts night to warn that the British were coming. William Dawes, Samuel Prescott, and more than 60 others also got on their horses to spread the word. Why then do we remember Revere's name but not the names of the many others who rode? According to Gladwell, it is because, like Grace Hopper, Paul Revere was a connector. His prominence in local Bostonian politics and in various revolutionary organizations allowed him to construct the groundwork for spreading the message in the months and years leading up to the fateful night.[55]

The epidemic metaphor is relevant to the dissemination of COBOL as well as to Grace Hopper's role as a connector. Instead of a virus with unique biological characteristics, there existed in 1960 a prototype of a common business language with certain design attributes. In the post-Sputnik, Cold War-era United States, the overall demand for computers was on the rise, as was the need for programmers. Into this environment stepped Hopper as a connector. With the ability to operate in a variety of different subcultures, connecting users with programmers and industry executives with senior military officers, she translated her computing vision into a language that each of these groups understood, communicating complex technology to technically savvy people and nontechnical people alike. Her special gifts and unique position allowed her to drive the COBOL "epidemic" forward.

COBOL STANDARDIZATION AND THE NAVY

On 1 January 1967, Commander Grace Hopper was placed on the Naval Reserve's retirement list. Two years earlier she had stepped down as Director of Automatic Programming in the UNIVAC Division of Sperry Rand. Though she remained with UNIVAC as a senior staff scientist, from all appearances the 60-year-old Hopper was slowly making the transition to retirement.

Hopper's 1966 report to the Navy recommending the full implementation of COBOL began with a two-page discussion of a general theory of language. She explained that a primary characteristic of intelligent life is the ability to communicate: "Man's brain enables him to learn an elaborate system of rules both for communication with others and for control of his own mental processes. Man, having created rules, added a generative potential—rules can produce consistent but flexible (i.e., contingent) systems—making languages possible." The elements of code that make up a language, following a system of rules, combine in almost unlimited combinations to creating meaning. But the key, according to Hopper, is to have orators and listeners agree on both codes and rules. "Surely," she writes, "the story of Babel is the lesson of the destruction of standards."[56]

For Hopper, computer languages were no different than any other human language. COBOL, in particular, was an artificial dialect, made up of English words and some parts of English syntax, that followed agreed-upon rules. The artificial language permitted humans to communicate an exact description of data and the algorithms or procedures to be followed in the solution of business problems by computer. What made it unique was that the language could also communicate by means of a compiler with a variety of computer hardware and translate exact descriptions into machine instructions.[57] Linguistic history shows that over time languages tend to standardize in order to increase the efficiency of communication between people. Hopper put it this way: "Thus it seems that COBOL is but one of many efforts in science and technology to standardize terminology and syntax in order to provide better communications between men concerning a particular class of activities."[58]

COBOL AND TECHNOLOGICAL CLOSURE

COBOL is distinctive within the history of technology, for it represents a technological artifact consciously and deliberately designed and selected by a number of social groups with competing interests. Although manufacturers, users, administrators, and engineers typically participate in what social constructivists refer to as the "closure" of artifact design,[59] technological stabilization is usually a much more random process, with standards organically emerging from the struggles between heterogeneous organizations and individuals.

The story of COBOL has some elements of randomness, but the intention of Hopper, Phillips, and the other CODASYL members was to create a forum to rationalize the design process and generate consensus apart from the marketplace. Not only was a standardized technology blueprint produced and approved by January 1960; the intermediate-term and long-term committees had grander visions. In effect, the intermediate-term committee was charged with inventing the next generation *following* the "state-of-the-art" design of the short-term committee. Even more ambitious, the envisioned long-term committee was supposed to then design the "ultimate" state of the art that would unify all programming languages into one.

In the end, the short-term committee's design, which was meant to be temporary, became the de facto COBOL standard.

Though individual manufacturers made changes to the language as the 1960s progressed, COBOL did not degenerate into a large number of dialects, as occurred with FORTRAN.[60] The intermediate-term committee had little influence over future COBOL developments, while the long-term committee was never even established. By the late 1970s, COBOL was the most extensively used computer language, and more than 80 percent of all business applications were written in the FLOW-MATIC-based language.

As the 1950s came to a close, Sperry Rand's director of programming research Grace Hopper conducted an "experiment" to demonstrate how far the field of software development had advanced in the 15 years since she wrote her first code. Hopper would attempt to turn a "trim, attractive blonde" into a computer programmer. Hopper's subject—Marilyn Mealey, a 19-year-old high school graduate from the Mayfair section of Philadelphia—was "prettier than average" and liked to swim and listen to records. According to Hopper, Marilyn was much like other young women who "window shop during their lunch hours and look forward to the evening's dates and dancing."[1]

The experiment's results were published in *Popular Electronics*, a magazine with an overwhelmingly male audience of gadget lovers who must have been amused at the thought of a young woman barely out of high school programming a computer. Anyone with even a limited knowledge of computers knew that communicating with multi-million-dollar mechanical brains was a task best left to highly educated professionals. Only the sharpest mathematical and scientific minds could write computer code, and there was no place in the growing industry for pretty blondes from the Mayfair section of Philadelphia.

Grace Hopper believed otherwise. In fact, Marilyn Mealey embodied Hopper's 15-year crusade to democratize the computer industry. Hopper invented the fundamental technologies that permitted humans to efficiently communicate with complex calculating machines. Subroutine libraries, pseudo-code (source code), decision branching, debugging routines, and compilers were the building blocks for all future high-end computer languages. But it was Hopper's relentless promotion of a "computer age" that gave her technological creations contextual meaning. If computers were merely a tool for the scientific elite, as her former boss Howard Aiken believed, then there was no need for automatic programming. Hopper envisioned a future wherein computers would be indispensable to a diverse set of people and organizations. In such a world, both elite mathematicians and high school graduates would need to converse with the machines.

Hopper's example runs counter to the well-known adage that necessity is the mother of invention. Hopper "invented" not because of a glaring need in her immediate present, but because of a "potential" need in a "possible" future. To complicate matters, the probability of success of that possible future was dependent on not only the technologies Hopper invented but also on her relentless promotion of a particular future that incorporated those technologies. An inventor not only invents a technology but also formulates a future need for that technology. In this light, Hopper's skills in writing and in oratory were as important as her technical and mathematical acumen.

Marilyn Mealey also represented Hopper's continued struggle to keep the new technical field gender neutral. Computers were not only for men, nor were they just for exceptional women such as Hopper. By purposefully picking a young, attractive blonde, Hopper aimed to shatter stereotypes. "New opportunities for women in electronics have been created by the wide scale application of computers to business and scientific work," she wrote in the *Popular Electronics* article.[2] By connecting the growing electronics industry with new opportunities for women, Hopper aimed to expand a legacy that she had worked so hard to create.

HOPPER'S CAREER IN THE CONTEXT OF THE HISTORY OF PROGRAMMING

In many ways, Hopper's career mirrors the rise in prominence of the programming profession. Howard Aiken and Presper Eckert did not foresee the difficulties inherent in the operation of their machines. Fortunately, Grace Hopper, Richard Bloch, Betty Snyder (Holberton), John Mauchly, and others brought the hardware to life. Initially responding to wartime necessity, these pioneers developed early coding techniques, debugging practices, subroutine principles, and batch processing procedures that confirmed the utility of the new technology at a time when the computer's future success was far from inevitable.

As the technology was transferred from the laboratory to business and government installations in the late 1940s and the early 1950s, Hopper believed programming to be the chief technical bottleneck that hindered the spread of electronic computers.[3] The costs associated with defining an application and writing and debugging the necessary programs began to outstrip the price of the hardware. Hopper first attempted to deal with this mounting programming crisis through better organization, training, and maximum personal effort. At Harvard University and at the Eckert-Mauchly Computer Corporation (and later at Remington Rand), her superior managerial skills were employed to train and organize new programmers in order to make the machines more productive.

But by the fall of 1951 Hopper was searching desperately for a technical solution that would help computers "educate" themselves. Her eloquent solution, which she named a compiler, was a master program that could call on relevant subroutines and could manage address and memory allocation, thus relieving the human programmer from the most difficult and menial "housekeeping" tasks.

Compilers, Hopper believed, were the key to "democratizing" computers. They would enable many more people—even the likes of Marilyn Mealey—to communicate with the mechanical giants. Instead of forcing the human to learn machine language, she made the computer learn English, French, German, or any other human language. This concept was embedded into Hopper's business language FLOW-MATIC, which would serve as the blueprint for COBOL (still the most widely used computer language).

LESSONS OF TECHNICAL INNOVATION

There is much to learn from Grace Hopper's approach to invention and innovation. Some lessons are apparent; others are quite unexpected. If we view Hopper's early career as a case study in innovation, we can glean some principles that help to explain her success in rapidly advancing the field of computer programming while also providing compelling guidelines for present-day innovators.

EMPOWER YOUTH

Hopper had the habit of assigning the most difficult technical problems to the youngest and least experienced members of a team. Mildred Koss, shortly after arriving at the Eckert-Mauchly

Computer Corporation, was handed the task of having the UNIVAC automatically edit its data for printing. The result was Koss's "editing generator," a sophisticated piece of code that created margins, titles, headings, and page numbers on the fly and represented the first attempt to use a computer for word processing. Harry Kahrimanian, just out of college, got an even more daunting assignment: he was asked to create a program that could automatically solve differential equations. Kahrimanian's differentiator was a watershed in applied mathematics. The user had merely to enter the equation and indicate the number of n derivatives; the computer did the rest. Kahrimanian's achievement was even more impressive in light of Hopper's own long and arduous experience working alongside the famed mathematician John von Neumann to solve differential equations on the Harvard Mark I. Had Kahrimanian's differentiator been available to von Neumann and Hopper, they could have solved the Manhattan Project's implosion problem in days instead of months.

Common sense would dictate that the most experienced programmers should have been assigned to these difficult tasks, but, as Hopper glibly explained, young people did not know that they were supposed to fail. On a deeper level, Hopper understood that "experts," be they senior engineers, experienced programmers, or business executives, have difficulty seeing beyond the borders of their specialty. Education, tradition, and community culture create a stable mental framework that helps to explain reality yet also hinders one's ability to see alternative approaches or adjust to ever-changing circumstances. Hopper felt that young, inexperienced programmers often had the ability to look beyond "what is" and grasp "what could be."

LEARN FROM THE MARGINS

Since youth is fleeting, Hopper discovered that one could maintain a "youthful," creative outlook by constantly broadening one's own knowledge base. Her self-education began during her days as a professor at Vassar College and continued through her stints at Harvard and Remington Rand. At Vassar, Hopper stretched beyond mathematics and audited classes in astronomy, physics, chemistry, geology, biology, zoology, economics, architecture, philosophy, and the history of scientific thought. Besides educating herself in computer hardware and programming while at Harvard, Hopper became quite an expert in military affairs, and was one of the first women to attend the prestigious Naval War College. During her lengthy corporate career, the adaptable Hopper mastered the machinations of a variety of diverse industries, ranging from insurance to aerospace engineering. As a result, her mind was informed enough to transcend her own intellectual discipline. She had freed herself from any particular methodology, and could approach problems from a variety of angles. In a sense, Hopper's flexible intellect mirrored that of a general computer, for both could adapt to the changing needs of the customer. After learning how a given business or other organization functioned, Hopper could outline detailed computer applications to automate or streamline aspects of the business, from payroll and accounting to industrial process control. Her analysis was captured in code, which turned the general computer into one specifically configured to meet the customer's needs. Herein lies the true power of the computer revolution: generalized hardware that could be specialized in a thousand different ways by software. Hopper not only grasped this relationship; she helped to invent it.

DISTRIBUTED INVENTION: THE MORE MINDS, THE BETTER

Despite how developed and flexible her own mind had become, Hopper recognized that the more brainpower working together on a given technical problem, the better the outcome. I refer to Hopper's organizational approach to innovation as *distributed invention*. Learning from the Harvard Computation Laboratory's unconstructive tendency to isolate itself from other computer research programs, Hopper understood that, in the long term, a distributed network of inventors, each with his or her particular technical perspective, could sustain a faster rate of innovation than an individual inventor or an isolated team of inventors.

The development of the compiler serves as a case study in distributed invention. Though Hopper created the original A-0 compiler on her own between October 1952 and May 1953, she soon shared her prototype with a number of programmers and users. Through the summer and fall of 1953, personnel at the Census Bureau, the Air Force Air Comptroller, the Army Map Service, the David Taylor Model Basin, Lawrence Livermore Laboratory, New York University, and the Bureau of Ships were experimenting with Hopper's compiler. This network generated a continuous stream of feedback and rewritten code that led quickly to the more advanced A-1 and A-2 versions of the program.

Hopper's system of invention differs substantially from the notion of the inventor as a heroic genius working alone in a laboratory or a basement. Such a vision is embedded deeply in the American sense of individualism, and is institutionalized in the many awards and prizes that are bestowed on individual inventors and scientists. Hopper believed that the process of invention should not be confined to herself, her staff, or even her company. Information flowed smoothly between her team and other organizations, with Hopper serving as the conductor of invention rather than its dictator. Today's freeware and open source movements preserve this doctrine. The roots, however, go back to Hopper and her team of distributed inventors.

PROACTIVE INVENTION: INVENTOR AS SALESMAN

It is important to note the two roles that Grace Hopper played during the development of what she referred to as automatic programming. First, she was the inventor. She wrote the first compiler, and she directed her programming staff and others to improve and expand on her initial invention. This led to A-0 through A-3, MATH-MATIC, and FLOW-MATIC. Hopper's second role, however, was as important as the first. She applied her collaborative skills and became the chief marketer of the automatic programming concept. During the 1950s, much of her energy was spent spreading the gospel of automatic programming through lectures, articles, and conference presentations. She was responsible for setting up a series of conferences and workshops dedicated to teaching others how to apply her inventions. Hopper's example confirms the theories of the historians Thomas Hughes and W. Bernard Carlson, who have proposed that famous innovators such as Elmer Sperry, Thomas Edison, and Elihu Thomson were responsible not only for the invention of new technologies but also for the integration of those technologies into the economic, political, and social fabric of society. Proactive invention extends well beyond the initial moments of creative inspiration; it involves the patient, time-intensive construction of a sustainable infrastructure that supports the new technology. Hopper, like other elite inventors, successfully nurtured her creations through the precarious early stages of technological development. Eventually they became self-sustaining technological systems that influenced the development of the whole computer industry.

HOPPER'S PLACE WITHIN THE PROGRAMMING COMMUNITY

Paradoxically, Hopper's drive to automate programming threatened to make the very profession she had pioneered obsolete. Back in 1944, when Hopper joined Robert Campbell and Richard Bloch as a "coder" on the Harvard Mark I, what a programmer was, what one did, and how one did it had not yet been defined. Through their efforts during and after the war, Hopper and Bloch in particular created the framework for the profession. They defined the techniques (subroutines), invented the language (debugging), and contributed to the culture (midnight "hacking") that would be the foundations of the budding profession.

By training others to be programmers, Hopper expanded the community one person at a time. Though she left Vassar to join the Navy in 1943, Hopper never abandoned her calling as a teacher. She conducted classes on programming at the Harvard Computation Laboratory, at the Eckert-Mauchly Computer Corporation, at the University of Pennsylvania through the 1950s and the 1960s, and at George Washington University from 1971 to 1978. Much of her time was also spent lecturing potential users, and her more than 50 papers and articles on programming and computer applications served as the literary foundation for the field.[4]

Hopper also helped to establish the premier organization for computer professionals: the Association for Computing Machinery, which today has 80,000 members in more than 100 countries. Founded in 1947 by the crewmembers of the Harvard

Computation Laboratory, the ACM fostered lateral communication within the nascent industry through conferences, newsletters, and journals. Hopper headed the ACM's nomenclature committee in 1953 and 1954, served from 1956 to 1958 as an ACM council member, and in 1957 and 1958 was a member of the editorial board of the association's main publication, *Communications of the ACM.*

Finally, Hopper organized many of the early formal meetings of programmers. After the "hardware-oriented" 1947 Harvard Symposium on Large-Scale Digital Calculating Machinery, Hopper took it upon herself to create forums for the discussion of issues and concerns relevant to programmers. After leaving Harvard, she maintained her connections with the Navy and co-sponsored a series of conferences during the 1950s centered on programming rather than hardware. Hopper also saw the need to educate business leaders and managers about the utility of computers, and she created a series of workshops in the 1950s that explained how general hardware coupled with automatic programming had become an essential business and decision-making tool. Computers, combined with automatic programming, would usher in an information age that allowed humans to make better, more timely decisions.

COBOL: THE QUINTESSENCE OF DISTRIBUTED INVENTION

Hopper's boldest organizational feat involved creating the groundwork for the 28 May 1959 meeting of the Committee on Data Systems and Languages (CODASYL). Hopper's efforts helped 40 representatives from seven government agencies, eleven companies (users), and ten computer manufacturers put aside their differences in the name of creating a common business language. "I don't think ever before or ever since have I seen in one room so much power to commit men and monies as I saw that day," said Hopper, reflecting on the first organizational meeting that led to the COBOL programming language.[5]

CODASYL was the physical embodiment of Hopper's inventive style. Her collaborative nature predictably led her to a distributed view of invention that transcended organizational boundaries. In 1951 Hopper created the A-0 compiler on her own, but she immediately released it to an ever-growing community programmers, users, and managers. Throughout the 1950s she played the role of facilitator, gathering technical, economic, and social feedback about automatic programming and embedded what she learned in the next iteration of design. For her, the invention of a computer language was an ongoing, organic process that was always adapting to the changing needs of the computing profession.

Such an open system of innovation seems foreign today, when large, competitive software firms race to patent and protect technology. With the unbundling of software from computer hardware by IBM in 1969, the software industry flourished, but so too did a proprietary form of innovation. In comparison, Hopper's inventive style echoes her academic sensibilities: collegial collaboration, an openness to knowledge dissemination, a healthy skepticism (even of one's own work), and the belief that the advancement of knowledge can come from a variety of people and sources. In this light, today's open source movement is less a revolution than a return to the past. Though the Internet offers the programming community a far more powerful collaborative tool, the current open source community's goals of distributed peer review reflect the outlook of Grace Hopper and her colleagues half a century before.

AMAZING GRACE 2.0

On 1 January 1967, Commander Grace Hopper was placed on the Naval Reserve's retirement list. Two years earlier, she had stepped down as Director of Automatic Programming Development in the UNIVAC Division of Sperry Rand. Though she remained with UNIVAC as a senior staff scientist and served as a visiting associate professor at the University of Pennsylvania, from all appearances the 60-year-old Hopper was slowly making the transition to retirement. Not surprisingly, 25 years on the cutting edge of the information revolution led to numerous awards. In 1962, she had been elected a fellow of the Institute of Electrical and Electronic Engineers, and in 1964 she had received an achievement award from the Society of Women Engineers. The highlight of these tributes came in 1969 when the Data Processing Management Association named Hopper the first ever Computer Sciences "Man of the Year."[6]

But to the surprise of everyone except probably Hopper, "retirement" merely signaled the beginning of a new productive phase in her life. The Navy was experiencing difficulties fully implementing COBOL, and Hopper was once again called upon to develop a COBOL certifier program. What began as a 6-month active duty appointment extended for 20 years. Hopper was named director of the Navy Programming Languages Group, and she remained in that position until 1977. She officially retired from Sperry Rand in 1971, and in 1973 she was promoted to the rank of captain. She also served as an associate professor in management science at George Washington University starting in 1971.[7]

From 1977 to 1983, Hopper was assigned to the Naval Data Automation Headquarters (NAVDAC) in Washington, where she

Rear Admiral Grace Hopper, 1983. Courtesy of Harvard University Archives.

monitored the state of the art in computing and recommended which technologies should be applied to the Navy's existing systems. It was during this period that Hopper developed the fleet-wide tactical data system for nuclear submarines, an effort for which she was awarded the Navy's Meritorious Service Medal. She spent her final three years in the service touring and lecturing, and in 1986 she retired as the oldest active officer in the Navy. Hopper was immediately hired as a senior consultant by the Digital Equipment Corporation. She worked for Digital until her death in 1992 at the age of 86.[8]

Today, with the computer industry dominated by Bill Gates and Steve Jobs, it is easy to overlook the role that pioneering woman like Grace Hopper played in shaping the information age. Her ability to transcend organizational gender bias and to elevate her career to uncharted heights was a combination of ability, serendipity, and force of will. Like any career woman during this period, Hopper had to face discrimination. In fact, by constantly placing herself in male-dominated environments, she courted conflict to some extent. Yet she found the strength of character to overcome, turning harassment into self-motivation. Hopper's confidence in her abilities, in her leadership skills, in her sense of humor, and (most important) in her collaborative skills enabled her to garner respect from even the toughest critics. Moreover, she created a safe work environment for other young, aspiring female programmers, thus tapping into an intellectual talent pool that was overlooked in other more mature industries.

Grace Hopper was many things to many people. She was an inventor, an academic, a naval officer, and a business leader. In her later years, she became a tireless public speaker who inspired a new generation of women and men in the computer industry to carry on her vision of a democratic information age.

NOTES

ABBREVIATIONS USED FOR ARCHIVAL COLLECTIONS

CHP Carl Hammer Papers, Charles Babbage Institute, Center for the History of Information Technology, University of Minnesota, Minneapolis

COH-SI Computer Oral History Collection, Smithsonian Institution, Archive Center, National Museum of American History, Washington

EBP Edmund Berkeley Papers, Charles Babbage Institute, Center for the History of Information Technology, University of Minnesota, Minneapolis

GHP Grace Murray Hopper Collection, Archive Center on the History of Technology, Invention, and Innovation, Archive Center, National Museum of American History, Washington

HAP Howard Aiken Papers, Harvard University Archives, Harvard University, Cambridge, Massachusetts

HCL Harvard Computational Laboratory, Harvard University Archives, Harvard University, Cambridge, Massachusetts

HOL   Francis Holberton Papers, Charles Babbage Institute, Center for the History of Information Technology, University of Minnesota, Minneapolis

HPL   History of Programming Languages Conference Records, Charles Babbage Institute, Center for the History of Information Technology, University of Minnesota, Minneapolis

ISP   Isaac Auerbach Papers: Charles Babbage Institute, Center for the History of Information Technology, University of Minnesota, Minneapolis

JCPP   James Conant Presidental Papers, Harvard University Archives, Harvard University, Cambridge, Massachusetts

JMP   John Mauchly Papers, Van Pelt Library, University of Pennsylvania, Philadelphia

MFP   Margaret Fox Papers, Charles Babbage Institute, Center for the History of Information Technology, University of Minnesota, Minneapolis

NBS   National Bureau of Standards Collection, Charles Babbage Institute, Center for the History of Information Technology, University of Minnesota, Minneapolis

OHC-CB   Oral History Collection, Charles Babbage Institute, Center for the History of Information Technology, University of Minnesota, Minneapolis

WFGP   Women in the Federal Government Oral History Project, Schlesinger Library, Radcliffe College, Cambridge, Massachusetts

NOTES TO CHAPTER I

1. John Mauchly received 65,000 hits, J. Presper Eckert Jr. 29,000, John von Neumann 750,000, Howard Aiken 35,000, and Bill Gates 13 million.

2. Margaret A. M. Murray, *Women Becoming Mathematicians: Creating a Professional Identity in Post-World War II America* (MIT Press, 2000), 4–5.

3. Though the historian Jennifer Light charges that the differences in status between early hardware and software developers on the ENIAC project exemplify women's discounted value in the history of science and technology, Hopper's experiences at Harvard and at the Eckert-Mauchly Computer Corporation do not support her thesis. See Light, "When Computers Were Women," *Technology and Culture* 40, no. 3 (July 1999): 6.

4. Holberton and Bartik, interview, 27 April 1973 (COH-SI), 118; Holberton, interview, 14 April 1983 (OHC-CB, OH-50), 204–206; John Backus, "Programming in America in the 1950s—Some Personal Impressions," in *A History of Computing in the Twentieth Century*, ed. N. Metropolis, J. Howlett, and G.-C. Rota (Academic, 1980), 127–128.

5. William Aspray, *John von Neumann and the Origins of Modern Computing* (MIT Press, 1990); Nancy Stern, *From ENIAC to UNIVAC: An Appraisal of the Eckert-Mauchly Computers* (Digital, 1981); Paul Ceruzzi, *Reckoners: The Prehistory of the Digital Computer* (Greenwood, 1983); Michael S. Mahoney, "The History of Computing in the History of Technology," *Annals of the History of Computing* 10, no. 2 (April 1988): 113–125.

6. Michael S. Mahoney, "Software: The Self-Programming Machine," in *From 0 to 1: An Authoritative History of Modern Computing*, ed. A. Akera and F. Nebeker (Oxford University Press, 2002).

7. It took place in Palo Alto and was sponsored by the Charles Babbage Institute (located at the University of Minnesota), an archive and a

research center dedicated to preserving the history of information technology and promoting and conducting research in the field. As a conference participant, I noted that historians of technology and computers were well represented, but pioneers in the field once again presented many of the papers.

8. Most early programmers were formally trained in mathematics. Furthermore, a number of these programmers were women. See Light, "When Computers Were Women," 455–483.

9. Grace Hopper and John Mauchly, "Influence of Programming Techniques on the Design of Computers," *Proceedings of the I.R.E.* 41, no. 10 (October 1953): 1250–1254.

10. Aiken, interview, 26–27 February, 1973 (COH-SI), 107.

11. EMCC was purchased by Remington Rand in 1950 and functioned from 1950 to 1955 as a semi-autonomous division of the parent company. Remington Rand merged with Sperry Gyroscope in 1956, and EMCC division was renamed the UNIVAC division of Sperry Rand.

12. Grace Hopper, "The Education of a Computer," *Symposium of Industrial Applications of Automatic Computing Equipment* (January 1953); Grace Hopper, "Compiling Routines," *Computers and Automation* (May 1953); Grace Hopper and John Mauchly, "Influence of Programming Techniques on the Design of Computers," *Proceedings of the I.R.E.* 41 (1953), no. 10: 1250–1254.

13. These advances include the use of pseudo-code, iterative routines, editing routines, interpreters, and compilers.

14. Thomas Hughes's term "reverse salient" describes the critical lag point that hinders a given technological system from advancing. "Salient" is a military term for a bulge that occurs when, in the advance of a battle line, a segment of the army moves more rapidly than the surrounding units.

15. Jean Sammet, "Conference Chairman's Opening Remarks: Organization of the Conference," in *History of Programming Languages I*, ed. R. Wexelblat (ACM Press, 1981), xvii–xx.

16. A finding aid for the Computer Oral History Collection is available at http://invention.smithsonian.org.

17. See Francis Trevelyan Miller, *Thomas A. Edison, Benefactor of Mankind: The Romantic Life Story of the World's Greatest Inventor* (John Winston, 1931); Mervyn Kaufman, *Thomas Alva Edison, Miracle Maker* (Garrad, 1962); H. Gordon Garbedian, *Thomas Alva Edison, Builder of Civilization* (J. Messner, 1947); John McMahon, *The Wright Brothers: Fathers of Flight* (Little, Brown, 1930).

18. Hugh G. J. Aitken, *Syntony and Spark: The Origins of the Radio* (Wiley, 1976, 1985); Thomas P. Hughes, *Networks of Power: Electrification in Western Society, 1880–1930* (Johns Hopkins University Press, 1983).

19. Among them were David Nye's *Electrifying America: Social Meanings of a New Technology, 1880–1940* (MIT Press, 1990), Claude Fischer's *America Calling: A Social History of the Telephone to 1940* (University of California Press, 1992), John Law's "The Olympus 320 Engine: A Case Study in Design, Development, and Organizational Control," *Technology and Culture* 33 (1992), 409–440, and Gabrielle Hecht's "Political Designs: Nuclear Reactors and National Policy in Postwar France," *Technology and Culture* 35 (1994), 657–685.

20. David Nye, *The Invented Self: An Anti-Biography, from Documents of Thomas A. Edison* (Odense University Press, 1983).

21. Donald Reid, *Paris Sewers and Sewermen* (Harvard University Press, 1991).

22. For more on Grace Hopper's military career from 1967 to 1985, see Kathleen Broome Williams, *Grace Hopper: Admiral of the Cyber Sea* (Naval Institute Press, 2004). Kathy and I worked closely through

the years, sharing resources and insights as we uncovered the story of this remarkable woman, and I am happy with how we divided the historical terrain.

NOTES TO CHAPTER 2

1. Grace Hopper, interview by Uta Merzbach, 15 July 1968 (COH-SI), 24.

2. Murray, *Women Becoming Mathematicians*, 1–17.

3. Hopper, interview, 15 July 1968 (COH-SI), 7–8.

4. Murray, *Women Becoming Mathematicians*, 110–111.

5. Ibid., 5, 111. According to statistics gathered by the mathematician Margaret Murray, only 15.7% of the doctoral degrees awarded in mathematics between 1930 and 1934 went to women. More troubling, the percentage of women receiving doctorates in mathematics decreased for the next 60 years, not reaching 1934 levels until 1989 (16.7%).

6. Williams, *Grace Hopper: Admiral of the Cyber Sea*, 11–12. Williams shared details via e-mail of her conversation with Grace Hopper's sister, Mary Murray Westcote, before Westcote's passing.

7. Hopper, interview, 15 July 1968 (COH-SI), 23.

8. Ibid,16.

9. Ibid., 18–19.

10. Ibid., 19–20.

11. Murray, *Women Becoming Mathematicians*, 100.

12. Hopper, interview, 15 July 1968 (COH-SI), 21.

13. Ibid., 21–22.

14. Constance Reid, *Courant in Göttingen and New York: The Story of an Improbable Mathematician* (Springer-Verlag, 1976); Alan D. Beyerchen, *Scientists Under Hitler: Politics and the Physics Community in the Third Reich* (Yale University Press, 1977). During the late 1930s, Courant also helped other mathematicians who were fleeing Nazi Germany to obtain positions in the United States.

15. Hopper, interview, 15 July 1968 (COH-SI), 28.

16. Ibid., 24–25.

17. Ibid.; Williams, *Admiral of the Cyber Sea*, 20.

18. Ibid.

19. Grace Hopper, interview by Beth Luebbert and Henry Tropp, 5 July 1972 (COH-SI), 9–10.

20. Elizabeth Allen Butler, *Navy Waves* (Wayside, 1988).

21. Hopper, interview, 15 July 1968 (COH-SI), 25.

22. Ibid., 25–26.

23. Ibid.

24. Ibid., 26–27.

25. Ibid., 27–28.

26. Ibid.

27. For more on Aiken, see I. Bernard Cohen, *Howard Aiken: Portrait of a Computer Pioneer* (MIT Press, 1999).

28. Grace Hopper, interview by Christopher Evans, 1976, 2 (OHC-CB); Anthony G. Oettinger, "Retiring Computer Pioneer—Howard Aiken," *Communications of the ACM* 5, no. 6 (1962): 298–299.

29. Cohen, *Howard Aiken*, 146, During the dedication ceremony, on 7 August 1944, a rift developed between Aiken and IBM CEO Thomas Watson Sr., which would persist for the rest of their lives. For more on the strained relationship between IBM and Aiken, see Cohen, *Howard Aiken*.

30. Traditionally, ships are referred to as feminine. Aiken considered the Mark I to be a ship and thus used feminine pronouns when referring to it.

31. Grace Hopper, interview by Uta Merzbach, 27 July 1968 (COH-SI), 29.

32. Ibid.

33. Robert Campbell, interview by Henry Tropp, 11 April 1972 (COH-SI), 66.

34. Grace Hopper, "Keynote Address" (speech given at the History of Programming Languages Conference, Seattle, WA, 1–3 June 1978) (HPL, 3/8), 41–42; Hopper, interview, 27 July 1968 (COH-SI), 29.

35. In the summer of 1944 other computing projects were underway, namely the ENIAC at the University of Pennsylvania and the Colossus in Britain, but as of July 1944 these projects were classified and Lieutenant (j.g.) Hopper did not have clearance.

36. Maurice Wilkes, director of the Mathematical Laboratory at Cambridge University, is credited with coining the term "programmer" in the late 1940s.

37. Hopper, interview, 1976 (OHC-CB), 6; Hopper, interview, 27 July 1968 (COH-SI), 29.

38. Campbell, interview, 11 April 1972 (COH-SI), 13–16.

39. All problems were given letter designations for security reasons.

40. Cohen, *Howard Aiken*, 112. As it turned out, King was unable to gain access to the generated results—the problem was completed after the machine came under the Navy's jurisdiction, and King lacked the necessary security clearance.

41. Campbell, interview, 11 April 1972 (COH-SI), 11–13.

42. Grace Hopper, interview, 5 July 1972 (COH-SI), 8.

43. Richard Bloch, interview by William Aspray, 22 February 1984 (OHC-CB), 15.

44. Ibid., 7.

45. Ibid., 8.

46. Ibid.; Richard Bloch, interview by Henry Tropp, 12 April 1972, 3–5.

NOTES TO CHAPTER 3

1. "Technical style" is a concept developed by Thomas Hughes to describe the mental framework that a particular inventor operates from when creating new technical artifacts. Evidence of the inventor's style is embedded within the artifact itself. See Hughes, *Elmer Sperry: Engineer and Inventor* (Johns Hopkins University Press, 1971).

2. Richard Bloch, interview by Henry Tropp, 12 April 1972 (COH-SI), 5–7.

3. For more on this, see Ceruzzi, *Reckoners: The Prehistory of the Digital Computer.*

4. *IBM Automatic Sequence Controlled Calculator* (GHP, 1-3); Volta Torrey, "Robot Mathematician Knows All the Answers," *Popular Science*, October 1944: 87–89.

5. Grace Hopper and Howard Aiken, "The Automatic Sequence Controlled Calculator, Part I," *Electrical Engineering* 65 (1946): 384–391.

6. Bloch, interview, 12 April 1972 (COH-SI), 13.

7. Ibid., 15.

8. Grace Hopper, interview by Uta Merzbach, November 1968 (COH-SI), 2–3.

9. Jennifer Light, examining the ENIAC project at the University of Pennsylvania from 1942 to 1946, has argued: "The ENIAC project made a fundamental distinction between hardware and software: designing hardware was a man's job; programming was a woman's job. Each of these gendered parts of the project had its own clear status classification. Software, a secondary, clerical task, did not match the importance of constructing the ENIAC and getting it to work." Light does well to highlight the important contributions the ENIAC women made, but she overstates the gendered nature of computing and reads it into the difference in status between early hardware and software designations. See Light, "When Computers Were Women," 6.

10. Note that the ENIAC was constructed before the concept of the stored program was invented.

11. Robert Campbell, interview by Henry Tropp, 11 April 1972 (COH-SI), 83.

12. Hopper, interview, November 1968 (COH-SI), 4.

13. Hopper, interview, 1976 (OHC-CB), 10.

14. Ibid., 11.

15. Hopper, Interview, November 1968 (COH-SI), 7.

16. Generally it is not possible to solve differential equations with exactitude. Courant's method demonstrated that differential equations could be solved numerically by solving a related approximate problem.

17. Harry Goheen, interview by Henry Tropp, 1972 (COH-SI), 9.

18. Grace Hopper, interview by Beth Luebbert and Henry Tropp, 5 July 1972 (COH-SI), 46.

19. In his 1999 book *Howard Aiken*, I. B. Cohen dedicates an entire chapter to "the mystery of the number 23." In this chapter he speculates why Aiken insisted on designing a machine capable of accuracy to 23 decimal places, suggesting that he intended to compute planetary orbits. Hopper's simple explanation is that such accuracy is generally necessary when working with partial differentials. Hence, the mystery is a matter of mathematical practicality.

20. Hopper, interview, 5 July 1972 (COH-SI), 46.

21. Bloch, interview, 22 February 1984 (OHC-CB), 9.

22. The Harvard Computation Laboratory staff included four enlisted personnel who were familiar with IBM punch-card machines. These "I" specialists were an official navy "rate" during the war and wore an "I" embroidered on their uniforms. A "rate" constitutes the job specialization of an enlisted person in the Navy.

23. The difference between officers and enlisted personnel runs deeper than dress and etiquette protocol. A Lieutenant (O-3) earns about three times more than a Seaman First class (E-3).

24. Sometimes the six women associated with the ENIAC are referred to as the first "programmers." Not only is the term "programmers" anachronistic; on the basis of the descriptions in this chapter, the work done by the original "ENIAC Girls" correlates more with the "operators" at Harvard than with the coding work of Hopper and Bloch.

25. Robert Burns, interview by Henry Tropp, 2 August 1972 (COH-SI), 57.

26. Grace Hopper, Problem L Operating Instruction, 1944 (GHP, 1–9).

27. The "starting tape" could be thought of as the most rudimentary form of a "boot disk."

28. Hopper, interview, November 1968 (COH-SI), 2.

29. Ibid.

30. Time sharing, which originated at MIT, permits multiple users to use the same computer simultaneously.

31. Frederick Miller, interview by Henry Tropp, 14 April 1972 (COH-SI), 5; Miller notes that reliability of the ENIAC was about 20%. Robert Campbell also highlights the efficiency of Aiken machines as compared to the operational problems surrounding ENIAC; Campbell, interview, 11 April 1972 (COH-SI), 60.

32. Hopper, "Keynote Address" (HPL, 3–8), 15.

33. Hopper, interview, 5 July 1972 (COH-SI), 10.

34. Because of how "hackers" have been depicted in recent movies and fiction, many equate the term with computer crime. In proper usage, however, "hacker" refers to a person who enjoys exploring the details of programmable systems and how to stretch their capabilities.

35. Hopper, interview, 5 July 1972 (COH-SI), 5.

36. Ibid., 4.

37. Hopper, interview, November 1968 (COH-SI), 6.

38. Maurice Wilkes, *Memoirs of a Computer Pioneer* (MIT Press, 1985), 145.

39. Campbell, interview, 11 April 1972 (COH-SI), 29.

40. Hopper, interview, November 1968 (COH-SI), 2.

41. Ibid.

42. Bloch, interview, 12 April 1972 (OHC-CB), 11.

43. Hopper, interview, 5 July 1972 (COH-SI), 22.

44. Miller, interview, 14 April 1972 (COH-SI), 38.

45. Scott McCartney, *ENIAC: The Triumphs and Tragedies of the World's First Computer* (Walker, 1999), 23–25.

46. Eckert discovered that reducing the voltage below the amount for which the tube was designed significantly prolonged its life. In the end he ended up running tubes at less than 10% of the standard voltage.

47. Campbell, interview, 11 April 1972 (COH-SI), 30.

48. Hopper claimed that Bloch could write code in ink and it would run the first time.

49. Campbell, interview, 11 April 1972 (COH-SI), 59. Both Campbell and Bloch would go on to make significant contributions to the practice of automated checking at Raytheon in the late 1940s. Bloch's major contribution was the original concept of the parity check.

50. Robert Burns, interview by Henry Tropp, 2 August 1972 (COH-SI), 21.

51. Ibid., 15.

NOTES TO CHAPTER 4

1. Aiken to Weaver, 5 September 1940 (HAP). For a more complete depiction of Aiken's journey, see Cohen, *Howard Aiken*. This book, however, contains new material about Aiken that is not covered in Cohen's book.

2. Aiken to Weaver, 5 September 1940 (HAP).

3. Cohen, *Howard Aiken*, 17.

4. Aiken to Weaver, 5 September 1940 (HAP); Cohen, *Howard Aiken*, 18–19; Robert Burns, interview by Henry Tropp and I. Bernard Cohen, 2 August 1972 (COH-SI), 6–8.

5. Saunders to Conant, 8 December 1939 (JCPP 165).

6. Calculating Machine Committee, 18 December 1939 (JCPP 165), 2.

7. Van Vleck to Chase, 19 March 1940 (JCPP 165).

8. Saunders to Chase, memorandum, 5 March 1940 (JCPP 165).

9. Chase to Conant, memorandum, 20 April 1940 (JCPP 165).

10. Ibid.

11. Conant to Aiken, 26 April 1940 (JCPP 165).

12. Aiken to Conant, 2 May 1940 (JCPP 165); Aiken, interview, 26–27 February 1973 (COH-SI), 7.

13. Aiken to Weaver, 5 September 1940 (JCPP 165); Cohen, *Howard Aiken*, 14.

14. "Problem of Dr. Aiken's Future," 12 March 1940 (JCPP 165).

15. Cohen, *Howard Aiken*, 119.

16. Robert Campbell, interview by Henry Tropp, 11 April 1972 (COH-SI), 32.

17. Cohen, *Howard Aiken*, 119–120.

18. Grace Hopper, interview by Beth Luebbert and Henry Tropp, 5 July 1972 (COH-SI), 16.

19. Burns, interview, 2 August 1972 (COH-SI), 22.

20. Ibid., 18–19.

21. Frederick Miller, interview by Henry Tropp, 14 April 1972 (COH-SI), 62; Aiken, interview, 26–27 February 1973 (COH-SI), 55.

22. Hopper, interview, 5 July 1972 (COH-SI), 18–19.

23. Cohen, *Howard Aiken*, 238–239.

24. Hopper, interview, 7 January 1969 (COH-SI), 18.

25. Miller, interview, 14 April 1972 (COH-SI), 23–24.

26. Hopper, interview, 5 July 1972 (COH-SI), 8–9.

27. Wilkes, *Memoirs of a Computer Pioneer*, 129.

28. Miller, interview, 14 April 1972 (COH-SI), 46–47.

29. Burns, interview, 2 August 1972 (COH-SI), 56.

30. Ibid., 20–21.

31. Hopper, interview, 5 July 1972 (COH-SI), 26.

32. Burns, interview, 2 August 1972 (COH-SI), 42.

33. Cohen, *Howard Aiken*, 162–163.

34. Thomas J. Watson Jr. and Peter Petre, *Father, Son & Co.: My Life at IBM and Beyond* (Bantam, 1990), 190.

35. Hopper, interview, 5 July 1972 (COH-SI), 24.

36. Ibid., 23–24.

37. Ibid.

38. Grace Hopper, interview by Uta Merzbach, July 1968 (COH-SI), 33–34.

39. Hopper, interview, 5 July 1972 (COH-SI), 25.

40. Hopper, interview, July 1968 (COH-SI), 34.

41. Burns, interview, 2 August 1972 (COH-SI), 42.

42. Hopper, interview, 5 July 1972 (COH-SI), 47.

43. Aiken, interview, 26–27 February 1973 (COH-SI), 44.

44. Hopper, interview, 5 July 1972 (COH-SI), 27–28.

45. Ibid., 26.

46. Ibid., 9.

47. Ibid., 15.

48. Report, Berkeley to U.S. Naval Proving Ground, 27 May 1946 (EBP, 76-2).

49. Hopper, interview, 5 July 1972 (COH–SI), 20.

50. Ibid., 10.

51. Aiken to Wood, 24 August 1944 (HAP).

52. Hopper, interview, 5 July 1972 (COH–SI), 29.

53. Aiken, interview, 26–27 February 1973 (COH–SI), 62.

54. Aiken also signed many of his patent rights away when contracting with IBM on the Mark I. Such was not the case with the Mark II.

55. USN Ordnance Contract NORD-8555 (HAP); Williams, *Hopper*, 58.

56. Ibid.; Cohen, *Howard Aiken*, 201.

57. Harry Goheen, interview by Henry Tropp, 1972 (COH–SI), 1–2.

58. Ibid., 3–4.

59. Ibid., 7–8.

60. Confidential Memorandum U.S. Naval Proving Ground from Lt. Cdr. Edmund Berkeley, 27 May 1946 (EBP, 76-2).

61. Ibid.

62. Goheen, interview, 1972 (COH–SI), 18–19.

63. Ibid.

64. Grace Hopper, "Keynote Address" (at the History of Programming Languages Conference, Seattle, 1–3 June 1978) (HPL, 3/8), 14.

65. Maurice V. Wilkes, David J. Wheeler, and Stanley Gill, *The Preparation of Programs for an Electronic Digital Computer, with Special Reference to the EDSAC and the Use of a Library of Subroutines* (Addison-Wesley, 1951).

66. John von Neumann, "First Draft of a Report on the EDVAC, Contract No. W-670–ORD-4926, 23 June 1945," in *The Origins of Digital Computers: Selected Papers*, ed. B. Randell, third edition (Springer-Verlag, 1982).

67. Wilkes, *Memoirs of a Computer Pioneer*, 108–109, 116–126.

68. Ibid., 127–142.

69. Ibid., 143–153; Hopper, "Keynote Address" (HPL 3/8), 15.

70. Ibid. Hopper acknowledges in an internal UNIVAC report dated November 1958 that Wilkes and the EDSAC crew should be given credit for consolidating and formally systematizing subroutine concepts. See Grace Hopper, "Automatic Programming: Present Status and Future Trends" (NBS, 32/717/1).

71. Grace Hopper, interview by Christopher Evans, 1976 (OHC-CB), 13.

72. Ibid.

73. Grace Hopper, interview by Uta Merzbach, November 1968 (COH-SI), 1.

74. Richard Bloch, interview by Henry Tropp, 12 April 1972 (COH-SI), 20–21.

75. Richard Bloch, interview by William Aspray, 22 February 1984 (OHC-CB), 9.

76. Human computers at Los Alamos also solved the implosion problem during the fall of 1944, but they computed values to six decimal places, while the Mark I produced results out to 18 decimal places and a smaller interval size (Cohen, *Howard Aiken*, 164–166).

77. Bloch, interview, 22 February 1984 (OHC-CB), 10.

78. Hopper, interview, 1976 (OHC-CB), 14.

79. John A. N. Lee, "Howard Aiken's Third Machine: The Harvard Mark III Calculator or Aiken-Dahlgren Electronic Calculator," *IEEE Annals of the History of Computing* 22, no. 1 (January 2000): 62–81.

80. The Mark III was the first of a series of early machines to use magnetic drums as primary storage. Among the others were SWAC, MADDIDA, Manchester Mark I, and ERA. Those members of the computing community with RADAR experience during the war turned to mercury acoustic delay lines as their primary storage technology (BINAC, UNIVAC, EDSAC, EDVAC, ACE). Eventually magnetic core memory developed by Jay Forrester while working on the Whirlwind project at MIT would become the standard memory technology.

81. Hopper, interview, November 1968, 3–4.

82. The Mark III's "stored-program" concept was different from that associated with the von Neumann computer architecture. First, the Mark III had one drum for instructions and a separate drum for data, whereas von Neumann architecture stores instructions along with data and treats the two in a like manner. Even though separate instructions and data made debugging less problematical, the Mark III lacked the flexibility to take an instruction from memory, manipulate it, and execute the changed instruction. With the success of EDSAC, UNIVAC,

and the IAS computer (at Princeton), the von Neumann architecture became the standard within the industry.

83. Lee, "Howard Aiken's Third Machine," 68.

84. Ibid.

85. Tom Standage, *The Victorian Internet: The Remarkable Story of the Telegraph and the Nineteenth Century's On-Line Pioneers* (Walker, 1998); Hughes, *Networks of Power*; Edward W. Constant, *The Origins of the Turbojet Revolution* (Johns Hopkins University Press, 1980).

86. Trevor Pinch and Wiebe Bijker explore the concept of "technological closure" with their noteworthy discussion of how the modern form of the bicycle came to being. See Trevor Pinch and Wiebe Bijker, "The Social Construction of Facts and Artifacts," in *The Social Construction of Technological Systems*, ed. W. Bijker, T. Hughes, and T. Pinch (MIT Press, 1987).

87. Bijker et al., eds., *The Social Construction of Technological Systems*, 12–13.

88. The invitation was arranged by Aiken's colleague and friend Douglas Hartree. Hartree, a British professor of physics, trained a generation of British mathematicians and scientists, including Maurice Wilkes, on the use of differential analyzers. Hartree maintained active lines of communication between Harvard and Cambridge during the 1940s.

89. Wilkes, *Memoirs of a Computer Pioneer*, 124–125.

90. Hopper, interview, November 1968 (COH-SI), 4.

91. James W. Cortada, *Historical Dictionary of Data Processing: Biographies* (Greenwood, 1987), 62.

92. Ibid.

93. Leslie J. Comrie, "Babbage's Dream Comes True," *Nature* 158 (October 1946): 567–568.

94. Wilkes, *Memoirs of a Computer Pioneer*, 167.

95. In the preface, Aiken thanks Hopper for being the author, even though authorship is attributed to "Staff of the Computation Laboratory."

96. Ibid., 1.

NOTES TO CHAPTER 5

1. For a general discussion of technical communities of practice, see John Seely Brown and Paul Duguid, *The Social Life of Information* (Harvard Business School Press, 2000).

2. Robert Campbell, interview by Henry Tropp, 11 April 1972 (COH-SI), 49.

3. Grace Hopper, interview by Beth Luebbert and Henry Tropp, 5 July 1972 (COH-SI), 11, 31; President of MIT to President of Harvard, confidential memorandum, 7 February 1940 (JCPP, 165).

4. Ibid.

5. For more on the tensions between Thomas Watson Sr. and Howard Aiken, see Cohen, *Howard Aiken*.

6. Hopper, interview, 5 July 1972 (COH-SI), 39–40.

7. Von Neumann, "First Draft of a Report on the EDVAC."

8. For more on the von Neumann/Eckert-Mauchly controversy, see Stern, *From ENIAC to UNIVAC*; McCartney, *ENIAC*; Herman H. Goldstine, *The Computer from Pascal to von Neumann* (Princeton University Press, 1972), 191.

9. Stern, *From ENIAC to UNIVAC*; McCartney, *ENIAC*, 196. The paper was not distributed widely, for it was deemed "Confidential" by the US Army. The historical controversy over the "First Draft" had real-world ramifications during the summer of 1971, for the document was successfully held up as evidence against Eckert's and Mauchly's bid for a computer patent.

10. Cohen, *Howard Aiken*, 164.

11. Howard Aiken, interview by Henry Tropp and I. B. Cohen, 26–27 February 1973 (COH-SI), 33, 183.

12. Hopper, interview, 5 July 1972 (COH-SI), 13.

13. Richard Bloch, interview by William Aspray, 22 February 1984 (OHC-CB), 12.

14. Grace Hopper, interview by Uta Merzbach, 7 January 1969 (COH-SI), 9–10.

15. Cohen, *Howard Aiken*, 165; Bloch, 22 February 1984 (OHC-CB), 18.

16. Ibid.,16.

17. Hopper, 7 January 1969 (COH-SI), 10.

18. Bloch, 22 February 1984 (OHC-CB), 12.

19. Goldstine, *The Computer from Pascal to Von Neumann*, 182.

20. Ibid., 138.

21. Ibid., 141–149; McCartney, *ENIAC*, 61.

22. Goldstine, *The Computer from Pascal to Von Neumann*, 182.

23. Ibid., 111.

24. Ibid., 192.

25. Ibid., 198–200.

26. Ibid.

27. Ibid.

28. Mark I's sequential mode of operation,, as with all "von Neumann architecture" computers, inspects one instruction at a time before execution. The ENIAC performed many activities in parallel.

29. Von Neumann, "First Draft of a Report on the EDSAC."

30. Ibid.

31. Aiken, interview, 26–27 February 1973 (COH-SI), 34.

32. Grace Hopper, interview with Linda Calvert, 1 October 1982 (WFGP), 138; Hopper, interview, 5 July 1972 (COH-SI), 1.

33. Harvard University Press, Fall Releases 1946 (GHP).

34. Hopper, interview, 5 July 1972 (COH-SI), 1.

35. Ibid.

36. Ibid., 6. It appears that Hopper relied heavily on the following works: J. A. V. Turck, *Origin of Modern Calculating Machines* (Arno, [1921] 1972); Philbert Maurice d'Ocagne, *Le calcul simplifié par les procédés mécaniques et graphiques*, second edition (Gauthier-Villars, 1905), Philbert Maurice d'Ocagne, *Vue d'ensemble sur les machines á calculer* (Gauthier-Villars, 1922); Charles Babbage, *Passages from the Life of a Philosopher* (Longman, Green, Longman, Roberts, & Green, 1864).

37. [Grace Hopper], *A Manual of Operation for the Automatic Sequence Controlled Calculator*. Annals of the Computation Laboratory of Harvard University, volume 1 (Harvard University Press, 1946; reprint, MIT Press, 1985); Grace Hopper and Howard Aiken, "The Automatic Sequence Controlled Calculator," *Electrical Engineering* 65 (1946), 384–391, 449–554.

38. Ibid.

39. Ibid. Aiken would use a similar system of separating data from operational commands in all of his machines, a technique that was discarded in the von Neumann stored-program architecture.

40. [Hopper], *A Manual of Operation*; Cohen, *Howard Aiken*, 64.

41. On the relationship between Aiken and Babbage, see Cohen, *Howard Aiken*.

42. One copy of this book was inscribed "From one admirer of Babbage to another." L. J. Comrie to Howard H. Aiken. 8 March 1946. Comrie reinforced the Babbage-Aiken connection with his 1946 review of the *Manual of Operation* entitled "Babbage's Dream, Comes True."

43. Hopper, interview, 1 October 1982, 139–140.

44. *IBM Automatic Sequence Controlled Calculator* (GHP, 1-3).

45. Ibid.

46. Ibid.

47. Ibid. T. H. Brown had been a consulting member of the IBM Department of Education since 1928.

48. Ibid.

49. Ibid.

50. At the dedication, IBM freely donated a machine which cost the company $259,000 to build and four years to construct. Moreover, Watson personally dedicated another $100,000 to Harvard to help defray the costs of the machine's operation.

51. Ibid.

52. Ibid.

53. See Cohen, *Howard Aiken*; Cohen, "Howard H. Aiken, Harvard University, and IBM: Cooperation and Conflict," in *Science at Harvard University: Historical Perspectives*, ed. C. Elliot and M. Rossiter (Lehigh University Press, 1992).

54. Watson, *Father, Son & Co.* On the shift from independent inventor/ engineer approach to a more corporate approach to technological innovation, see Noble, *America by Design: Science, Technology, and the Rise of Corporate Capitalism* (Knopf, 1977).

55. *IBM Automatic Sequence Controlled Calculator* (GHP, 1-3).

56. Ibid.

57. For more on this version of technological advancement, see the writings of Joseph Schumpeter.

58. Hopper, interview, 5 July 1972, 2.

59. See I. B. Cohen, "Babbage and Aiken," *Annals of the History of Computing* 10 (1988): 171–193.

60. The steps Aiken took to turn his ideas into a functioning computing machine are well documented and will not be reviewed here. See Cohen, *Howard Aiken*.

61. Headlines from this period, from HCL: "Automatic Brain for Harvard: Navy Man Inventor of World's Greatest Calculator"; "Harvard Told Robot Brain Just a Starter"; "Robot Works Problems Never Before Solved"; "Highbrow Harvard Bows to a Robot Brain"; "Mechanical Einstein Calculator Has Mathematical World in Palm."

62. In President Conant's foreword, the machine is referred to as the "I.B.M. Automatic Sequence Controlled Calculator." See [Hopper], *A Manual of Operation*; L. J. Comrie, "Babbage's Dream Comes True," *Nature* 158 (26 October 1946), 567.

63. Comrie, "Babbage's Dream Comes True," 567. Comrie's comments suggest that he may not have been aware of the top secret British computer work at Bletchley Park during WWII that produced the Colossus.

64. Hopper's name appeared with Aiken's as co-author.

65. Hopper, interview, 5 July 1972, 35–36.

66. Howard Aiken to Hubert Livingston, 18 July 1946 (HAP).

67. Howard Aiken to Mr. W. H. Claflin, 1 October 1945 (HAP).

68. Hopper, interview, 7 January 1969 (COH-SI), 11.

NOTES TO CHAPTER 6

1. James Conant to Howard Aiken, 26 April 1940 (JCPP, 165).

2. According to I. B. Cohen, this grander vision never materialized. See Cohen, *Howard Aiken*, 201–202. For more on the modernization of Harvard, see Morton Keller, *Making Harvard Modern: The Rise of America's University* (Oxford University Press, 2001).

3. Bureau of Ordnance Contract, 27 August 1945 (HAP); Cohen, *Howard Aiken*, 201–202.

4. Grace Hopper, interview by Uta Merzbach, 7 January 1969, 6 (COH-SI). The Harvard Symposium of 1947 was the third postwar conference devoted to large-scale computing machinery. The first took place at MIT from October 31 to November 2, 1945. The second was a six-week course during the summer of 1946 at the Moore School of Electrical Engineering in Philadelphia. The Harvard Symposium far outstripped the first two meetings in attendance.

5. "Day of Triumph," *Harvard Alumni Bulletin* (January 1947): 337–339 (HAP).

6. Edmund Berkeley, "Report on the Symposium of Large Scale Digital Calculating Machinery at the Harvard Computation Laboratory," 13 January 1947 (EBP, 8-52).

7. Joseph Harrison to Commander J. H. Carmichael, 14 November 1946 (HAP).

8. Hopper, interview, 7 January 1969 (COH-SI), 6.

9. Conference List (HAP); Howard Aiken, interview by Henry Tropp and I. Bernard Cohen, 26–27 February 1973 (COH-SI), 37.

10. Howard Aiken to Richard Babbage, 17 April 1946 (HAP).

11. Ibid.; Babbage to Aiken, 25 April 1946; Babbage to Aiken, 19 June 1946; Aiken to Babbage, 24 December 1946; Babbage to Aiken, 14 January 1947; Aiken to Babbage, 22 January 1947; Babbage to Aiken, 31 January 1947; Babbage to James Conant, 15 February 1947; Babbage to Aiken, 15 February 1947; Babbage to Aiken, 27 February 1947; Babbage to Aiken, 22 March 1947; Babbage to Aiken, 11 December 1947; Babbage to Aiken, 6 April 1948; Aiken to Babbage, 13 April 1948 (HAP).

12. Berkeley, "Report on the Symposium," 13 January 1947 (EBP, 8-52).

13. Robert Campbell, interview by Henry Tropp, 11 April 1972 (COH-SI), 35.

14. Grace Hopper, interview by Uta Merzbach, November 1968 (COH-SI), 5.

15. [Grace Hopper], *Description of a Relay Calculator*, 1–41.

16. Harvard Symposium program, 7 January 1947 (HAP).

17. Berkeley, "Report on the Symposium," 13 January 1947 (EBP, 8-52).

18. Ibid.; William Blair, "Harvard Unveils Huge Calculator," *New York Times*, 8 January 1947.

19. Howard Aiken, "Opening Remarks," Harvard Symposium on Large-Scale Digital Calculating Machinery, January 1947 (HAP).

20. Babbage to Aiken, 11 December 1947 (HAP).

21. Howard Aiken, "Opening Remarks," 4–5; Berkeley, "Report on the Symposium," 13 January 1947 (EBP, 50-8-52).

22. Cohen, *Howard Aiken*, 205–207.

23. Ibid.; "Harvard's New 'Brain' Permits Social Studies," *Boston Herald*, 10 January 1947; Cohen, *Howard Aiken*, 207.

24. Hopper, interview, 7 January 1969 (COH-SI), 6.

25. Berkeley, "Report on the Symposium," 13 January 1947 (EBP, 8-52).

26. There has been much historical debate concerning who was responsible for the stored-program concept. See Stern, *From ENIAC to UNIVAC*.

27. Harvard Symposium program, 7 January 1947 (HAP).

28. "Calculation ad Infinitum," *Newsweek*, 20 January 1947, 58; Norbert Wiener, *Cybernetics, or Control and Communication in the Animal and Machine* (Cambridge. Mass.: MIT Press, 1948); Norbert Wiener, "A Scientist Rebels", *The Atlantic*, January 1947, 46.

29. R. C. Gibbs, Chairman, Division of Physical Sciences, National Research Council, to Members of the Committee on High Speed Calculating Machines, 18 November 1946 (HAP). Other members of the committee included Walter Bartky (Division of Physical Sciences, University of Chicago), S. H. Caldwell (Department of Electrical Engineering, MIT), E. U. Condon (National Bureau of Standards), J. H. Curtis (National Bureau of Standards), G. R. Stibitz (Bell Telephone Laboratories), and Warren Weaver (Rockefeller Foundation).

30. John von Neumann to Howard Aiken, 25 November 1946 (HAP).

31. Ibid.

32. Hopper, interview, 7 January 1969 (COH-SI), 7.

33. Ibid.; Aiken to Babbage, 22 January 1947 (HAP).

34. Hopper, interview, 7 January 1969 (COH-SI), 6–7.

35. Isaac Auerbach, interview by Henry Tropp, 17 February 1972 (COH-SI), 11.

36. On the interaction of government, academia, and business in the early history of the computing field, see James W. Cortada, *The Computer in the United States: From Laboratory to Market* (Sharpe, 1993).

37. "Day of Triumph," *Harvard Alumni Bulletin* (January 1947): 337–339.

38. Hopper, interview, November 1968 (COH-SI), 5.

39. Wilkes, *Memoirs of a Computer Pioneer*, 175.

40. Paul Morton, interview by Robina Mapstone, 12 October 1972 (COH-SI), 14.

41. Hopper, interview, November 1968 (COH-SI), 4.

42. Richard Bloch, interview by William Aspray, 22 February 1984 (OHC-CB), 18.

43. Frederick Miller, interview by Henry Tropp, 14 April 1972 (COH-SI), 61.

44. Ibid., 24.

45. Richard Bloch, interview by Henry Tropp, 12 April 1972 (COH-SI), 11–12.

46. It also runs counter to I. B. Cohen's account of Aiken's selection of relay technology over vacuum tubes (*Howard Aiken*, 40–44). Cohen expresses astonishment that, in a 1973 interview, Aiken declared that he had never been "wedded" to any particular technology. As Hopper, Wilkes, Miller, Campbell, and Bloch recalled it, this does not seem to have been Aiken's position in 1947.

47. Miller, interview, 14 April 1972 (COH-SI), 24.

48. William Blair, "Harvard Unveils Huge Calculator," *New York Times*, 8 January 1947.

49. Campbell, interview, 11 April 1972 (COH-SI), 49.

50. Miller, interview, 14 April 1972 (COH-SI), 45.

51. Campbell, interview, 11 April 1972 (COH-SI), 57–58.

52. Ibid., 66.

53. Bloch, interview, 22 February 1984 (OHC-CB), 20.

54. Ibid.

55. Hopper, interview, 7 January 1969 (COH-SI), 5–6.

56. Goheen, interview, 1972 (COH-SI), 20.

57. Grace Hopper, interview by Beth Luebbert and Henry Tropp, 5 July 1972 (COH-SI), 24.

58. Hopper, interview, 7 January 1969 (COH-SI), 2.

59. Hopper, interview, 5 July 1972 (COH-SI), 24.

60. Goheen, interview, 1972 (COH-SI), 11.

61. Robert Campbell, interview by William Aspray, 22 February 1984 (OHC-CB), 55–56.

62. Henry Tropp, "The 20th Anniversary Meeting of the Association for Computing Machinery: 30 August 1967," *Annals of the History of Computing* 9 (1988), no. 3: 251.

63. Aiken, interview, 26–27 February 1973 (COH-SI), 32–33.

64. Goheen, interview, 1972 (COH-SI), 14–15.

65. Ibid., 19.

66. Goheen's account states that the election was very close between Berkeley and an IBM man for secretary ("Memorandum for the Eastern Association for Computing Machinery," Report No. 2, 30 September 1947, MFP, 4-41).

67. Ibid.

68. Tropp, "The 20th Anniversary Meeting of the Association for Computing Machinery: 30 August 1967," 251.

69. John von Neumann to Edmund Berkeley, 15 September 1947 (MFP, 4-41).

70. Goheen, interview, 1972 (COH-SI), 16.

71. "Report to the Association for Computing Machinery," Report No. 4, 30 January 1948 (MFP, 4-41).

72. Campbell, interview, 22 February 1984 (OHC-CB), 57.

73. Ibid.

74. Upon his retirement, the Computation Laboratory was renamed the Howard Hathaway Aiken Laboratory of Computer Science.

75. Hopper, interview, January 1969 (COH-SI), 15.

76. Ibid.; Hopper, interview, 4 February 1969 (COH-SI), 1–2.

77. Conference Program, Association for Computing Machinery, Oak Ridge, Tennessee, 18–20 April 1949 (GHP, 5-5).

78. Hopper, interview, January 1969 (COH-SI), 16.

79. Ibid., 15–16.

80. Ibid.

NOTES TO CHAPTER 7

1. Edmund Berkeley to Grace Hopper, 20 November 1949 (JMP, 3: B: 1–4). This four-page "intervention letter" was sent to Grace Hopper and to her closest friends and relatives, including her new boss at EMCC, John Mauchly.

2. Ibid.

3. Ibid.

4. In 1946, apparently borrowing from the Harvard Mark I, von Neumann, with the assistance of ENIAC operator Jean Bartik, developed a paper tape/mechanical relay input system for ENIAC that alleviated some of the programming difficulties.

5. Mary, Mauchly's first wife of 16 years and the mother of their two children, drowned in a swimming accident on 8 September 1946. McNulty and Mauchly began to date about a year later.

6. Grace Hopper, interview by Linda Calvert, 3 September to 28 February 1982 (WFGP), 42.

7. "Brief List of Devices and Fields of Application of Devices" (memo, EMCC) (JMP, 3: C: 3–60); Hopper, interview by Uta Merzbach, 4 February 1969 (COH–SI), 2.

8. John Mauchly, interview by Uta Merzbach, 22 June 1970 (COH–SI), 96.

9. Stern, *From ENIAC to UNIVAC*, 90–91.

10. J. Presper Eckert Jr., Kathleen Mauchly, William Cleaver, and Jim McNulty, interview by Nancy Stern, 23 January 1980 (OHC–CB, OH11), 62.

11. A stored-program computer named EDVAC, built by the Moore School of Engineering after Eckert and Mauchly's departure, was completed after the UNIVAC.

12. Eckert, interview by Nancy Stern, 28 October 1977 (OHC–CB, OH13), 20; Eckert, interview, 23 January 1980 (OHC–CB, OH11), 98; John Mauchly, interview by Henry Tropp, 6 February 1973 (COH–SI), 2. Nancy Stern does not directly address von

Neumann's apparent ability to bypass security restrictions because of his prominent position in government circles, though she does note "that even after the security classification was lifted, Eckert and Mauchly failed to publish any report on the ENIAC" (*From ENIAC to UNIVAC*, 54).

13. See Stern, *From ENIAC to UNIVAC*, 96–99.

14. Maurice Wilkes's EDSAC at Cambridge University, inspired by the "First Draft," was operational before UNIVAC. See Electronic Control Company, *Plan for a Statistical EDVAC*, 13 May 1947 (MFP, 4-10).

15. Ibid. The laptop computer used to write this book, like the vast majority of computers today, uses the same serial fetch-and-execute architecture.

16. "An Introduction to The UNIVAC System" (GHP, 5-6).

17. Ibid. The system could read or write at 20,000 pulses per second, and each word required roughly fifty pulses.

18. For another interpretation of Eckert and Mauchly's fund-raising challenges, see Martin Campbell-Kelly and William Aspray, *Computer: A History of the Information Machine* (Basic Books, 1996), 108–110.

19. Ibid., 20–26, 47.

20. Ibid., 107–109; Stern, *From ENIAC to UNIVAC*, 102–106, 115.

21. Stern, *From ENIAC to UNIVAC*, 137.

22. Ibid., 137.

23. Raytheon's RAYDAC, under development by Hopper's former colleagues Robert Campbell and Richard Bloch, appeared to be the only competing commercial system. However, it was a one-of-a-kind

machine, much like the BINAC (Hopper, interview, 4 February 1969, COH-SI, 5, 10).

24. Her name does not appear in the general works of Campbell-Kelly, Aspray, and Ceruzzi; more surprisingly, Stern references her only once. See Campbell-Kelly and Aspray, *Computer;* Paul Ceruzzi, *A History of Modern Computing* (MIT Press, 2003); Stern, *From ENIAC to UNIVAC.*

25. Hopper, interview, 4 February 1969 (COH-SI), 1, 3.

26. Betty Snyder Holberton, interview by James Baker Ross, 14 April 1983 (OHC-CB, OH-50), 4.

27. Ibid., 3. Margaret Murray's book *Women Becoming Mathematicians* also highlights the prejudice faced by the majority of the women who received degrees in mathematics as they attempted to create a professional identity in postwar America. Murray, however, only covers the success stories. Betty Snyder's experience reminds the reader that for every Winifred Asprey or Susan Hahn, there were other women who were discouraged from becoming mathematicians.

28. Francis E. Holberton and Jean Bartik, interview by Henry Tropp, 27 April 1973 (COH-SI), 2.

29. Ibid., 11–12.

30. Ibid., 2. Snyder's perspective differs significantly from that of Jennifer Light, who suggests that the six women selected for the ENIAC project were the best and brightest of the 200 BRL computers ("When Computers Were Women"), Light may have reflexively augmented the status of the ENIAC women in order to defend her thesis that the women and their accomplishments were systematically overlooked by a gender-biased society.

31. Holberton and Bartik, interview, 27 April 1973 (COH-SI), 15.

32. Ibid.

33. Holberton and Bartik, interview, 27 April 1973 (COH-SI), 109–110. Holberton's remarks shed some light on Mauchly's behavior during the less-than-cordial break between Eckert, Mauchly, and the Moore School administration. See Stern, *From ENIAC to UNIVAC.*

34. Ibid., 114.

35. Hopper, interview, 4 February 1969 (COH-SI), 3.

36. Arthur Katz, "Flow Chart Symbols," 15 June 1950 (GHP, 5-7).

37. "Outline for Second Lecture: Programming Course for EMCC's Engineers," 11 April 1950 (GHP, 5-7).

38. Goldstine, *The Computer from Pascal to Von Neumann*, 266–268.

39. Holberton, interview, 14 April 1983 (OHC-CB, OH-50), 9; Goldstine, *The Computer from Pascal to Von Neumann*, 166–167; Hopper, interview, 4 February 1969 (COH-SI), 3–4.

40. The "10" in the name C-10 stood for the tenth iteration of the UNIVAC operational code (UNIVAC Conference Transcript, 17–18 May 1990, OHC-CB, OH-200, 86; Holberton, interview, 14 April 1983, OHC-CB, OH-50, 23).

41. Frances Elizabeth Snyder, "UNIVAC Instructions Code C-10," 6 May 1949 (GHP, 5-6).

42. Hopper, interview, 4 February 1969 (COH-SI), 10.

43. Ibid., 10–11.

44. Ibid., 7–8.

45. Ibid., 8.

46. Hopper, interview, 1 October 1982 (WFGP), 32.

47. "EMCC Request for Comments on Traits and Abilities which Coding and Programming Personnel Should Have," 28 September 1949 (JMP, 3:C:1, 1).

48. Wilkes, *Memoirs of a Computer Pioneer*, 146.

49. Ibid., 167.

50. Snyder's sort-merge generator contributed to Hopper's concept of compilers.

51. Holberton and Bartik, interview, 27 April 1973 (COH-SI), 122.

52. Frances Elizabeth Snyder, "UNIVAC Instructions Code C-10," 6 May 1949 (GHP 5-6); Hopper, interview, 4 February 1969 (COH-SI), 8.

53. John Mauchly, "President's Report to the Shareholders," 15 December 1949 (JMP, 3: C: 1, 1)

54. Ibid.

55. Stern, *From ENIAC to UNIVAC*, 146.

56. Watson, *Father and Son Inc.*, 198.

57. Ibid., 192–193.

58. Ibid.

59. Ibid., 134–135.

60. Ibid., 199.

61. Ibid., 198–199.

62. Eckert further explained that, besides the emotional attachment to each other, the two held patents jointly, which made it difficult to separate at that point in time (interview by Nancy Stern, 28 October 1977, OHC-CB, OH-13).

63. John Mauchly, interview by Uta Merzbach, 22 June 1970, 75 (OHC-SI); Watson, *Father and Son, Inc.*, 194.

64. Hopper, interview, 1 October 1982 (WFGP), 131–133; Hopper, interview, 4 February 1969 (COH-SI), 12–13.

65. Berkeley to Hopper, 20 November 1949 (PENN, 3: B: 1, 4)

66. Ibid.

67. Ibid.

68. Ibid.

69. Ibid.

70. Ibid.

71. Ibid.

72. John Mauchly, "Recent Events," 14 May 1953 (JMP, 3: C: 3, 57); Stern, *From ENIAC to UNIVAC*, 46.

73. In the 1890s, as a young bank clerk, Rand invented and patented an index system of dividers and tabs that enabled documents to be placed in vertical file cabinets and located rapidly.

74. UNIVAC Conference Transcript, 17–18 May 1990 (OHC-CB, OH-200), 13.

75. Holberton, interview, 14 April 1983 (OHC-CB, OH-50), 14.

76. UNIVAC Conference Transcript, 17–18 May 1990 (OHC-CB, OH-200), 89–90; Hopper, interview, 1 October 1982 (WFGP), 7–9.

77. Stern, *From ENIAC to UNIVAC*, 149.

78. Ibid.; Eckert, K. Mauchly, Cleaver, and McNulty, interview, 23 January 1980 (OHC-CB, OH11), 122.

79. UNIVAC Conference Transcript, 17–18 May 1990 (OHC-CB, OH-200), 61.

80. Hopper, interview, 1 October 1982 (WFGP), 41; Hopper, interview by Christopher Evans, 1976 (OHC-CB), 22–23. Hopper's claim concerning tolerance of "color" did not appear to apply to EMCC personnel as of 1949, although Bob Shaw was an albino.

81. Holberton and Bartik, interview, 27 April 1973 (COH-SI), 135; Holberton, interview, 14 April 1983 (OHC-CB, OH-50), 20. A similar organizational atmosphere existed in the early Ford Motor Company, according to Thomas Hughes. See Thomas P. Hughes, *American Genesis: A Century of Invention and Technological Enthusiasm* (Penguin, 1989).

82. Holberton and Bartik, interview, 27 April 1973 (COH-SI), 205–209; Holberton, interview, 14 April 1983 (OHC-CB, OH-50), 11–12.

NOTES TO CHAPTER 8

1. The nature of invention has been considered by Thomas Hughes, W. Bernard Carlson, Wiebe Bijker, Trevor Pinch, Janet Abbate, Stewart Leslie, and John Law.

2. See Ceruzzi, *A History of Modern Computing*; Campbell-Kelly and Aspray, *Computer*; Grace Hopper, interview by Christopher Evans, 1976 (OHC-CB, OH-81), 14; Hopper, "Keynote Address," 1–3 June 1978 (HPL, 3-8), 21.

3. Hopper, interview by Uta Merzbach, 11 February 1969, 13 (COH-SI); Hopper, "Keynote Address" (HPL, 3-8).

4. On 17–19 May 1990, a three-day conference on the UNIVAC computer was held under the sponsorship of the Smithsonian Institution. The conference brought together 30 computer pioneers to discuss their UNIVAC experiences. The historians of technology Michael Mahoney and Paul Ceruzzi moderated the discussions.

5. Shuler had to take personal leave in order to visit Eckert-Mauchly and see the machine firsthand. UNIVAC Conference, 17 May 1990 (OHC-CB, OH-200), 8.

6. Frederick Miller, interview by Henry Tropp, 14 April 1972 (COH-SI).

7. John Mauchly to Al Seares, December 1950 (John Mauchly Papers, 3:C:1); Mauchly, "Recent Events," 14 May 1953 (JMP, 3:C:3, 57).

8. Mitchell to Sales Division, Remington Rand, 16 November 1950 (HOL, 94-23)

9. Jean Bartik and Frances Holberton, interview by Henry Tropp, 27 April 1973 (COH-SI), 138–139.

10. Ibid., 138; UNIVAC Conference, 17 May 1990 (OHC-CB, OH-200), 13.

11. Adele Mildred Koss, interview by Kathy Kleiman, 19 May 1993 (WFGP), 25.

12. Grace Hopper, interview, 1 October 1982 (WFGP), 42.

13. Grace Hopper, interview by Christopher Evans, 1976 (OHC-CB, OH-81), 19.

14. Hopper appears to have learned from the mistakes of Mauchly and Eckert, and to have vigorously documented the development of automatic programming from its inception. Her primary motivation, however, was to spread her ideas to the programming community rapidly.

15. Grace Hopper, "Keynote Address," (HPL, 3-8), 24.

16. Grace Hopper, "The Education of a Computer," presented at meeting of Association of Computing Machinery, 2–3 May 1952 (GHP, 5-10).

17. Ibid.

18. Ibid.

19. It seems reasonable to speculate that the factory metaphor was a direct result of her experiences at the Harvard Computation Laboratory. Aiken (who had worked in the electric-power industry) often stated that the process of "makin' numbers" was no different than generating electricity.

20. Hopper, "The Education of a Computer" (GHP, 5-10).

21. In the case of UNIVAC I, the compiler produced Holberton's C-10 machine code.

22. The word "catalogue" most likely comes from Wilkes. On page 25 of *The Preparation of Programs*, Wilkes describes a loose-leaf binder that his team used to keep track of subroutine information. A loose-leaf binder was used so that new sheets could be inserted as subroutines were added to the library.

23. Hopper, "The Education of a Computer" (GHP, 5-10).

24. Ibid.

25. Hopper, "The Education of a Computer" (GHP, 5-10).

26. Richard Ridgway, "Compiling Routines," presented at meeting of Association of Computing Machinery, 8–9 September 1952 (GHP, 6-1).

27. Ibid.

28. Ibid.

29. Ibid.

30. Grace Hopper, "Developments in Compiling Techniques to 31 December 1953," memorandum, 31 December 1953 (GHP, 6-1).

31. Hopper, "Keynote Address," 1–3 June 1978 (HPL, 3-8), 24.

32. "The A-2 Computer System Operating Manual," 15 November 1953 (GHP, 6-1), 53.

33. Ibid.

34. Hopper, "Keynote Address," 1–3 June 1978 (HPL, 3-8), 25.

35. "The A-2 Computer System Operating Manual," 15 November 1953 (GHP 6-1); Nora Moser to Margaret Harper, 22 January 1954 (HOL, 94-13)

36. Grace Hopper, "Compiling Routines," *Computers and Automation* 2, no. 4 (May 1953) (GHP, 5-11), 1–5.

37. Ibid.

38. Grace Hopper, interview by Christopher Evans, 1976, 14 (OHC–CB, OH-81). Though this quote comes from an interview during the 1970s, Hopper's vision that programming had to become more democratic, that is, available to more users, was a central theme in most of her writing during the 1950s.

39. Hopper, "Compiling Routines."

40. İbid., 3.

41. Hopper, "Keynote Address," 1–3 June 1978 (HPL, 3-8), 27.

42. Emil Schell to Grace Hopper, 14 December 1953 (GHP, 6-1).

43. Nora Moser to Grace Hopper, 15 February 1954 (HOL, 94-13).

44. Margaret Harper to Nora Moser, 10 February 1954 (HOL, 94-13).

45. "Second Workshop on UNIVAC Automatic Programming," 1 December 1953 (GHP, 6-1).

46. On the concept of "technological framework," see *The Social Construction of Technological Systems*, ed. Bijker et al.

47. Adele Mildred Koss, interview by Kathy Kleiman, 19 May 1993, 23 (WIC); Hopper, "Compiling Routines," 4; Grace Hopper and John Mauchly, "Influence of Programming Techniques on the Design of Computers" *Proceedings of the I.R.E.* 41, no. 10 (October 1953): 1253.

48. The differentiator was Kahrimanian's doctoral thesis at Temple University.

49. Hopper, "Developments in Compiling Techniques to 31 December 1953" (internal Remington Rand report; GHP, 6-1).

50. Carl Hammer, interview by James Ross, 15 April 1983 (OHC-CB, OH-56), 16.

51. Ibid.

52. Herb Grosch is best known for "Grosch's Law," which states that computer power increases at the square of the cost. In business terms,

this means that in order to perform a computation twice as cheaply one must do it four times as fast.

53. Hopper, interview, 1976, 16, 19 (OHC-CB, OH-81). On technological momentum, see Thomas P. Hughes, "The Evolution of Large Technological Systems," in *The Social Construction of Technological Systems*, ed. Bijker et al.

54. John Backus, "Programming in America in the 1950s—Some Personal Impressions," in *A History of Computing in the Twentieth Century*, ed. Metropolis et al., 127–128.

55. Hopper, interview, 1976 (OHC-CB, OH-81), 14.

56. Hopper, "Developments in Compiling Techniques to 31 December 1953" (GHP, 6-1).

57. Ibid.

58. Ibid.

59. Ibid.

60. Ibid.

61. Hopper to Nora Moser, 10 February 1954 (HOL, 94-13).

NOTES TO CHAPTER 9

1. Richard Thomas DeLamarter, *Big Blue: IBM's Use and Abuse of Power* (Dodd, Mead, 1986), 36.

2. See Delamarter, *Big Blue*; Franklin M. Fisher, James W. McKie, and Richard B. Mancke, *IBM and the U.S. Data Processing Industry: An Economic History* (Praeger, 1983); Charles Bashe et al., *IBM's Early*

Computers (MIT Press, 1986); Cortada, *The Computer in the United States*; Emerson W. Pugh, *Building IBM: Shaping an Industry and Its Technology* (MIT Press, 1995).

3. DeLamarter, *Big Blue*, 34. DeLamarter, an economist by training, worked for the antitrust division of the U.S. Department of Justice from 1974 to 1982. In the book's introduction he openly admits his frustration with the government's decision to dismiss the case against IBM. Also note that in reality the sales of the 701/702 were modest.

4. See Fisher, McKie, and Mancke, *IBM and the U.S. Data Processing Industry*.

5. Campbell-Kelly and Aspray, *Computer*, 122–123.

6. Watson, *Father, Son & Co.*, 228.

7. UNIVAC Conference, 17 May 1990 (OHC-CB, OH-200), 116.

8. Cortada, *The Computer in the United States*, 92.

9. Ibid., 13.

10. Ken Garrison, interview by Robina Mapstone, 28 June 1973 (COH-SI), 7.

11. Fisher, McKie, and Mancke, *IBM and the U.S. Data Processing Industry*, 44–45.

12. UNIVAC Conference, 17 May 1990 (OHC-CB, OH-200), 9–11.

13. Ibid., 9.

14. Ibid., 42–43.

15. Ibid., 90.

16. Ibid., 81.

17. On the connection between labor scarcity and technology, see Cowan, *A Social History of American Technology*; Hopper, "Developments in Compiling Techniques to 31 December 1953" (GHP, 6-1).

18. Grace Hopper, Reflections on the History of Computer Programming, audio tape of lecture by G. Hopper presented at U.S. Military Academy, West Point, 1971, transcribed by Kurt Beyer (GHP).

19. During the 1990s, historians of technology studying the computer industry arrived at similar conclusions. See Pugh, *Building IBM*; Cortada, *The Computer in the United States*; Thomas P. Hughes, *Rescuing Prometheus* (Pantheon, 1998).

20. Hughes, *Rescuing Prometheus*, 16–17.

21. Ibid., 30–32; Pugh, *Building IBM*, 199–207.

22. Watson, *Father, Son & Co.*, 232.

23. During World War II, German engineers experimented with ferrite cores (Hughes, *Rescuing Prometheus*, 35–36).

24. Robert R. Everett, "Whirlwind," in *A History of Computing in the Twentieth Century*, ed. Metropolis et al.

25. Watson, *Father, Son & Co.*, 231. Emerson Pugh's research suggests that Watson Jr.'s assessment was correct. See Pugh, *Building IBM*, 207–209.

26. Ibid., 208.

27. Ibid., 208–209; Hughes, *Rescuing Prometheus*, 49.

28. Watson, *Father, Son & Co.*, 243.

29. Hughes, *Rescuing Prometheus*, 51.

30. IBM's commercial success with computers incorporating Whirlwind technology led almost inevitably to litigation concerning patent rights. In the end, IBM paid MIT a lump-sum licensing fee of $13 million. Even though this constituted a substantial amount of money in the late 1950s, it represented a fraction of the value of magnetic core memory to IBM and the computer industry in the next 20 years (Hughes, *Rescuing Prometheus*, 38).

31. Cuthbert C. Hurd, "Computer Developments at IBM," in Metropolis, *A History of Computing*, 411–414.

32. Watson, *Father, Son & Co.*, 243.

33. Pugh, *Building IBM*, 209–210.

34. Hughes, Rescuing Prometheus, 55–57.

NOTES TO CHAPTER 10

1. Donald Knuth and Luis Pardo, "The Early Development of Programming Languages," in *A History of Computing in the Twentieth Century*, ed. Metropolis et al. (Academic, 1980), 237.

2. Ibid., 241.

3. John Backus, "Programming in America in the 1950s—Some Personal Impressions," in *A History of Computing in the Twentieth Century*, ed. Metropolis et al., 128.

4. Grace Hopper, "Keynote Speech," Symposium on Advanced Programming Methods for Digital Computers, Washington, 28–29 June 1956. (NBS), 32, 65–66.

5. Adele Mildred Koss, interview by Kathy Kleiman, 19 May 1993 (WFGP), 25.

6. Pseudo-code, as used by Hopper and other programmers during the 1950s, is equivalent to what is referred to today as source code.

7. Grace Hopper, "The Interlude 1954–1956," in *Symposium on Advanced Programming Methods for Digital Computers* (Office of Naval Research, 1956) (HOL, 94-2), 1–2.

8. Sammet, *Programming Languages*, 310; Hopper, Reflections.

9. John Backus, "Paper: The History of FORTRAN" 1978 (HPL), 26–27.

10. Ibid., 26.

11. Ibid.

12. Knuth and Pardo, "The Early Development of Programming Languages," 241.

13. Ibid., 30.

14. Ibid., 241.

15. Backus had discovered that more than 50 percent of compiler computer time was spent testing and debugging.

16. Campbell-Kelly and Aspray, *Computer*, 190.

17. Grace Hopper, interview, 1 October 1982 (WFGP), 15.

18. Mary Hawes, "Automatic Routines for Commercial Installations" (NBS, 94-23)

19. Ibid.

20. Hopper, Reflections.

21. Ibid.

22. Ibid. Hopper's quote serves more to highlight her sense of the dramatic rather than to represent management's position.

23. The development of FLOW-MATIC pseudo-code appears to be one of the first instances of the intersection between programming and linguistic theory. Hopper and her team had to define and construct a standardized data-processing language from scratch.

24. Hopper, interview, 1 October 1982 (WFGP), 16.

NOTES TO CHAPTER 11

1. Grace Hopper, "Glossary of Computer Terminology: Memo to ACM Members," 10 February 1954 (EBP, 50-19)

2. John Markoff, "Rear Adm. Grace M. Hopper Dies; Innovator in Computers Was 85," *New York Times*, 3 January 1992; Richard Pearson, "Adm. Hopper Dies; Pioneer in Computers," *Washington Post*, 4 January 1992.

3. Campbell-Kelly and Aspray, *Computer*, 191–192; Jean Sammet, "Brief Summary of the Early History of COBOL," *Annals of the History of Computing* 7, no. 4 (October 1985): 288–301; Jack Strong, "The Tale of the Near Demise of COBOL at Birth," *Annals of the History of Computing* 7, no. 4 (October 1985): 327.

4. "Common Business Languages for ADP: A Progress Report," *John Diebold and Associates Newsletter* 4, no. 10 (1959): 1–3 (GHP, 5-12); Charles Phillips, "Report from Committee on Data Systems Languages," 1 September 1959 (HOL, 94-2).

5. Hopper's Navy service record and obituary verify Phillips's assertion that she was associated with the University of Pennsylvania during 1959. Hopper's position as "Visiting Lecturer to Adjunct Professor, Moore School of Electrical Engineering, University of Pennsylvania," was held for one year. During that time, Hopper remained the director of UNIVAC's automatic programming division. See Elizabeth Dickason, "Remembering Grace Murray Hopper: A Legend in Her Own Time," *CHIPS* 7, no. 2 (April 1992): 4–8; Charles Phillips, "Reminiscences (Plus a Few Facts)," *Annals of the History of Computing* 7, no. 4 (October 1985): 304–308; Phillips, "Report from the Committee on Data Systems Languages," 1 September 1959 (HOL, 94-2).

6. Contrary to Phillips's and Hopper's recollection of events, Jean Sammet, a programmer who represented Sylvania on the CODASYL short-range committee, has written that Mary Hawes of the Burroughs Corporation requested the 8 April 1959 meeting. See Jean Sammet, "Brief Summary of the Early History of COBOL," *Annals of the History of Computing* 7, no. 4 (October 1985): 288–301.

7. Grace Hopper, interview, 1 October 1982 (WFGP), 18.

8. Hopper, Reflections.

9. Mary Hawes and Benjamin Cheydleur, "Suggestions for Consideration at the Washington CBL Conference," 22 May 1959 (HOL, 94-2).

10. Ibid., 306; Hopper, Reflections.

11. Phillips, "Reminiscences (Plus a Few Facts)," 306.

12. Ibid.; Phillips, "Report from Committee on Data Systems Languages," 1 September 1959 (HOL, 94-2).

13. Phillips, "Reminiscences (Plus a Few Facts)," 305.

14. Hopper, Reflections; "Common Business Languages for ADP: A Progress Report" (GHP, 5-12), 1–3.

15. Phillips, "Report from Committee on Data Systems Languages"; Phillips to Mr. Benjamin Cheydleur, 18 May 1959 (HOL, 94-2).

16. Agenda for CODASYL meeting, 28–29 May 1959 (HOL, 94-2).

17. Ibid.

18. Hopper, interview, 1 October 1982 (WFGP), 19.

19. Francis Holberton, handwritten notes from 28–29 May 1959 (HOL, 94-2).

20. Ibid.

21. E. J. Albertson, "Current Developments in Common Language Programming for Business Data Systems" (paper presented at the Computer Applications Symposium, Chicago, Illinois, 28 October 1959) (GHP, 5-12), 3–6. Hopper supported words over symbols for business languages.

22. At the time, the efficiency of machine language was difficult to quantify. See Jean Sammet, "The Early History of COBOL," in *History of Programming Languages*, ed. Wexelblat; Charles A. Phillips, "Report from Committee on Data Systems Languages," Oral presentation to Association for Computing Machinery, Boston, September 1, 1959.

23. Francis Holberton, handwritten notes (HOL, 94-2).

24. "Results on Questionnaire on Programming Languages" (HOL, 94-2); Albertson, "Current Developments" (GHP, 5-12).

25. Jean Sammet, "Report #1: Task Group on Statement Language," 29 June 1959 (HOL, 94-2).

26. Alfred Asch, "Minutes of Committee Meeting on Data Systems Languages Held at Bureau of Standards, June 23–24 1959" (HOL, 94-2); Nora Taylor to Dr. Larry Polachek, 24 July 1959 (HOL, 94-2)

27. Grace Hopper, Sperry Rand Statement on Common Data Processing Language, 28 July 1959 (HOL, 94-2)

28. Hopper, interview, 1 October 1982 (WFGP), 20–22.

29. Programmers of the von Neumann-type stored program computer got used to treating operations and data equally in memory. Returning to a method used at the Harvard Computation Laboratory, Hopper's FLOW-MATIC differentiated between the two types of information in order to make debugging easier.

30. Jean Sammet, "Answers to Written Questions from the ACM History of Programming Languages Conference," 1 February 1979 (HPL, 19-3), 16.

31. His programmers were writing an AIMACO compiler for the IBM 705, which allowed AIMACO source code to run on either the UNIVAC 1105 or the IBM 705; Sammet, *Programming Languages*, 324.

32. The Justice Department cited "product pre-announcement" as an abuse of market power in its 1952 lawsuit against IBM.

33. Sammet, *Programming Languages*, 325.

34. CSC, one of the first "software" companies, has become one of the largest companies in the world.

35. Jack Strong, "The Tale of the Near Demise of COBOL at Birth," *Annals of the History of Computing* 7, no. 4 (October 1985): 327.

36. Ibid.

37. Sammet, "Paper: The Early History of COBOL," 209.

38. Howard Bromberg, "Howard Bromberg Tells the Story of Sending the COBOL Tombstone to Charlie Phillips," *Annals of the History of Computing* 7, no. 4 (October 1985): 309.

39. IBM's technique of bundling software with hardware products came under attack by the U.S. Department of Justice in the 1960s, prompting IBM to "unbundle" in December 1968. IBM's action decoupled software from hardware, thus transforming it into a commodity. This transformation ignited the explosive growth of the software industry. See Campbell-Kelly and Aspray, *Computer.*

40. Hopper admitted in an interview years later that one of her motivations for supporting a COBOL standard was to block IBM from developing the business language standard. Aside from Jean Sammet's opinion that there was a certain amount of anti-IBM sentiment within the CODASYL organization, documents from the period do not confirm Hopper's later beliefs; Hopper, interview, 1 October 1982 (WFGP), 23.

41. Hopper, Reflections; Bromberg, "COBOL Tombstone," 309.

42. Phillips, "Reminiscences," 307.

43. Bromberg, "Howard Bromberg Tells the Story of Sending the COBOL Tombstone to Charlie Phillips," 309.

44. Wegstein to Phillips, 20 November 1959 (HOL, 94-2).

45. Gaudette to Phillips, 30 November 1959 (HOL, 94-2).

46. Howard Bromberg, "The COBOL Conclusion: End of the Beginning"; Sammet, *Programming Languages,* 332.

47. Jean Sammet, "General Views on COBOL," 2 December 1960 (GHP, 5-12). Since Hopper had a copy of Sammet's report in her possession, and based on the intended audience for the document, one can only assume that it was distributed among CODASYL members as well as represented users and manufacturers.

48. Nelson to Phillips, January 26 1960 (HOL, 94-2).

49. Ibid.

50. Howard Bromberg, "Report to NBS," 1967.

51. Edmund C. Arranga et al., "In COBOL's Defense: Roundtable Discussion," *IEEE Software* 17, no. 2 (March-April 2000): 70–72.

52. Francis Holberton, handwritten notes from 28–29 May 1959 (HOL 94-2).

53. See *The Social Construction of Technological Systems*, ed. Bijker et al.

54. "Computer Science" was not a term used to describe computer-oriented education until the late 1960s.

55. Malcolm Gladwell, *The Tipping Point: How Little Things Can Make a Big Difference* (Little, Brown, 2000), 56–59; David Hackett Fischer, *Paul Revere's Ride* (Oxford University Press, 1995). Fischer confirms Gladwell's interpretation of Revere.

56. Grace Hopper, "Draft Report on COBOL," 1966 (HOL, 94-2).

57. Ibid.

58. Ibid.

59. "Closure" is the term used to describe the stabilization of an artifact and the disappearance of technological problems that the artifact

addresses. According to the social constructivists, a technological standard does not emerge because the artifact is the most logical way to solve a given problem, but rather the influential social groups believe the problem to be solved. See Trevor Pinch and Wiebe Bijker, "The Social Construction of Facts and Artifacts: Or How the Sociology of Technology Might Benefit Each Other," in *The Social Construction of Technological Systems*, ed. Bijker et al.

60. This can be attributed in part to Hopper's work with the Department of Defense in the late 1960s. Her assignment was to standardize COBOL for the military.

NOTES TO CHAPTER I 2

1. Grace Hopper, "We Teach Computers to Think," *Popular Electronics*, 1959.

2. Ibid.

3. See Hughes, *Networks of Power*.

4. Naval Service Record Biography, "Captain Grace Murray Hopper, July 1981" (OBC).

5. Hopper, interview, 1 October 1982 (WFGP), 19.

6. Naval Service Record Biography, "Captain Grace Murray Hopper, July 1981" (OBC).

7. Ibid.

8. Kathleen Williams, *Improbable Warriors* (Naval Insititute Press, 2001), 209–212.

INDEX